THE LIMITS OF EUROPEAN INTEGRATION

The Limits of European Integration

Paul Taylor

CROOM HELM
London & Canberra

© 1983 Paul Taylor
Croom Helm Ltd; Provident House, Burrell Row,
Beckenham, Kent BR3 1AT

British Library Cataloguing in Publication Data

Taylor, Paul
    The limits of European integration.
    1. European federation   2. European Economic
    Community Countries—Economic integration
    I. Title
    337.1'42   HC241.2

    ISBN 0-7099-2423-2

Printed and bound in Great Britain
by Billing and Sons Ltd, Worcester.

CONTENTS

Acknowledgements

Introduction

To Janetta

ACKNOWLEDGEMENTS

My primary debt is to the Students at the London School of Economics, both graduate and undergraduate, with whom much of this book has been discussed. For their help with the preparation of the manuscript I am deeply indebted to Philippa Sandford, Marie Williams, Anita LeaKer and Hilary Parker. Larry Trachtenberg also provided invaluable assistance with both academic and technical advice: the process of producing the manuscript was considerably eased by his understanding of the mysteries of the word processor.

INTRODUCTION

This volume is an account of European integration in the last decade or so. It explores the pattern of relations between the member states of the European Communities and identifies limits imposed by the states upon incursions into their arrangements by the European Communities. The main question which is addressed is: where did the states choose to defend their sovereignty in this period?

This is a question which concerns the whole extent of the interface between the state and the European Communities, and it was obviously impossible to deal with such a range in one volume. I was therefore impelled to develop a procedure by which particular areas and problems could be selected for closer examination: this procedure hardly deserves the title of theory though it determines the overall shape of the volume. Rather is it an approach or method of work. The starting point is an account of the major dynamics of integration: what are the major pressures which might impinge upon states and integrate them more closely? Since the theories of the Neofunctionalists constitute the most sophisticated account of these dynamics I have focussed in the first chapter upon presenting and analysing these; and I contrast the dynamics derived from these theories with some which I have developed from the Functionalism of David Mitrany. Together they constitute a reasonably comprehensive account of the range of conceivable challenges to the autonomy of the modern state. One important point which emerges is that the dynamics which might be thought important in integration vary with the theoretical perspective of the observer.

In the second chapter I suggest a number of questions about international integration in Western Europe which are derived from the dynamics previously examined. These questions are organised into three sets. They concern: first, the degree of "supranationalism" in the institutions of the Communities (questions derived from both theories); second, policy making in the Communities, involving both national governments and the regional institutions (questions derived from Neofunctionalism); and third, the status of the legal systems of member states and the extent of the challenge to the authority of member governments, (questions derived, according to my interpretation in Chapter 1, from the ideas of the older Functionalists). In presenting these questions I am obviously indicating the main areas where the limits imposed upon integration by the states are to be sought. In the rest of the second chapter I concentrate upon locating the limits in empirical terms: I am not here attempting to test or refute the theories but am concerned with locating the limits imposed within the state upon the dynamics which they suggest.

The remaining chapters of the volume are also arranged in the three groups suggested by the sets of questions, though in these I am more concerned with the task of explaining the limits described in the second chapter rather than with their description. The various chapters represent points of focus and inevitably touch upon questions which are also raised from a different perspective in other chapters: this approach follows from the nature of the area of study which defies a clear cut categorisation. Aspects of the theories illuminate aspects of the arguments throughout the volume. But, although the existing theories are amended and developed, the primary focus is empirical.

Chapters 3, 4 and 5 are concerned primarily with the limits upon the development of the central institutions in the European Communities. The broad theme in each chapter is the way in which the supranational potentials of the early phase of integration were limited and the role of the institutions altered. In Chapters 6, 7 and 8 I deal more closely with the policy-making process in the Communities from the perspective of national decision-makers. Pressures which impinged upon national civil servants and executives are discussed in order to explain the limits imposed upon the dynamics which I derived from the theories of the Neofunctionalists. In this context three areas were chosen because they seemed to be particularly revealing in the late 1970s about these limits. They are the diplomacy concerning the European Monetary System in 1978 and later; the pattern of development of the Communities' involvement with a range of social policies; and problems concerning the Communities' Budgetary arrangements, and the Common Agricultural Policy, in particular as they affected Britain's relations with her partners. I discuss further in Chapter 9 the legal bases of the Communities and the claims and counter-claims about the nature of the obligations of Community membership. As I indicate in Chapter I, the questions dealt with here, though relevant to both Neofunctionalism and the Functionalism of David Mitrany, are of more central importance in the latter. It should perhaps be stressed again that there are in the volume a number of inter-related points of focus and that the materials to which they relate inevitably overlap.

The structure of the volume reflects its primary concern with the question of where the states chose to defend their sovereignty in the 1970s and early 1980s. A second theme is, however, taken up in Chapter 3 and is touched upon in other chapters: that integration in Western Europe in the 1970s had a discernable overall shape. Between 1970 and 1973-4 there were still uncertainties about the direction of development of the Communities. There remained some encouragement for those who favoured a more supranational Europe. In 1974, however, these uncertainties were clarified and in the late 1970s states began to impose clearer limits upon integration. Indeed there was then some evidence to suggest that states were entrenching their defences against incursions from the Communities into their domain. In Chapter 10, therefore, I also consider some of the ways in which the problems which had emerged in the way of further integration might be overcome.

The volume is intended to constitute a summary of the limits imposed upon integration within the state by a variety of mechanisms and in a variety of contexts. Its perspective is one of looking from the state outwards towards Europe. But - perhaps rather treacherously - having examined the defences of the citadel from within, it proposes in Chapter 10 to those who may be interested, ways of pressing the attack in favour of further integration.

Chapter One

THE CONCEPT OF COMMUNITY AND THE GRADUALIST PROCESS OF INTEGRATION

Among the problems which face the student of the process of international integration, such as that between the member states of the European Communities, is that of finding a way among the various theoretical approaches to the subject. The theoretical approach which one adopts is certain to affect ones understanding of the integration process, and each approach has its own implications for the kind of strategy which is thought to be appropriate in seeking further integration. This chapter seeks both to illustrate these points and to clarify some aspects of integration. In particular it is intended to describe some of the main pressures towards integration which were identified in the two major theories of gradualist integration among states, namely, Functionalism and Neofunctionalism. This is a necessary prelude to the more detailed discussion in Chapter 2 of the empirical limits upon integration defined in these terms which were imposed by the states in the 1970s.

The approach of the Neofunctionalists involved the attempt to use the analogy of national government in interpreting the existing structure and process of European institutions and in suggesting possible ways of furthering integration; it looked to national governmental institutions and methods of control as a model for understanding and strengthening the powers of the central institutions of the Communities. The other, which might be termed a Functionalist approach, in the style of the older Functionalists (such as David Mitrany), distinguished between the desirable end-situation and the methods of achieving it, between the conditions of the stable state which should result from integration, and the

1

requirements of the strategy for achieving those conditions.(1) It suggested that the analogy of the national government might not be appropriate, and indeed, that its use might suggest courses of action, and lead to the attachment of significance to observed developments, which would lessen the chances of its being appropriate later on.

Some observers, particularly the Neofunctionalists and the Federalists saw in the European Communities an emerging bi-polarity of power and authority.(2) On the one side there was the community method, centred upon the Commission, which had competence and took decisions in its appropriate sphere; and on the other side, the residue of power and authority was left in the hands of the national governments. An important part of the integration process in this analysis was the transfer of decision-making powers from the national governments to the European institution, that is, the Commission; the Court sustained the Commission's decision-making by establishing and protecting the supremacy of Community Law over National Law in the integrated areas. The progress of integration in this case lay in the expanding competence of the European institutions, particularly the Commission. In 1967 Lindberg detected the beginnings of a European political system; and, in doing so, he counted those fields in which the European institutions took decisions, and those which remained the preserve of governments.(3) His analysis was highly illuminating on many aspects, but it accepted implicitly certain assumptions about the nature of sovereignty and authority which would be challenged by those who take a different theoretical approach to the subject.

There are, of course, several different views on the nature of sovereignty. One view - the older one - lays primary stress upon the legal aspect: that power is sovereign which has the legal right to act and 'whose acts are not subject to the legal control of another human will'.(4) In this case it is the possession of the legal right to undertake certain activities, such as the defence of the realm, which is the most important aspect of sovereignty. Another view, however, goes beyond this to demand as a condition of sovereignty that the power should be based on a popular consensus, upon a community or nation; the power of government should receive the sanction of popular approval and support before that government can be said to be sovereign. And the same general distinction can be made about authority: authority of governments can be based upon a recognition of competence expressed through the approval of the mass of the citizens. Authority in this second case derives from a general agreement that the government should have the right to act; in the first case it comes from a legal dispensation.

I should indicate at this point the sense in which I use the word community, as Functionalists and Neofunctionalists have rather different views of this concept. Where I am not talking specifically about the European Communities, in the sense of its institutions and methods of work, I mean community in the sense of a community of beliefs, values, attitudes and loyalties. I call this a socio-psychological community, and would distinguish it from, for instance, the political community of Etzioni(5) or the system of co-existing but different interests which Haas discusses.(6) The socio-psychological community is very similar to the community with which Deutsch was concerned in his discussion of the nation and in his discussion of amalgamated and pluralistic security communities.(7) This type of community is, of course, similar to that detected by Tonnies when he made his distinction between Gemeinschaft and Gesellschaft at the end of the nineteenth century.(8) Gemeinschaft is translated as community, and Gesellschaft as society. Society, Tonnies suggested, is characterized by competitiveness and the transactions within it are based on contract. Community, on the other hand, describes a sense among the individuals forming it of belonging together, of having common loyalties and values, of kinship; and tasks performed within a community are not performed because of reciprocal arrangements such as contracts, but because of a feeling of duty, a sense of contributing something worthwhile to the good of the whole. An example of society in Tonnies's sense is the firm; an example of community is the family, the church, or the nation.

It is interesting that the Gaullist view of sovereignty which became fundamental in the attitudes of the French government towards the European Communities, was similar in many respects to that of the older Functionalist theorists such as David Mitrany. The Functionalist argument seemed to be that sovereignty was vitally dependent upon the loyalties of citizens; that institution was sovereign which attracted popular loyalties. The dynamic of integration for the Functionalists was the learning process of citizens who were gradually drawn into the co-operative ethos created by functionally specific international institutions devoted to the satisfaction of welfare needs, which were defined in a rather broad sense as the maintenance of adequate economic and social standards. Functionally specific international institutions which escaped from the bonds of national frontiers were thought to be capable of satisfying these needs more efficiently in that they could be tackled in an area, and in a fashion, which was more closely related to their character, rather than determined by political, or ideological considerations; and in doing so the new institutions could attract the loyalties of citizens by convincing them of the advantages of co-operation. Citizens would learn to co-operate from their experience that co-operation brought them greater benefits.

This very brief discussion of the integrative dynamic of the older Functionalists is sufficient to bring out two major aspects of their attitude towards sovereignty; first, sovereignty was in their view conditional upon the appearance of popular loyalties which focussed upon the governing institutions; and secondly, the functionally specific institutions were thought to attract loyalties by efficiently carrying out the task of satisfying welfare needs. A number of successful international institutions could gradually erode the loyalties of citizens towards national governments and refocus loyalties upon themselves: there was to be an accumulation of partial transfers which would bring about a 'translation of the true seat of authority'.(9) This in turn would lead to a 'sharing of sovereignty' and the imposing of restraints upon national governments. But, most importantly, the transfer of the function was but the beginning of the process of transferring sovereignty, and creating a new basis for the authority of international institutions(10); the process was one of building a socio-psycholgical community which transcended the nation state.

Similarly, writers such as Rosenstiel, who might be said to represent a kind of idealised French position, argued that sovereignty was vitally linked with its sociological base.(11) They argued that in Europe the national governments attracted the overwhelming loyalty of the majority

4

of their citizens. The nations continued to
provide the sovereign base of the national
governments; and in the consequential absence of a
European nation European institutions could not be
sovereign; the term 'supranational' was a misnomer.
They must be viewed rather as an extension of the
juridical and administrative arm of the national
governments. As to the older Functionalists,
sovereignty to, for instance, the Gaullists, was
vitally dependent upon a community of values,
beliefs and attitudes which sustained it.
Similarly, in their view, institutions could not be
said to possess authority unless they had been
legitimized by receiving the support and reflecting
the values, attitudes and beliefs of citizens.

It hardly needs pointing out that the
Gaullists and the Functionalists drew very
different conclusions from these similar
assumptions about the relationship between
community and sovereignty. The Gaullists saw the
continued vitality of the different European
nations as a reason for resisting the encroachment
of Europe. The Functionalists' argument, when
applied to Europe, suggested a strategy for
creating the conditions under which sovereignty
could be transferred.

The Neofunctionalists and, indeed, the
Federalists, on the other hand, shared a suspicion
of the Tonnian view of community, and accepted a
pluralist model of society.(12) For instance,
Professor Haas rejected _Gemeinschaft_ and
substituted for it a kind of community of competing
interests which co-existed because of an agreement
about the rules of the game within a constitutional
system. The Neofunctionalists' view upon the major
characteristics of society within the modern state
was the starting point of their amendment of the
older Functionalism: the older Functionalists
seemed to point to the element of agreement or
consensus in society; they saw the essence of
stability in the underlying homogeneity of society.
The Neofunctionalists on the other hand argued that
social life was dominated by competition among
interests. They recognized stability in the
efficient management of conflict in a pluralist
society. It is, of course, a question of stress:
the older Functionalists did not deny the
competitive aspects of society; neither did the
Neofunctionalist position deny the crucial
importance of the role of consensus. But, whilst

5

The Gradualist Process of Integration

Functionalism saw integration as being primarily about consensus-building, Neofunctionalism saw the best chance of obtaining international integration in the harnessing of pressures produced by the competing elements in society.

It was logical, therefore, that interest groups should be allocated an important place in the Neofunctionalist view of integration; the gains from integration were seen as stimulating the demands of interest groups for further integration. And integration was supported by shifting coalitions of interest groups, parties and officials. The expectations and demands of groups were channelled towards integration, not because of the perception of a general gain as with the older Functionalism, but because of each group's perception of its own particular advantage. Such interests included 'every group-backed demand that enters the market place of political competition'(13) - from economic interests to political interests, and even religious interests. Cooperation among groups was seen to be the result of a convergence of separate perceptions of interests and not 'a spontaneous surrender to the myth of the common good.'(14)

The main motor of integration was to be found, however, in the institutional structures and in the changing behaviour of elites within those structures. Haas described integration as 'the process whereby political actors in several distinct national settings are persuaded to shift their loyalties, expectations and political activities towards a new and larger setting'(15) and elsewhere he explained that 'integration is conceptualised as resulting from an institutionalized pattern of interest politics played out within existing international organizations."(16)

The essential elements in the integration process which are indicated here were the changing attitudes of key actors, such as national civil servants, and the framework of existing institutional structures; in Europe, of course, the latter were the Communities' institutions which linked Brussels in a web of interactions with national governments. Indeed, 'the decision-making process, in its institutional setting, stimulated parties to work out common positions; it creates pressures on high national civil servants to get to know and establish rapport with their opposite numbers; it sharpens the sensitivities of the legal profession.'(17)

If Functionalism was more concerned with a substantive community - a consensus about interests - the Neofunctionalist theory of international integration was centred around the requirements of a procedural consensus; groups were persuaded to pursue their interests through an agreed framework which was an essential element in the end situation of the integration process: a political community was formed which has as its 'central feature ... the likelihood of internal peaceful change in a setting of contending groups with mutually antagonistic claims'.(18) And the emergence of the political community was to lead interest groups to articulate supranational solutions to their problems and to begin to address their demands to the supranational institutions. The attitudes and expectations of political actors were pushed in a supranational direction by their own involvement in the work of the supranational institutions and these were reinforced by the resulting changes in the expectations and calculations of the interest groups.

The Neofunctionalists stressed the psychology of elites in an integration process ideally culminating in the emergence of a new political system, whereas Functionalism stressed a popular psychological community. The difference in focus is evident: the Neofunctionalists were much more interested in decision-making and formal structures as frameworks of elite behaviour(19) and concentrated upon the patterns of fusion of existing international and national political systems; Mitrany on the other hand was more concerned with changes in popular attitudes as the test of effective integration, and aimed to subsume existing national political systems in a new international one. For him institutions were essentially the trigger of major changes which were to take place elsewhere; that is one reason why Functionalism says little about the details of the institutional structures which were proposed, apart from the broad dictum that 'form should follow function.'

Neofunctionalism and Functionalism were both process theories; they both contained a sophisticated view upon the causal links which were expected to lead from one level of integration to another. But in an article written in 1967 Haas

7

described European integration without mentioning the possible changes in popular attitudes towards integration(20): he stressed the state of relations between the Commission and national governments and he implictly accepted this as the most significant aspect of integration. Although Haas elsewhere accepted that a new centre could attract the general support of citizens as a result of their satisfacton with the performance of crucial functions(21), this, to the Neofunctionalists, was not one of the key elements of the process. In contrast in an analysis of the European experience from the point of view of the older Functionalist theory - if it were misapplied to an example of regional political integration - it would be demanded that the effective work of the former should change the attitudes of the latter so that a new European community of interests emerged. The two theories lead to the attachment of significance to quite different aspects of the integration process.

A concern with types of decision-making was a characteristic of the Neofunctionalist' view on the process of integration: it followed from their search for procedural consensus. Haas distinguished what he called three modes of accommodation and each of these was both an indicator of a particular level of integration and a causal element leading to further integration.(22) They were, first, the technique of finding the minimum common denominator: bargaining partners located the areas where positive agreement was immediately possible and struck their deal only on that basis; secondly, there was the technique of splitting the difference: bargaining partners positively located both an area of agreement and an area of disagreement and agreed to divide the ground which separated them. This technique was usual where values could be readily identified, as, for instance, in the case of negotiations about financial question. And thirdly there was the technique - common within political communities - which was described as upgrading the common interest: bargaining partners agreed to stress what they had in common and to postpone the settlement of disagreements. The expectation was that agreement in the short term would increase the chances of agreement in the long term; the environment would be changed so that in the long term the procedural consensus was maintained.

The Gradualist Process of Integration

The distinguishing of these three modes of accommodation as part of the process of integration again revealed the importance of elites and procedures in an institutional framework in the Neofunctionalist analysis of the process of integration. Professor Haas concluded: 'Broadly speaking international institutions maximizing decision making by means of the second and third modes yield the greatest amount of progress towards the goal of political community.'(23)

Yet the changes which were necessary in order to lead to a higher style of bargaining in the integration process were not to be found in Neofunctionalist thinking precisely in the functional areas within which an agreement had been struck; neither were they to be found entirely in the changing attitudes of actors. The progress towards political community (the causal links between one level of integration and the next in Neofunctional theory) was to be understood rather in terms of a subtle relationship between the two: this relationship was summed up in the term spill-over. Neofunctionalism was a process theory; spill-over was a way of describing the central dynamic of that process. Spill-over was a product of the mode of accommodation, and was to lead to a higher mode which in turn would take the process nearer political community.

Spill-over was the process whereby successful integration in an area of lesser salience would lead to a series of further integrative measures in linked areas so that the proces wouuld become increasingly involved with issues of greater political importance. Integration would be led closer to sovereignty - its level would increase - and to involvement with such 'high political' questions as defence policy and foreign policy. The essential dynamic of the process was seen to derive from an increasing preference for solving problems arising in the management of activities, which were immediately adjacent to areas which had been integrated, by a further act of integration. The preference was in the attitudes of decision-makers, bureaucrats, politicians, - who had learnt that integration was a possible way of solving technical problems, and who were supported by interested non-governmental organizations, which had themselves realized that integration was capable of producing rewards. Bureaucrats were reinforced in their disposition to take integrative decisions by their increasing involvement with each

other in the various national administrations and
the institutions of the Communities. This was a
process known as <u>engrenage</u>. Most politicians, most
of the time, were thought to be subject to
'incremental decision making', - they tended to
have no overall plan and responded to immediate
problems - and they were, therefore, vulnerable to
the pro-integration pressures which had been
generated within their national administrations.
Spill-over amounted to a process of accumulating
implications of previous acts of integration and
worked in particular through the changing attitudes
of decision-makers.

Haas wrote that 'many decisions are
integrative in their immediate consequences as well
as in the new expectation and political processes
which they imply.'(24) There was an element of
accumulation; but 'functional contexts are
autonomous' and 'there is no dependable cumulative
process unless the task assigned is inherently
expansive and thus capable of overriding the
built-in autonomy of functional contexts.' But
'if actors on the basis of their interest-inspired
perceptions desire to adapt integrative lessons
learned in one context to a new situation the
lesson will be generalized.' The circumstances in
which the actors might be led to desire to adapt
integrative lessons and to generalize these lessons
are clearly of relevance to the concept of
spill-over: they determine whether spill-over is
effective. The most favourable circumstances are
obtained when the functional area is specific and
not trivial.(25) And the functional area must be
conducive to an involvement with political areas.
The decision-making process leads to an
accumulation of integrated areas which persuades
decision-makers to an increasing preparedness to
deal with issues which lie closer to the heart of
sovereignty.

It was the 'institutionalized pattern' which
was significant to the Neofunctionalists, and not
the development of a socio-psychological community.
Institutional spill-over and the learning process
of bureaucrats together with the support of
interest groups are the equivalent of the changing
values of citizens in Functionalism.(26) And, as
they concentrated on decision-making and not upon
the emergence of socio-psychological community,
they implicitly accepted the view that sovereignty
was confered by extending a legal competence. The
sovereignty of the regional institutions followed

upon the granting of a legal competence by national governmental institutions, and the existence of a socio-psychological community was not seen to be immediately relevant; community was not viewed as the essential base of sovereignty, although, of course, it was hoped that a community of competing interests would follow from the transfer of sovereignty. Indeed, it was not until 1971 that Haas came to focus upon the problem of 'authority-legitimacy transfer' to the international institution as part of the process of regional integration. This is indicative of the Neofunctionalist tendency not to address directly the problem of the transfer of sovereignty.(27) Before then the implication was in his analysis that the authority of the international institution derived from the recognition by national governments of an institutional competence, which in Europe resided in the Commission or even in an Assembly; it did not depend upon the prior appearance of Gemeinschaft which could sustain the international institutions.

These two differing views of community, and their relationship with sovereignty and authority, profoundly affected attitudes on the status of the decisions of the existing European institutions. If socio-psychological community was accepted as the essential basis of sovereignty and authority, and if there was no European community, even the decisions of institutions which had been granted a significant range of formal powers were each, in effect, dependent upon the decision of national governments to allow implementation. This would continue to be the case no matter how long the international institutions exercised their formal powers; the decisions of the European insitutions were thus of a different and lower kind when compared with those of national governments. They could not be compared on a like-to-like basis. Although they were not explicitly stated, the latter assumptions seem to form one of the starting points of the Neofunctionalists' analysis.

In their acceptance of the pluralist model of society the Neofunctionalists agreed with the European Federalists. Federalism can be viewed either as providing a political solution, a way of managing different interests within a single political framework; or it can be viewed as an administrative convenience, a method of governing a homogeneous society within which there is a high degree of consensus. The Neofunctionalists seemed

11

to fall squarely into that tradition which sees
Federalism as providing a political solution; it
was not necessary to the stability of the political
system that it should be coextensive with a
socio-psychological community. The Federalists, in
the absence of a European socio-psychological
community, also found this argument plausible, and
it reinforced their determination to place a high
priority upon developments at the institutional
level and upon finding a political solution.(28)

Mitrany, on the other hand, was suspicious of
Federalism; he wrote about the dangers of seeking
solutions to societal conflict in formulas such as
Federalism.(29)   It could not provide a political
solution to the problem of divisive interests, and
might in the absence of socio-psychological
community add to the divisions in society. A
suspicion of Federalism as a political solution was
also to be found in Rosenstiel's argument.(30)

I will return to these different approaches to
the fundamental problems of the integration process
in the other sections of this chapter. But, in
preparing to do this, I must first consider the
relationship between the capacity of international
institutions and the level of community feeling.
As I show later in this volume this relationship is
of some importance in the problems which emerged in
the communities in the 1970s, such as those in
relations between Britain and the other member
states. Capacity has been defined as the ability
to receive, understand and act upon the demands fed
into an organization from its environment; it is an
indicator of performance.(31)   Low capacity
indicates that the organization is not able to
satisfy all the demands made upon it; a high
capacity suggests the ability to respond quickly
and adequately.

The level of capacity required in a stable
state has been thought to vary with the strength of
the community within it. If there is only one
community in the state a government needs only
moderate capacity in order to maintain the
stability of that state. A failure of response
does not generate the belief in individuals and
groups that their interest cannot be satisfied at
some future time by that government. If capacity is
consistently low, however, the community might
disintegrate into a number of communities. On the
other hand, where an institution has the task of
responding to the demands of several different
communities, only a high level of capacity can

12

maintain stability. Different communities remain
together in a single state framework when their
different interests are recognized and satisfied
quickly by the government. In this situation the
Functionalist argument is that the various
communities in the state will slowly integrate into
a single community. Deutsch mentions that many
existing nation states contain remnants of older
nations(32): the British government in general
maintained a relatively high level of capacity and
this contributed to the appearance of a relatively
homogeneous community. The government of
Austro-Hungary, on the other hand, lacked adequate
capacity and was unable to prevent the various
nations from eventually breaking away.
    The older Functionalism was deeply concerned
with the problem of capacity; the success of their
approach depended crucially upon the ability of the
various international institutions to perform their
tasks efficiently in order to attract the loyalties
of citizens, and without a high degree of capacity
the approach would fail. It was for this reason
that Mitrany was concerned to stress that experts
could often formulate the technical arguments for
increasing the scope and level of integration; and
their researches could lead to the discovery of new
areas where integration would increase the
prosperity and strengthen the economic and social
security of citizens. Within the framework of
functional institutions experts could play a
leading part in the creation of a
socio-psychological community which would transcend
the framework of the nation state. Indeed, as part
of a strategy for international integration - the
traditional forms of government only being
appropriate when socio-psychological community had
appeared - Functionalism envisaged something which
was surprisingly similar to what we now call
technocracy.(33)
    I hope that this brief discussion has brought
out some of the general characteristics of the
various theoretical approaches to international
integration; I have not attempted a detailed
discussion. But enough has been said, I hope, to
clarify two broad approaches to the subject. The
Neofunctionalists had distinctive views on the
relationship between community, and sovereignty and
authority, and they were mainly concerned with
developments in decision-making among and within
institutions. And the Neofunctionalists'
acceptance of the pluralist model of society fits

easily with the Federalists' belief that a unified
Europe could provide a political solution. In the
older Functionalism, on the other hand, it was
insisted that the development of
socio-psychological community was the essential
precondition of sovereignty; and that without such
a community Federalism could not work.
Institutions with high capacity were more likely to
attract popular loyalties.

I now turn to an examination of the
implications of the two gradualist theories for
understanding various aspects of the Communities
development. The differing views on relationships
between community and sovereignty affected views on
the nature of the decision-making process in the
European Communities, the community method. When
first examined the method may have seemed like a
very haphazard series of interactions between
international civil servants (the Commission),
national governments, and a variety of more or less
organized interested groups. But Functionalist
theory on the one hand, and Neofunctionalist theory
on the other hand, each make a different kind of
sense of the method; and this affected views on
strategies which were available to the Commission
in working towards further European integration.
The Neofunctionalists concentrated upon
relationships between governments and the
Commission.(34)   The Commission proposed;
governments were persuaded, sometimes by direct
consultation on particular problems and sometimes
by the use of a peculiar kind of diplomatic
technique which relied for its success upon the
self-interest of governments, namely the
Commision's presentation to the Council of a
package of proposals. And the whole process was
lubricated by the interpenetration between national
bureaucracies and the Commission - the process
which involved national civil servants in the
Community - and by the logic that held that partial
integration produced problems which could best be
solved by further integration. From the process of
interaction with governments, the Neofunctionalist
argument ran, the Commission increased the range of
its formal powers; and it increased its capacity to
act in areas affecting the interests of groups
within the state. It is worth repeating that, in
this analysis, the main dynamic of integration lay
in the inter-relationship between governments and
Commission. The transfer of formal powers enabled
the Commission to increase its capacity and the

emergence of a European focus for group interests
was expected to follow from this. The community
method viewed from this vantage point can be
summarized diagrammatically as follows:

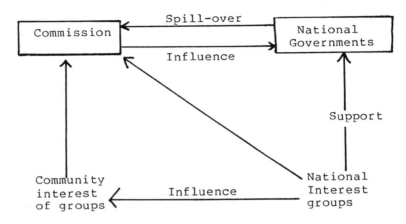

The older Functionalism stressed different
aspects of the method. And President de Gaulle's
opinions and actions would suggest that he was more
concerned with the likely effects of this method.
The community method from this perspective was much
more of a circular set of interactions; its main
dynamic was the growth of a socio-psychological
community among citizens. The process may be
broken into at any point, but if I start with the
role of the Commission the resulting steps are as
follows:

1. The Commission, having been allocated areas of
    competence and some formal powers by the
    agreement of governments, sought to maximize
    its capacity to act in these areas.
2. As a result of the Commission's activities the
    group interests were activated and attracted
    to the Commission. A change of interest in
    favour of further integration was generated
    and directed at national governments; at this
    stage a re-focusing of loyalties away from
    national governments towards the European
    institutions could be expected.

3. National governments, subjected to a series of
    influences and pressures from within the
    state, were persuaded to allow the Commission
    greater powers; the possibilities for
    independent action by national governments
    were reduced by the weakening of internal
    loyalties and citizens' changing expectations.
4. The Commission's greater powers and increasing
    range of functions allowed it to increase its
    capacity; and the circle began again.
    This view of the community method may be
    represented as follows:

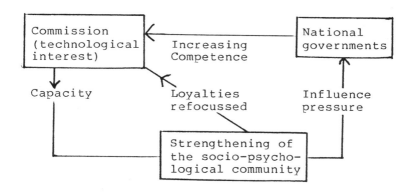

President de Gaulle, as one might have
expected from his views on the nation and its
importance to sovereignty, was aware of the dangers
of this method. Hence his attempts to restrict the
Commission's public relations activities and his
insistence on restricting interactions at the
Communities level to those between the Commission
and national governments. I consider some examples
of his efforts in this direction later in this
chapter. He was probably more frightened by the
possibility of the erosion of the French system
from within than by direct attack on it by the
Commission. He saw the danger to French
sovereignty of a redefinition of the interest of
groups of citizens in line with the general
interest of the Community as defined by the
Commission.
     The point which I am stressing here is that
the significance attached to particular

developments varies with the approach followed - a
simple point which is frequently overlooked; that
some developments might be judged as favouring
integration from the point of view of one approach,
but unfavourable from the point of view of the
other; and that the two approaches also have
implications for the choice of strategies for
obtaining further integration. Perhaps I should
add here that I am at this stage deliberately
misapplying some of the ideas contained in
Functionalism. I consider its view of the dynamics
of integration and the relationship between
sovereignty and the loyalties of citizens in order
to illustrate and clarify one possible line of
argument about Europe; but the end-situation to
which I relate this dynamic, a united Europe, is
not one which Mitrany welcomed. His ideas,
however, do point to one possible way of obtaining
that goal.

The Neofunctionalist and Federalist approaches
lead to the view that progress towards greater
integration should be measured by the Commission's
acquisition of formal powers from national
governments, and by corresponding reinforcement of
its supporting institutions, such as the Assembly.
The various ways for improving the methods of
control by the Assembly over the Commission, such
as the "advise and consent" procedures in relation
to individual appointments, which were recommended
by the Vedel and the Tindemans Reports,(35) or for
improving the Assembly's powers to dismiss the
Commission, or to decide upon legislation, or to
alter the Budget in the face of Council opposition,
are to be judged in this approach as representing
progress towards further integration. They
represent a strengthening of the supranational
elements in the Communities' institutions, and the
corresponding weakening of the decision making
structures of the member states. In general this
strategy reflects a concern with changes in
institutions and the behaviour of elites rather
than a concern with the nature of the different
community interests. Sovereignty is separable from
the socio-psychological base; it can be transferred
from governments to international institutions by
the formal granting of a legal competence. The
failure to move to majority voting in the Council
of Ministers is in this perspective, therefore,
identified as a major setback in the path of
integration, as was the Commission's limited
success in expanding the range of those independent

powers which it was granted under the Rome Treaty, particularly those concerning the day-to-day management of the Common Agricultural Policy, the supervision of the competition policy under the terms of Article 85 and 86 of the Rome Treaty, and the representation of the Communities in the conduct of external commercial relations (for instance, with the Japanese) after the completion of the Common External Tariff (which was accomplished in 1969).(36)

From the perspective of the older Functionalism, and of main-stream French political thinking — as I have pointed out — the transfer of sovereignty can only follow from the appearance of a socio-psychological community; it follows that in helping to create this, stress should be placed upon building up the capacity of the Commission and upon increasing its efficiency, both in administration and in research; and, in the absence of a community base of interests and attitudes it would be inappropriate for it to seek to take on any of the character of the national governments.

The Commission's failure to develop its reputation for efficiency, its technocratic elements, in the 1970s is here identified as a major problem in the way of developing a stronger socio-psychological base for its activities. A belated recognition of these failures was reflected in the unsuccessful attempt made in the mid-1970s to develop the "Human Face" of Europe, and to become more noticeably involved in activities which seemed to generate rewards for all citizens and which affected them directly.(37) The Functionalist approach also suggests that there would have been dangers in making the Commission more dependent upon the Assembly in the 1970s because this would have made it easier for the Commission or individual Commissioners to be voted out of office by the Assembly at a time when there was no developed socio-psychological community. Responsibility to a directly elected Assembly, far from helping the Commission, could in some circumstances tend further to reduce its efficiency. It might, for instance, have resulted in a lowering of the calibre of the members of the Commission, on whom so much of its reputation depended, because elected officers tend to lose their reputation for impartial efficiency; they tend to be successful in maintaining their position more through political machination than technical skill and expertise. Furthermore the representation of particular party interests is damaging to the efficiency of technocracy; it tends to detract from its impartiality and to drag it into the area of politics. And, anyway, in the absence of a community of interest what kind of interest could be represented? On what kind of consensus could a Commission which was responsible in the traditonal sense base its decisions?

The relationship between socio-psychological community and these two broad strategies for the integration of Europe is an interesting one. Neither strategy denied the importance of community for the stability of the integrated state; but the first, the Neofunctionalist, saw its emergence as one of the possible results of the transfer of formal powers and of 'sovereignty' from national governments to the Commission; and it was not to be a community of common loyalties and values but, rather, a community of competing interests contained within an accepted constitutional framework. Integration resulted from the Commission's ability to convince national governments that it was capable of attaining those objectives which they preferred, or came to prefer, and as a result of the spill-over between functional areas. (Part of the Neofunctionalist rationale for creating a technological community was that success here would produce pressures upon governments to harmonize - and integrate - their defence policies.) The technocratic/Functionalist strategy, on the other hand, saw socio-psychological community as the essential condition of the transfer of real power and sovereignty to the international institution. Until that stage was reached any transfer of formal powers was likely to be misleading; it would continue to be the governments who were expected to act in crisis situations and they would continue to attract new tasks to themselves. In this case the main dynamic of integration lay in the development and strengthening of identitive relationships between the Commission and citizens and groups within the state. One of the essential differences between the Neofunctionalist/Federalist and the Functionalist approaches was this: the Functionalist strategy saw integration as a process which passed through several stages which were different from the end-situation, but which it must pass through in order to reach the end-situation; the Neofunctionalist/Federalist approach, on the other hand, sought to involve the end-situation as far as possible in the present one.

These considerations again point to the need in evaluating the progress of integration in the Communities in the 1970s to focus both upon developments in institutions and decision-making, and upon the implications of changes in attitudes and values. Development in each of these areas may take place at different rates and the significance of each is altered with the theoretical perspective.

This point may be illustrated with reference to the Luxembourg Accord of January 1966 which concluded the crisis in the Communities caused by the French withdrawal from participation in the major committees of the communities in June 1965.(38) These accords may be judged from a Neofunctionalist perspective as fundamental to the pattern of development of the Communities' institutions in the 1970s, in that they confirmed in Articles (b) 1. and 2. that there would be no movement to majority voting in the Council of Ministers, as had been stipulated in the Treaty of Rome, in the third transitional period which had begun in January 1966. This decision had the effect, as I argue below, of hastening the development of intergovernmentalism in the Communities: it meant that the style of decision-making came to focus upon building a consensus among governments rather than upon building an adequate majority in the Council. This stress inevitably reinforced the role of the Committee of Permanent Representatives and weakened that of the Commission. The latter had to be more cautious in putting forward 'European' initiatives, and in attempting to get its way in relations with the Council. It is striking, though, that although this is undoubtedly a valid interpretation of the accords, it does not exclude another interpretation which holds that the French government's main concern then was to impose restrictions upon the Commission's procedures and public relations activities when it tried to develop support for its position among groups and people within the states. The Commission had to be restrained from using public relations activities and links with organised groups to generate more positive support for its positions, thereby limiting national governments' freedom of manoeuvre by undercutting their position before they had made a decision in particular cases. Article (a)1. read: 'Before adopting any particularly important proposal it is

desirable that the Commission should take up the
appropriate contacts with the Government of the
Member States through the Permanent
Representatives, without this procedure
compromising the right of initiative which the
Commission derives from the Treaty.'   Article (a)2.
held that : 'Proposals and any official acts which
the Commission submits to the Council and to the
Member States are not to be made public until the
recipients have had formal notice of them and are
in possession of the texts'.(39)   In both of these
Articles, which occurred in the first section ofthe
Accords, it was the Commission's ability to pursue
what was essentially a Functionalist strategy which
was being challenged by de Gaulle: the Commission
had to be restrained from using its public
relations facilities to generate support for itself
in opposition to governments.   It was these
restraints which from the Functionalist point of
view were the more damaging achievements of French
diplomacy at Luxembourg: this point is reinforced
by the fact that very few people, even in the
Commission, really thought that the Council would
move to majority voting in 1966.   The institutional
arrangements from this perspective were seen as
procedural adjustments, necessary in order to avoid
friction later, and to make it easier for the
governments to do what they would have to do
anyway, but essentially superficial when compared
with the more fundamental task of preventing the
Commission from building its 'supranational' base
in popular attitudes and values.
     The two theoretical perspectives are also
relevant to the interpretation of the events prior
to the Luxembourg Accords.   On the one hand is the
view that de Gaulle was moved to come to the
conference table in January 1966 by such factors as
the cost of withdrawal or continuing disturbance to
French agriculture (after the July crisis, French
farmers calculated that the abandonment of the
Common Agricultural Policy would cost them about
2,500-5,000 million new Francs per year(40), and
the surprising level of support for the
pro-European candidate, Mitterand, in the
Presidential elections of Decomeber 1965 (Mitterand
had attracted sufficient support to deny de Gaulle
victory at the first ballot: he was compelled to
follow the - for him - somewhat undignified course
of action of going to a second ballot)(41).   On the
other hand, however, the Presidential elections
could also be seen as having demonstrated to de

Gaulle that even the French people were not immune
from contamination by pro-Europeanism. Mitterand's
support was, in other words, an indication to de
Gaulle that action was needed to counteract the
Commission's public relations activities. The
French nation may have been one of the irreducible
political realities of Europe, but its leaders had
the obligation to ensure that this destiny was
manifest. This obligation was reflected in the
first part of the Luxembourg Accords of January
1966, and, of course, on this interpretation of
French policy it is a mistake to attach undue
importance to the confirmation of the principle of
unanimity in the Council of Ministers.

I have argued that the progress of European
integration through the Seventies needs to be
evaluated over a rather wide range of dimensions,
which are suggested by the major theories of
gradualist integration; but that the theories do
not merely allow us to put together a more complete
picture of regional integration, but also alter the
perspective from which the picture is viewed.
Although I have assumed in this chapter that both
Functionalism and Neofunctionalism may help us to
understand the pattern of regional integration, and
may indeed suggest typical strategies for achieving
this, it should not be forgotten that David Mitrany
was opposed to the idea of developing a new
regional state in Europe, and that a Functionalist
pattern of evolution may also lead to an
end-situation which is different from that
suggested by the Neofunctionalst approach. In
brief a Functionalist order in Western Europe would
possess a high degree of socio-psychological
community and a large number of international
organisations administering common tasks. There
would be a wide range of interdependencies and a
large number of common endeavours. But there would
be no requirement for a central government: indeed
the existing governments would survive and perform
residual functions.(42) One of the implications of
Neofunctionalism, however, was that the outcome of
a regional integration process would be a new
state.

I now turn in the succeeding chapters to an
examination of the limits placed by the member
states of the Europan Communities upon the wide
range of these dimensions of regional integration.
I also attempt to judge the progress of that
integration from a variety of perspectives.

NOTES

1. David Mitrany, <u>A Working Peace System</u>, Chicago, Quadrangle Books. The volume reprints the original essay, under the same title, of 1943 with additional new essays and an <u>Introduction</u> by Hans Morgenthau.

2. The term Neofunctionalist is normally applied to those writers who criticized and developed the older Functionalist propositions. (See Karl Kaiser's use of the term in his article 'The US and the EEC in the Atlantic System: The Problem of Theory', <u>Journal of Common Market Studies</u>, June 1967). Their founding member was Ernst B. Haas, but Leon Lindberg, Lawrence Scheingold, J.P. Sewell, Lawrence Scheinman and J.S. Nye, also made significant contributions to the development of the theory.

3. Leon L. Lindberg, 'The European Community as a Political System', <u>Journal of Common Market Studies</u>, June 1976.

4. Grotius, quoted in J. Herz, <u>International Politics in the Atomic Age</u>, Columbia Paperback edition, 1962, p.50.

5. Amitai Etzioni, <u>Political Unification</u>, London, Holt, Rinehart & Winston, 1965, p.4. Etzioni's political community possesses three kinds of integration: it has a monopoly on the control of force, it has a single centre for decision-making; and it is the dominant focus of identification for members.

6. See Ernst B. Haas, <u>The Uniting of Europe</u>, Stanford University Press, 1958, pp. 30-35.

7. See Karl W. Deutsch, <u>Nationalism and Social Communication: an inquiry into the foundations of nationality</u>, the M.I.T. Press, 1953 and 1966.

8. See F. Tonnies: <u>Fundamental Concepts of Sociology: Gemeinschaft and Gesellschaft</u>, New York, 1940.

9. David Mitrany, <u>A Working Peace System</u>, p. 31.

10. See Ernst B. Haas, <u>Beyond the Nation State</u>, Stanford, 1964, Chapter 1.

11. J. Rosenstiel, 'Some Reflections on the Notion of Supranationality', <u>Journal of Common Market Studies</u>, November 1963, pp. 127-39.

12. It would, however, be inaccurate to say that Professor Haas was for all practical purposes a Federalist.

13. <u>Beyond the Nation State</u>, op. cit., p. 34.

14. Ibid., p. 34.

15. Haas stated this central hypothesis in several of his writings: see 'International Integration: The European and the Universal Process' in Dale Hekius, C.G. McLintock, Arthus L. Burns (Eds.) International Stability, Wiley, 1964, p. 230.

16. Beyond the Nation State, p. 55.

17. Ernst B. Haas, 'International Integration, the European and the Universal Process', op. cit., p. 236.

18. Ibid., p. 230.

19. See Professor Haas' restatement of Functionalism in Beyond the Nation State, pp. 47-50.

20. Ernst B. Haas, 'The Uniting of Europe and the Uniting of Latin America', Journal of Common Market Studies, June 1967, pp. 315-343.

21. Beyond the Nation State, p. 50.

22. 'International Integration, the European and the Universal Process', op. cit., p. 231.

23. Ibid. p. 233.

24. 'International Integration, the European and the Universal Process', op. cit., p. 236.

25. 'International Integration, the European and the Universal Process', op. cit., p. 237.

26. Ernst B. Haas, Beyond the Nation State, Stanford, 1964, p. 35.

27. Ernst B. Haas, 'The Joys and Agonies of Pretheorising.'

28. See Pierre Duclos 'La Politisication: Trois essais', Politique, April-June 1961.

29. David Mitrany, A Working Peace System, p. 31.

30. Rosenstiel, op. cit.

31. The older Functionalists would view power, also, as an indicator of legal competence and would distinguish this from power legitimized by a socio-psychological community; it then becomes 'authority'.

32. Karl W. Deutsch, Nationalism and Social Communication, The M.I.T. Press, 1953 and 1966, p. 105.

33. David Mitrany, A Working Peace System, pp. 121-8.

34. This analysis of the community method is not based on any single Neofunctionalist writing; the same is true of the Functionalist one which follows. Each is a projection and interpretation of a range of ideas which are contained in a number of writings.

24

35. Commission of the European Communities, Bulletin of the European Communities, Supplement 4/1972; Commission of the European Communities, European Union: Report by Leo Tindemans to the European Council, Bulletin of the European Communities, Supplement 1/76.

36. See Chapter 5. below.

37. See Chapter 7 below.

38. See Leon N. Lindberg, "Integration as a Source of Stress on the European Community System", International Organisation, Volume XX, No. 2. Spring, 1966, pp. 233-265.

39. See text of Luxembourg Accords in Sweet and Maxwell's European Community Treaties, Sweet and Maxwell, London, 1972, pp. 234-235.

40. Agence Europe, September 1, 1965.

41. See Lindberg, Loc. cit., p. 241.

42. See my account of Functionalism, in Paul Taylor and A.J.R. Groom, International Organisation: a Conceptual Approach, Frances Pinter, London, 1978.

Chapter Two

THE LIMITS OF GRADUALIST INTEGRATION

        In this chapter I evaluate the progress of
integration among the member states of the European
Communities in the 1970s in the light of the
predictions of the Neofunctionalists and those
derived from the ideas of the older Functionalists,
which I discussed in Chapter 1. My purpose is to
look at the dimensions of integration which are
stressed in the two approaches and to discuss the
limits which have been placed upon them in the
Communities' development. Integration is
understood to refer to the process whereby an
international organisation acquires responsibility
for taking an increasing number of decisions in
areas which were previously reserved to the state.
The international institution might be seen to
increase the level and scope of its authority and
to have its formal powers and working methods
correspondingly adjusted; whilst the state might be
seen to lose its capacity for independent decision
-making. The gradualist processes identified in
the two approaches are, in other words, expected to
lead to a quality of supranationalism in the
international institution, and to the erosion of
some aspects of the sovereignty of the member
states.
        Beloff wrote that 'what supranationalism
means is that there is a recognised interest within
a political grouping of several nations which is
different from, or distinguishable from, the
interests of any one of them and which thus claims
institutional expression.'(1) Such a recognition
was fundamental in the circumstances of
supranationalism; it affected the authority of the
international institution, the role allowed to it
by the states, and its methods of taking decisions.
Beloff added that 'the difficulty lies not in the

conception of policy but in its authorisation and execution.'(2) Supranationalism depended upon the states' willingness to allow the international institution a range of powers and an area of independent initiative which were commensurate with the allocated task.

There were two facets of state sovereignty on which the processes of gradualist integration impinged. The first was the facet of the exclusive competence of a government within its territorial frontiers in legal and constitutional questions which was generally understood and widely accepted as fundamental in sovereignty. In the United Kingdom it meant that laws passed by Parliament prevailed within the frontiers of that country, and that laws passed by, for instance, the French government, had no legal standing and would not be upheld by British courts. A discussion of gradualist integration should be concerned with the extent to which challenges to this exclusive competence had developed.

The second facet concerned the integrity of decision-making structures in the state - the extent to which they were insulated from pressures from outside the state which required or compelled behaviour. It is possible to conceive of circumstances in which the decision-making structures of the state are so affected or controlled by outside forces that the legal effect of exclusive competence disguises a de facto subjection to external control. The elites of one state may subscribe to an ideology which disposes them normally to follow detailed instructions from another 'government' or agency outside its frontiers. It is conceivable that the members of one government could in effect be placed in office by another government, and, habitually follow the other's instuctions because of loyalty, physical dependence, or bribery. An example of this would be the Vietnam-dominated government of Cambodia after the invasion of the mid 1970s. The exclusive competence of the government to make laws for its territory was preserved, but the integrity of the government had been so undermined that the legal forms concealed a de facto breach of sovereignty. It is conceivable that a breach of integrity of national decision-making structures could result from an accumulation of pressures and interventions from international institutions, like the IMF, or international non-governmental institutions, like the oil companies, or large foreign corporations,

like Lockheed. It is, however, extremely difficult
to judge the point at which a government's ability
to control its own affairs has been so reduced that
it could be said that it faced serious challenge to
this aspect of its sovereignty. A situation in
which more than 50% of a national budget was
allocated according to the wishes of foreign
businessmen, who were bribing national officials,
might be accepted as constituting such a challenge.
But a single intervention, such as the much
discussed letters sent to the International
Monetary Fund (IMF) by the British Government in
1967, and 1976, which allowed IMF inspection of
British Treasury activities, was surely not enough.
An increasing range of interventions in the
internal affairs of states could, however, have
implications for sovereignty which were similar to
those which followed from the placing of personnel
by an outside power, or the subjection of the
state's own personnel to an ideology through which
they could be manipulated.

The second facet of sovereignty is essentially
concerned with the degree of self containment
within national systems of procedures and
structures related to decision-making. It may be
challenged, therefore, by the range of developments
which have been placed by interdependence theorists
under the headings of transnationalism and
intergovernmentalism(3), and which were also a
primary focus of Neofunctionalism. The integrity
of decision-making is seen to be challenged by the
development of transnational interest groups,
parties, and by 'engrenage', and the like. The
first facet is, in contrast, primarily concerned
with the factors which sustain constitutional and
legal self containment, which in turn involve the
degree to which the legal system has been formally
established at the regional level, as well as the
socialization of the norms of the new system. The
latter may be indicated in mass attitudes towards
the new regional arrangements and in what Haas has
called 'authority-legitimacy transfer'.(4)

The extent to which pressures, which were
recognised in the two approaches of gradualist
integration (Neofunctionalism and Functionalism)
had been successful in increasing the level and
expanding the scope of integration in the European
Communities' institutions, is, therefore, to be
considered, first in relation to the growing
supranationalism of the Communities' institutions,
and second in relation to the two facets of

sovereignty on which they could have impinged. I
am concerned with the nature of the limits upon
these pressures; those which are recognised in both
approaches are examined in relation to the
supranational character of the central
institutions. Pressures which impinged upon the
exclusive competence of the states acquired
particular significance in the context of
functionalism, whilst those about challenges to the
integrity of national decision-making systems are
more important in the Neofunctionalist approach.
As I have shown, Functionalism was particularly
concerned with the question of attitude change in
states. In 'open' societies the loyalties of
citizens are one of the bases of the exclusive
legal competence of national governments. The
Neofunctionalists, on the other hand, focussed upon
the building of transnational regional political
systems which could challenge the integrity of the
national systems.

The questions which seem helpful in discussing
the points of resistance to these pressures and
which I consider in this chapter, - though not in
strict succession - are as follows:

1.   Concerning the extent to which the
      Communities' institutions were
      supranational.
      a.   How far could the Commission of the
            European Communities take decisions
            which were binding upon governments,
            or enforceable within their
            territories, without regard for the
            positive approval of each member
            government?
      b.   How far could the Council of
            Ministers take decisions by majority
            vote which were binding upon
            dissenting governments?
      c.   How far were the Communities
            financially independent of the
            member states? Did the Commission
            have a right to its own finance?
      d.   How far did the Commission use, and
            develop, the right to initiate
            measures of further integration
            which was given it in the Treaty of
            Rome? To what extent did the
            Commission define European policies,
            and general approaches to common
            problems?

2. Concerning the extent to which national
governments have become involved in
Communities' decision-making, - as
defined earlier - and the integrity of
the former has been challenged.
   a. How far were national civil servants
   involved with each other in the
   course of their work? How much of
   this time was spent on Community
   business?
   b. How far did the attitudes of civil
   servants reflect an expectation of
   further integration? What were the
   limits upon their preparedness to
   cooperate?
   c. How far had transnational lobbies
   and political parties developed?
   What were the limits upon their
   development?
   d. What was the scale of the resources
   at the centre as a proportion of the
   total? How valuable was the
   Regional Fund, the Social Fund and
   the Investment Fund compared with
   national resources?

3. Concerning the development of challenges
to the exclusive competence of states
within their territorial frontiers.
   a. How far were national legal systems
   penetrated by the transnational
   legal systems of the Communities?
   What was the significance of this
   penetration?
   b. How far had popular loyalties and
   expectations moved to the new
   centre? Could they form a 'security
   community'? Were they eventually
   determined by 'utilitarian'
   considerations'(5) or was there
   evidence of a sense of involvement
   in a 'great enterprise'?
   c. How far did the central institution
   acquire 'authority'?

The governing bodies of international
institutions normally have two major elements, a
group of international civil servants, and a group
of state representatives, where decisions are taken
on the basis of either unanimity or majority

voting. A third element is sometimes found: an assembly of delegates from national parliaments which support one or other of the main bodies, provide additional expertise, and in some cases try to ensure accountability. Distinctive, supranational features, have been found in each of these elements. In this chapter I am more concerned with the first two elements than with the third.

1. The powers of the institutions

In the case of the group of international civil servants factors conducive towards supranationalism are those which allow the definition and pursuit of policies which reflect the longer term common interests of member states and which transcend their short-term individual interests. Support for supranationalism is found, first, in the condition of independence of the secretariat. In the case of the European Communities the independence of the members of the High Authority and of the Commission was required by the founding Treaties of Paris and of Rome. The Treaty of Paris, which established the European Coal and Steel Community (ECSC), contained one of the few instances of the actual use in a treaty of the term supranationalism, and it is significant that it is used in the context of discussing the requirement of independence of members of the High Authority: they 'will refrain from any action incompatible with the supranational character of their duties. Each member state undertakes to respect the supranational character.'(Article 9 (ECSC). In the Treaty of Merger of April 1965, under which the High Authority of the ECSC and the Commission of the European Economic Community (EEC) and EURATOM were merged, members were still told that they should 'in the general interest of the Communities be completely independent in the performance of their duties,' (Merger Treaty, Article 10, paragraph 2); and that 'they should neither seek nor take instructions from any government or from any other body', and should refrain from any action incompatible with their duties.'(Merger Treaty, Article 10, paragraph 2). As Mathijsen has pointed out these conditions underline the requirement that the High Authority and the Commission should represent 'the Communities' general interest and must be in a position to take a stand against any government

which tries to put national interests first.(6)
The independence of the staff of the Commission
from government control was also reinforced by the
requirement that they should formally affirm their
loyalty to the organisation. This was a procedure
that was found in a number of international
institutions including the Secretariat of the
United Nations.

The Commission's task of defining a common
European interest was rightly seen by those who
drew up the Treaty of Rome as being facilitated by
a right to initiate policy. Although a right to
initiate was laid down in several places in the
Treaty, it was protected in particular by Article
149 which held that : 'Where, in pursuance of this
Treaty, the Council acts on a proposal from the
Commission, unanimity shall be required for an act
constituting an amendment to that proposal.'
Unless there was general assent, the Council could
not simply take over a Commission proposal: the
Commission was required to reconsider and return to
the Council later. Its right to initiate was
thereby protected.

But through the 1960s and 1970s the
Commission's role as the Communities' main
initiator of proposals for cooperation was
challenged and weakened as the intergovernmental
machinery became stonger. As David Coombes has
pointed out, the 1965 crisis helped to weaken the
norm-defining, initiating character of the
Commission and contributed towards the
strengthening of its administrative role.(7)
Writing in 1980, Robert Marjolin, who had himself
been a member, and Vice-President of the
Commission, concluded that the Commission had 'lost
a great deal of ground ... precisely in its role as
originator of the proposals that are debated and
decided upon by the Council of Ministers.'(8)
Marjolin argued that the main reason for this was
that increasingly the problems being discussed in
Brussels, monetary or energy problems for instance,
were outside the scope of the Treaty; and in these
fields the Commission did not enjoy the exclusive
power of making proposals which was granted to it
by the Treaty. There had been 'a change in the
objective situation'. One crucial element, of
course, was the economic recession and the
'protective' reaction of the governments.
Initiatives now more frequently sprang from the
Council of Ministers or from the European Councils
of Heads of Government, which were incorporated

formally as a Community institution in 1974. I
would add, however, that the method of work between
the Commission and the Council remained in the late
1970s in its procedural aspects very much as it had
been in the early 1960s: the Commission was now
more frequently asked to work on initiatives that
came from outside itself, but then developed and
sent them to the Council in the way which I
describe in Chapter 4. Behind this procedural
similarity, however, lay a significant change in
the distribution of powers among the Communities'
institutions. Marjolin concluded that 'the balance
of power within the Community has shifted
appreciably during the late 1960s and the 1970s.
The decline of the "supranational principle" went
further. As a matter of fact I should stop using
an expression which does not correspond to any kind
of reality any more.'(9)

The Commission seemed less capable of defining
and projecting 'supranational' proposals: it became
less concerned with schemes which reflected a
general European interest and more with interests
defined by governments. This change represented a
departure from the tendency in intra-Communities
bargaining in the mid- and early- Sixties which had
been labelled by the Neofunctionalists as
'up-grading the common interest'.(10) Increasingly
the Commission allowed its proposals to be drawn
into the diplomatic process between governments at
an early stage: such a tendency had been noticed in
1971(11) but, as I argue below, in the mid-1970s,
it was taken much further.(12) By that time the
Commission's role as initiator, and norm-defining
activities which though linked are by no means
identical - had very considerably declined.

A further condition of independence of the
Secretariat and one which may be of great
importance in allowing it to strive actively for
the general interest is a measure of budgetary
independence. In the case of the European Coal and
Steel Community this independence was established
from the beginning by allowing the Community the
right to its own finance from a tax directly levied
on the coal and steel industries of member states.
In the case of the EEC the acquiring of a right to
independent finance took a considerable number of
years: the EEC and EURATOM depended upon the
contributions of member governments until the mid
1970s. It was only with the Council of Ministers'
decisions of 21 April, 1970, that steps were taken
towards the granting to these two institutions of

their 'own resources'.(13)   The financial activity
of the Communities may be conveniently examined in
this context from three major perspectives; that of
the raising of finance, that of the disposal, or
spending of the resources that are raised, and that
of the regulation of financial and related
activities in states.   In the raising of finance it
might be thought that the Communities had made some
progress towards the establishment of supranational
authority in that they possessed a right to their
'own resources' - <u>resource propre</u> - according to
the terms of the Council Regulation of April
1970.(14)   The states seemed to have agreed to a
system under which the central 'government' had a
measure of financial autonomy: these resources
belonged in law to the Communities rather than to
the member states.

There were, however, a number of differences
between the Communities' way of raising resources
to finance those operations with which they had
been entrusted, and the way in which this was done
in most systems of government where there was an
effective central power.   In the latter the
principle generally was that the centre had a
greater capacity to raise revenue than was strictly
necessary for the successful perfomance of the
tasks allocated to it.   In the USA where expression
of this principle is rather weak by the standard of
modern federations, the Federal Government had the
backing of the Supreme Court in its use of the
power to raise taxes in the general welfare in
order to finance activities which were reserved to
the states, such as social welfare, agricultural
support or industrial reorganisation.(15)   In other
federations, such as Canada or Australia, the
centre was even more powerful in that its tax laws
were regarded as having priority over regional law
which meant that the centre could by this means
prevent the regions from performing those tasks
which had been allocated to it under the
constitution.   In the US, though 'taxing power is
subordinate to the distribution of power laid down
in the Constitution'(16), the centre could in
effect use its power to raise resources to get the
states to do what it thought was in the general
welfare.

The revenue raising powers of the Communities
fell short of this in one crucial respect.   The
centre had a right to its own resources but it had
no clear right to resources which were adequate to
perform those tasks which had been required of it.

It could be said that the revenue raising powers of the Communities fell rather behind the rather limited range of tasks it needed to perform. The Communities regularly needed to collect resources above that proportion of its own resources to which it had an undisputed right, because commitments on some rather large items were very difficult to evaluate precisely; the main item of this character related to market interventions in the context of the common agricultural policy. In this area pricing arrangements and the level of spending were subject to unpredicatable political forces, and, of course such variables as the size of the harvest. The guarantees remained largely 'open-ended' and to that extent out of effective control. The Communities were, therefore, a victim of frequent Supplementary Budgets under which the Council allocated additional revenue up to the total agreed proportion of VAT.(17) These supplementary budgets should be seen as being made up of grants from national exchequers, although they were nominally 'own resources', being a proportion of the VAT which had been allocated, rather than as an element of supranational finance: it was in practice up to the Council to decide how much of these so-called own resources should be allocated to the Community's Budget. Each time they occurred they ran the risk of a veto by one of the member governments of the Council: they were in fact a measure of the dependence of the centre upon the regions. This procedure was in sharp contrast to the pattern which was normal where there was an independent central authority, where, as Wheare has pointed out, 'general governments receive little by way of grants from the regional governments whether compulsory or voluntary.'(18) Indeed, modern federations have in general shown a tendency towards the marked expansion of the scale of voluntary grants from the centre to the regions. The problem in the Communities was compounded, as Denton pointed out, by the fact that the scale of own resources in relation to commitments, was at best uncertain. The receipts from the Common External Tariff were likely to decline, because of a worldwide lowering of tariffs, and agricultural levies fluctuated wildly. Indeed in the early 1980s it looked as if receipts from the agreed maximum rate of VAT, 1%, would soon not be sufficient to cover all Communities expenditure.(19) It was likely that states would need to increase their own direct financing of

Communities activities within their frontiers.
The member states of the Communities were
jealous guardians of the principle that their right
to finance their own activities should take
precedence over that of the centre. Accordingly
there existed in the Communities no federal actor
which had the right to raise new taxes: the Council
of Ministers must be regarded in this context as
the agent of the states, rather than of the centre.
The centre did not have the power to <u>collect</u> its
own resources, but rather relied upon member states
for this, and paid them 10% of the common external
tariff revenue to cover the administrative costs.
('The powers of tax involves it may be assumed the
powers to lay taxes and also the power to collect
these taxes.')(20) and governments strictly
controlled the Communities' right to borrow and
invariably ensured that any funds thus obtained
were placed under inter-governmental control rather
than 'supranational' control. They insisted that
the loans raised in New York by the Commission
according to the scheme proposed by Commissioner
Ortoli, approved in 1978, should be placed under
the control of the Finance Ministers rather than of
the Commission.(See Chapter 6)The Communities were
also not permitted any form of direct taxation such
as income tax.
Views upon the way in which the resources of
the Communities should be spent indicated, if
anything, a move away from supranational principles
in the 1970s. In general US federal government was
not subject to any specific principle governing
shares of federal resources say, for welfare
provision, among the regions. There had emerged
during the first decade in the European Communities
a corresponding principle that discussion of
national shares was '<u>non-communautaire</u>'.(21)
Unfortunately, from the point of view of an
emergent federalism, the British government played
probably the decisive part in challenging this
development, when during its re-negotiation of the
Terms of Accession in 1975 it fought for the
principle of <u>juste retour</u>. At that stage this meant
that there would be a limit upon gross
contributions to the Communities fixed according to
the relative size of the gross national product of
the states. The weakening of the economies of some
member states in the mid-late 1970s led to the
extension of this principle to that of seeking a
balance of net contributions to the Communities;
that is, the states seemed to demonstrate a wish to

balance as far as possible what they got out
against what they put in. For instance: 'the UK
refusal in 1976 to allow the green pound to be
devalued, despite the wide gap that opened up
between this rate and the falling value of sterling
during that year, was supported by the argument
that since other aspects of the Community were
unfair to the UK, it was proper to claw back some
of the economic costs by taking advantage of this
somewhat accidental aspect of Community
agri-monetary arrangements.'(22) Other states
showed an increasing propensity to behave in a
similar fashion, so that by 1979 some commentators began to argue that the whole system of fair
national shares should be explored and explicit
criteria laid down.

It is generally accepted that the centre's
right to establish the framework of rules within
which finance, taxation, and monetary activities
are handled throughout the Union is a fundamental
aspect of federation. These rules refer to such
matters as control of the currency, regulation of
banking activities, and adjusting the various
regulators of economic activity such as interest
rates. It is apparent, however, that such a system
did not exist in the European Communities, and that
in so far as it was regulated as a unit this was a
result of the coordination of a de-centralised
system based upon national economies. Though this
point is fundamental it is not necessary to explore
it in detail here. But it is relevant in that the
lack of regulatory powers reinforced the centre's
dependence upon the states for its own finance in a
number of ways. The regulation of national
economies is naturally a consequence of the
continuing determination of governments to place
national economic interests ahead of those of the
collectivity of the Communities. Marjolin pointed
out that 'for years there were at every Common
Market meeting never-ending discussions and a
number of resolutions about the coordination of
economic financial and monetary policy, without any
concrete result to show.'(23) The rate at which
the size of the Communities Budget might be
expected to grow was essentially dependent upon the
calculations of the economic interest of national
governments, rather than of those of any central
agency in the light of general welfare as reflected
in the allocation of new tasks to the centre. As
Denton has suggested, the proposal that the EEC
budget should be allowed to grow by 2-2 1/2%, which

was recommended as a first step towards a federal budget in the McDougall Report was unlikely to be accepted by national governments: it was likely to lead to an increase in public expenditure of around 1% at national and Communities level combined(24), at a time when, because of adverse economic circumstances, states were reluctant to accept even this small additional burden and were determined to reduce the proportion of gross national product passing through national budgets.

Methods of exercising control in international institutions, in committees of intergovernmental representatives or international civil servants, are frequently thought to be good indicators of supranationalism. Reynolds wrote that 'the word supranational is of relatively recent origin and refers to institutions which have been created for the performance of specific functions, and which have power to take decisions binding on the members whether they have participated in the decision or not.'(25) He refered to the High Authority of ECSC as one example of such decision-making, and also the Committee of Ministers of Western European Union, which could, in certain circumstances, prevent, by majority voting, the United Kingdom from reducing the level of her forces in Western Germany below an agreed level. The voting arrangements of the Council of Ministers of the EEC, according to the original form of the Rome Treaty, would also qualify as evidence of that institution's supranationalism. There are, therefore, two situations in which a member could be said not to have participated in a decision taken by an international institution: the first would be when a binding decision is taken by a group of international civil servants; the second is when the decision is taken by a committee of representatives of national governments according to a system of majority voting. Conversely, member states participate in a decision when it is taken by a committee of governmental representatives on the basis of unanimity or on the basis of a system which gives them the right to say whether they will accept a decision which had been taken by other members. A binding decision is one which is not only taken according to the agreed forms and procedures, and is, therefore, binding in the legal sense, but is also effective in the sense that it is carried out.

Executive committees of international civil servants and of government representatives may take decisions which have two major kinds of effect: either the decision upholds a framework of policies or arrangements already approved by governments, for instance, in a founding treaty, or it initiates new arrangements and policies. The High Authority's decision-making role was the quasi-legal one of supporting arrangements already approved by governments rather than of initiating new elements of the framework. The High Authority was created by the Treaty of Paris and enforced the rules of that Treaty which had been laid down in some detail by the signatory states(26): the Treaty of Paris was, because of its completeness, called a Treaty of Laws by international lawyers. The Commission of the European Communities also possessed a power of this kind in that governments had agreed that the institutions should act directly in relation to individuals and groups within the state without immediate supervision by state authorities in agreed areas (the legal framework and its implications are discussed more fully in Chapter 9). The High Authority acted to impose the rules of the common market in coal, steel and scrap, as agreed by the states which signed the Treaty of Paris. Even in this role, however, the record of the High Authority was rather mixed: it failed, for instance, to obtain in the 1950s the rearrangement of West German coal selling cartels which seemed necessary to the proper working of the common market in coal. The Commission of the European Communities also took decisions independently only in areas already agreed by member governments.

In the Rome Treaty, however, the member states had agreed to be bound by qualified majorities in the Council, even in making decisions which would have the effect of creating new rules and policies: it was not merely a matter of imposing rules which had been agreed previously on the basis of unanimity, but of making new ones. For instance, according to Article 43, Regulations regarding the introduction of the Common Agricultural Policy were to be made on the basis of a qualified majority after the first two phases i.e. after 1966. (The implications of this Article were explicitly altered in the Luxembourg Accord between the member states in January 1966 which ended the 1965 crisis in the European Communities.) Article 69 allowed qualified majority regulations to be made in abolishing restrictions on the movement of capital between members in the third transitional phase and later; and Article 87 allowed the Council to act on the basis of a qualified majority in implementing Articles 85 and 86 (rules governing monopolies and cartels), three years after the entry into force of the Treaty of Rome. Had such procedures been used they would have represented a considerably more powerful form of supranationalism than that described in the Treaty of Paris: member states would have been obliged to accept measures of which they disapproved which filled out and developed the rules to which they had unanimously consented during the negotiating and signing of the Treaty. The Treaty of Rome was to be described as a 'framework Treaty'(27): it contained provision for filling out the framework of the Treaty, and in effect for completing and ratifying new treaties according to a system of qualified majority voting among member governments.

Member states, and, in particular, France, hesitated to accept this form of supranationalism. The French were the main instrument of plunging the Communities into a crisis in 1965 which was about the financial arrangements relating to the agricultural policy but also concerned the question of whether the Communities would really move towards majority voting in the Council and thereby incorporate a principle of supranationalism. They withdrew from the Communities' major institutions for a few months in part because President de Gaulle was anxious to avoid any further accretion of power to the Commission. One consequence of his action was the Luxembourg Accord of January 1966, according to which the member states accepted that important votes in the Council of Ministers would continue to be taken on the basis of unanimity. (See discussion of this in Chapter 1.) When the British joined in 1973, the principles of this Agreement were endorsed, for instance, in a statement by the Prime Minister, Mr. Heath to the House of Commons.(28) In this way the British when they joined the Communities' reinforced the model of the Communities' institutions on which President de Gaulle had insisted. Although a decision was taken in December 1974 at the Summit Meeting in Paris to return to majority voting wherever possible, this never amounted to anything: states made sure that nothing of any real importance could be decided on this basis, and consensus remained the rule. The Luxembourg Accord proved to be a realistic and durable arrangement.

2.   National decision-making and the Communities

I now turn to an examination of the extent to
which national decision-making was affected by
involvement in the European Communities. I am here
focussing on aspects of national decision-making
which the Neofunctionalists argued would be
modified during the integration process. As I have
pointed out, these aspects were placed by other
scholars under the headings of transnationalism and
transgovernmentalism and included changes in the
structure and procedures of interest groups,
political parties and civil servants. Limits upon
changes in these areas represented points of
effective resistance by the European states to the
major integrative dynamics which had been put
forward by Professors Haas, Lindberg, et al.(29)
Andrew Shonfield, though not a Neofunctionalist,
was also impressed by the extent of the
developments in these areas in the early 1970s. He
wrote that 'the dramatic improvement in
communications, the greatly increased mobility of
people and money, and also the huge concentration
of corporate power in the hands of international
businesses, taken together, demand the
establishment of a new dimension of international
public power ... at the same time there is a
parallel movement, less
obvious, but beginning to be significant, among the
associations of private and professional persons -
farmers, trade unionists, certain scientists, even
specialist professional civil servants, who find
that the natural links for much of what they wish
to accomplish are with their professional
colleagues abroad rather than with their own
national governments. The transnational lobbies
that are thus created look for some international
political counterpart'. 'Now I call this amalgam
of private groups and agencies transcending
national frontiers, together with the official
political agencies that have been established in
and around the European Community
supranational.'(30) Shonfield also pointed out
that these structures did not stand above
governments, but included parts of them.
The structures which developed across national
frontiers in Western Europe were certainly numerous
(about 300 examples of one type of structure,
interest groups, was counted in Brussels)(31) but
groups which were active in attempting to effect
the allocation of values still concentrated their

efforts at the national level, and had developed
rather weak umbrella organistions at the European
level. The term 'supranational', as applied to
such groups, was perhaps a misnomer in that they
were not frameworks within which national groups
worked out common positions which were then sought
within the Community system, and the national
groups had not refocussed their 'expectations and
loyalties' upon the international organisation.
Rather the Euro-groups were a forum for exchanging
information and helped national groups to define
the positions which they would follow in relations
with their own governments in national capitals or
with their governments' representaives in Brussels.
They also provided advice - though not always
agreed within the group - to the Commission as the
latter worked out its proposals. Frequently,
however, groups failed to coordinate their
positions: as Harrison pointed out, interest groups
in contemporary Western Europe often had leaders
who were 'part of a national leadership context'.
'The internationalisation of national group
leadership is not likely to be any easier than the
internationalisation of political leadership.'(32)
Having a presence in Brussels, and having a
transnational dimension, helped them to keep in
touch with developments, however, and allowed them
to exert pressure at a number of levels, and, if
circumstances allowed, in cooperation with groups
in other member states. But the interest groups
did not push strongly for integration in Brussels
or focus their energies primarily upon the European
institutions. Rather they reflected in their
structures and procedures the distribution of power
in the Communities and did not push to change it.
This tendency was reinforced by the small scale of
the funds available at the Communities level,
compared with national ones, which were available
to the groups. As I point out below (chapter 6)
the scale of funds available through the Regional
Fund, for instance, was very small compared with
that of the various states.
     Averyt pointed out that 'in spite of much
Community rhetoric, interest groups' representation
(whether Euro-group or national interest group) is
not institutionalised where the most important
matters are discussed.'(33) For instance, the
group of European food producers, COPA was excluded
from the crucial discussions among governments
about food price levels and was not represented in
the Management Committees which were set up to

supervise the market in particular agricultural
products.(34)   In some ways the Commission had a
rather ambivalent attitude towards the European
groups: on the one hand it had insisted on
consulting only with the European level groups and
actively encouraged their growth.   On the other
hand, its own proposals such as the Mansholt Plan
on agricultural reform of 1969, were frequently
very divisive in their effect on the Euro-groups.
Given that the groups themselves were already
divided, it was very difficult for the Commission
to act to encourage unity: the chances were that a
more active, initiating Commission would have had
an even more divisive affect on the European
interest groups.   Averyt added that even where
groups had established a reasonable degree of
cohesion 'the administrative agency (the
Directorate General in the Commission) is rarely
envisioned by itself or by the clientele group to
have the sole supreme aim of furthering the group's
interests.'(35)   The perception was that the
interest of the group might indeed by compromised
in new proposals for integration.   Cohesion in the
European group was not, therefore, a concomittant
of sympathy for the Commission and support for
integration.   And the Commission, on the other
hand, was anxious to avoid getting too close to a
group and thereby reducing its flexibility in
choice of policy.
     It might have been expected that interest
groups 'representation' would have been
institutionalised in the European Communities'
policy-making process through the Economic and
Social Committee (ESC).   The founders had intended
to involve social and economic groups in the
policy-making process, and the ESC was established
as one of the formal institutions of the
Communities with representatives of the employers,
of workers and of other social and economic
interests.   The ESC was, however, relatively
unsuccessful in representing non-governmental group
interests, because the other institutions were not
obliged to take account of its views, and because
they were only required to consult with it on a
limited range of issues.   Indeed it was not until
1974 that the Committee won the right to put
forward proposals on matters other than those which
were specifically named as requiring consultation
in the Treaty of Rome.   The members of the
Committee were also asked to serve in a personal
capacity rather than as representatives of the

groups to which they belonged. They were appointed for a four-year period by governments and this would suggest that they were liable to be people who would be unlikely to adopt a challenging stance in relation to their governments: in effect, the Economic and Social Committee was a quango.(36) The Committee was also faced with a procedural problem in that it tended to be consulted only at a late stage in the evolution of a Commission proposal or a Council decision, at which point it was usually too late to introduce any changes which the Committee might have recommended.

Lodge and Herman noted that after the Committee had acquired the right to initiate proposals in December 1974 it began to pronounce on more salient issues, for instance, on questions concerning grand economic policy in the Communities and in member states, as opposed to the rather technical opinions (e.g. on food additives, dangerous substances and so on) which had been its main product earlier. But, 'notwithstanding, the ESC's role remains minimal and the ESC recognizes that the internal procedures facilitating the emission of its own initiative opinions are convoluted and need refining.'(37) The ESC did not emerge therefore as the institution through which non-governmental interests could be fed into the Communities' system. There were a formidable range of difficulties in the way of strengthening the position of the ESC: these included not only the problem of obtaining agreement among the groups about questions of greater political sensitivity, but also - perhaps surprisingly - the ambivalent attitude of the Communities' institutions, including the Commission, towards developing its role. Cooperation seemed closest, and the interest of the groups most effective, in relation to technical, specialist questions.

In the 1970s, however, there was a noticeable expansion of the range of consultations within the Communities about ways of coping with the worsening economic situation and in particular, coping with inflation and the problems of unemployment. These consultations affected in particular the so-called 'social partners' in the form of the group which represented the employers, UNICE, and the workers, chiefly in the form of the European Trades Union Congress (ETUC). In 1975, for instance, the trade union groups decided that they would take part in the discussions of the so-called Tripartite Committee within the EEC which involved representatives of government, labour and management. The trade unions had previously opposed their participation in consultations of this type at the Communities level. In a number of meetings in the late 1970s rather bland recommendations on counter-inflationary policy, and on employment policy, were agreed, though these had little impact on policy at the European level. The Unions and management seemed to have some sense that their economic problems could be tackled effectively at the regional level, but in practice hesitated about going much further than orchestrating their attempts to influence their national governments. Nevertheless there was a significant expansion of the mechanisms for European level consultation. Kirchner commented, however, upon the 'inability of the Trade Unions to narrow sufficiently their national ideological political differences or to balance economic needs with European trade union principles in order to force the issue'.(38) ETUC was able to make a negative point by demonstrating the increasing concern of its members for their difficulties in the late 1970s when it organised a European day of action on 5th April 1978. 'By work stoppages, demonstrations, assemblies and special meetings in eighteen European countries, workers demonstrated their anxiety and determination in the face of the grave unemployment situation.'(39)

Trade Unions were also moved towards organising themselves at the regional level in order to cope with the activities in relation to labour of multi-national companies. Although regional coordination committees were established in some multinational corporations, such as Philips, Siemens, Volkswagen and Ford, effective regional action, for instance in collective bargaining or company-wide strikes, seemed to be rather distant. Kirchner concluded that 'most observers of transnational collective bargaining appear to agree on two characteristics. Firstly an attenuated form of international collective bargaining will probably develop on a regional level within the European Communities ... Secondly, it will not occur in the immediate future.'(40) Despite the increasing frequency of consultations about economic problems among the social partners in the late 1970s, this seemed to have no implications for the level of regional economic management among the member states of the European Communities, and consultations within the groups, such as ETUC, did not succeed in overcoming national differences.

But one interesting illustration of the way in which states imposed limits upon the Communities' role concerned the governments' and managements' refusal in the late 1970s to concede the unions' demands for effective negotiations on wages and conditions of employment in the tripartite Standing Committee on Employment, on which governments, trade unions, employers organisations and the Commission were represented. The unions had been reluctant to join this Committee, which was a Committee of the Council of Ministers, though they did so in 1975; but in the late 1970s they increasingly employed the strategy of attempting to use it as a framework for negotiation, rather than as a forum for discussion of intentions and principles. Governments and management consistently refused to become embroiled in this kind of activity at the Communities level – much to the unions' annoyance. The techniques which they used to reduce pressure upon them to do this included circulating papers for discussion before the meetings so that they had in effect been agreed before they took place, and not taking minutes of discussions or issuing any kind of communique: the only report or resume produced was in the form of the personal conclusions of the President of the Committee. He was normally a government official appointed by the government which held the Presidency of the Council of Ministers. The trade unions became increasingly irritated with these procedures, and with their failure to achieve their objective, and it seemed to some close observers that the tripartite approach at the Communities level was unlikely to survive for long.(41)

The experience of the European Communities, therefore, did not coincide with the expectations of Neofunctionalists that there would be a steady consolidation of European interest groups at the European level and a decline in the position of national ones. Indeed, the Commission found that in practice it became increasingly difficult to confine its consultations to Community level groups: national organizations had to be brought into the policy-making process. Indeed the distinctiveness of national groups was in some ways sharpened by the integration process: not only did national groups sometimes use the Communities' framework as another context within which to put pressure on their own governments, but the transnational links and the integration process itself helped to highlight the differences between the interests of the groups in the various national settings. National interest groups acquired their own direct representation at the Communities' level, though governments formally dominated the individual representatives: the tendency towards the building of transnational groups seemed by the 1970s to have been balanced against pressures towards the preservation of national groups.

Another kind of transnational organisation in the Communities, which I now discuss briefly, were the transnational party organisations. By the late 1970s these were of two major types. The oldest were the party groups in the European Parliament, of which there were six in 1980: Socialists, Christian Democrats, Liberals, Conservatives, Communists, and Progressive Democrats. (There was also a seventh group of independents.) They dominated the organisation of the work of the Assembly in the Committees and Plenary Meetings, tended to vote together rather frequently, and were the channel of financial support for the activities of members. Their development quite early on in the history of the European Assembly had indeed been hailed by many commentators as a major step towards the introduction of supranational party organisations. The second type was the party federations of which there were three principle examples, established largely in response to the prospect of direct elections to the European Parliament, which had been agreed in December 1974 at the Paris Summit, and which took place in the summer of 1979. These were the Confederation of Socialist Parties of the European Community, established in 1974, the Federation of Liberal and Democratic Parties of the European Community, (ELD), and the European Peoples Party (EPP) which involved Christian Democratic groups, which were both established in 1976. These groups held regional conferences and established small central offices. They helped the national parties during the direct elections of 1979, but did not fight the elections as European parties: the ELD was the more active of the three in coordinating and organising the campaigns of the national parties, but in all cases, it was the national parties themselves that dominated the campaigns.(42) In the late 1970s there remained various uncertainties about the future development of transnational groups: it seemed unlikely that they would emerge as European parties, and the corresponding groups in the European Parliament insisted upon maintaining their own identity.

The conclusion seemed unavoidable that the transnational party organisations were rather marginal. The Pridhams concluded that 'the one area where some breakthrough could occur in their acquisition of a more political role at the European level would be in the event of a uniform electoral law throughout the EEC, necessitating greater European coordination in the next elections for the European Parliament'.(43) Since such a development was unlikely the prospect for the party federations was not promising. The difficulty, of course, was essentially that the transnational parties had no obvious constituency. Issues were defined at the national level, and were understood by electorates essentially in the national political context.

The weakness of the European parties was essentially that of the European political system: there was an obvious chicken and egg problem in that European parties were unlikely to develop until there were European institutions with real powers, but real powers were unlikely to be granted to the central institutions in the absence of European interests and European constituencies. Indeed, in the absence of the latter, any increase in the powers of the centre were likely to be accompanied by an increasing challenge to the cohesion of transnational party organisations. In the late 1970s this difficulty also confronted the 'supranational' party organisations which had emerged in the European Assembly. National parties, particularly when they formed the government at the national level, were likely to attempt to strengthen their control over the transnational groups if new powers were in fact extended to the European Assembly. Indeed, the party groups developed in the 1960s in large part because of the relative powerlessness of that institution: they could be allowed to go their own way where they had little political significance. Conversely, greater powers in the Assembly would provoke national parties into creating stronger controls over the European groups. The positive correlation between the development of European interests, European structures, and powers, could be very easily upset if one moved ahead of the other. In this context the restrictions placed upon the transfer of further powers to the Assembly by the Danish and British Parliaments when they approved the legislation facilitating direct elections, and by the French Supreme Court, was seen to reflect a realistic appreciation of the difficulties of moving towards a higher level of integration in the Communities in this context in the mid 1970s. The limits upon the development of transnational party groups were another manifestation of the defensive shell of the state in the face of incursions from the European Communities in the decade.

The development of a system of transnational structures encourages the process of <u>legitimizing</u> the values of the regional institution. The arrangements mentioned by Shonfield encouraged the acceptance of goals which could be defined as 'European', into the political cultures of member states: the European solution was something which had become a generally acceptable option, even though it did not always prevail. It was possible for the bureaucrats in European states to consider 'general interest' solutions without putting themselves in danger of being thought to be 'selling out' and by the mid-1970s there was considerable evidence of 'complex interdependence' between the governments and administrations of member states. A large number of civil servants and politicians contacted colleagues in corresponding ministries in other states, or in Brussels, as part of the routine processes of decision-making. It was reported in the late 1970s that French and German administrations regularly exchanged senior civil servants(44): they were allowed to experience each other's work situation, though the nature of the restrictions placed upon their involvement was hard to discover. It is easy to overlook the remarkable character of this development. Conventions in communication had developed in the Communities between member countries themselves, which only a short while before would have been judged as a betrayal of the sacred interests of the separate nations.

Various pieces of evidence illustrated these developments and the limits upon them in structures and values in Western Europe. The picture of national bureaucrats presented by Feld and Wildgen's statistics was that national bureaucrats preferred specific or limited forms of integration;(45) a substantial group were, however, opposed to political union and rather resented long-term assignment to the Communities.(46)

One fear expressed by the bureaucrats was that if powers were shifted to Brussels they would lose the close relationship which they had developed with organised groups (clientele) in their own states.(47) But, although only around 5% of the respondents had been attached to the European Civil Service or had worked in the national delegations in Brussels, around a third (32%) had been involved in expert group activities in Brussels. This was one measure of the development of engrenage among the administrations in the European Communities. 45% of the national respondents considered, however, that any assignment to the Community would damage their careers.(48) Feld and Wildgen concluded that the limits imposed by bureaucrats upon their commitment to integration were explicable largely in terms of organisation pressures: they were seen to confirm the arguments of inter alia, Graham Allison.

Mennis and Sauvant illustrated the acceptance of the legitimacy of European solutions in their study of German business elite attitudes: they wrote that 'there are differences of opinion regarding the European Community, but for the most part they concern the degree of regional participation preferred and not the issue of the desirability or legitimacy of European integration itself'(49); 'the issue of "whether or not" Western European integration is probably a dead one'.(50) At the same time, though, German elites supported Europe because it served their current interests and rewarded material and value expectations defined in the existing national settings.(51) The view that European goals had been legitimized among the original Six (this, of course, does not mean that they were always thought to be correct) was also supported by the fact that the issue of membership in the European Communities played little part in national elections in the original six member states after the mid-1960s. It should be noted, though, that among the states which acceded to the European Communities in 1973, the question of 'whether or not membership' was by no means a dead one, especially in Britain and Denmark. The proposals of the Commission were accorded a far lower degree of legitimacy among elite groups, and the authority of the central institutions was more frequently disparaged.

Evidence from the attitudes and behaviour of administrators suggested that though there had been remarkable changes, which were indeed captured in

Keohane and Nye's concept of complex interdependence, there were nevertheless definite limits placed upon their commitment and involvement. Engrenage was by no means the linear process, involving positive feedback, which had been implied by the Neofunctionalists. The learning process proceeded to the point at which fears about the undermining of the role of the national organisation, and about career prospects, were raised. The same kind of fears probably arose, as Harrison implied(52) among other national elites. Integration in this context seemed in the 1970s to reach a plateau beyond which it was very difficult to travel.

3. Challenges to the member state's exclusive competence

I now turn to an examination of the challenges to the exclusive competence of states within their territorial frontiers. I do not mean to imply that such challenges have been effective, or that they have any necessary consequences for sovereignty. But there have been pressures which have been recognised by a number of authors as having implications for sovereignty which are conveniently examined as a group. I avoid the thorny question of how powerful they need to be, or what precisely needs to happen before sovereignty in the sense of the possession of an exclusive right to legislate has been ceded. The most obvious form of challenge to sovereignty is, however, the development of a rival legal system which has priority over the municipal law of the state within its frontiers. In a second form it consists of changes in attitudes at the popular level which indicate an increasing preparedness to accept the authority of the regional government, even if this clashes with the national one. This second form of the challenge to the exclusive competence of government touches on some of the arguments in the classic debate on sovereignty such as those contained in John Austin's Lectures on Jurisprudence.(53) In this case there is a general refocussing of attitudes and expectations. This might have the consequence of, for instance, transferring responsibility to the new centre to act in the event of a crisis. It involves the establishment of a kind of metaphysical relationship between government and people such as that which was characteristic of the Gaullist view of sovereignty.

There are, however, at least two other models of attitude change at the mass level though the links between these models are by no means clear. First there may be a movement towards what Karl Deutsch has called a <u>security community</u>, in which there is no refocussing of loyalties and expectations, but nevertheless a perception of the increasing unlikelihood of the use of violence as a means of settling conflicts between the peoples in the community.(54)   Consequences and illustrations of this would include the disappearance of military planning to cope with a possible attack by the other side, as in relations between Canada and the United States, or in Scandinavia, and the general weakening of restraints upon the movements of peoples and items across the common frontier. Secondly is a commitment to the common endeavour based upon utilitarian calculations: association with a particular people or organisation is seen to be developed and maintained because it is thought to bring specific practical advantages. This model of mass attitude change is, of course, quite different from that which could sustain a transfer of sovereignty or the development of a security community. I should stress again that I am not arguing here that these various models have any necessary causal relationship with each other.

The one extant example of the setting up of a rival legal system within the state was, of course, that of the European Communities, although lawyers were by no means agreed on how far this constituted a threat to national sovereignty (see Chapter 9 below). It was clear, however, that the member states of the European Communities accepted that law made by the institutions of the European Communities in Brussels should have direct effect in their territories: communities law was followed by domestic courts without the requirement of any special act of approval by national governments or national assemblies. Furthermore, under the terms of the Treaty of Paris (see, for example, articles 41, 42, 43, 44 and 92) and of the Treaty of Rome (article 177) it was the Court of the Communities which met at Luxembourg which was the final court of appeal on Communities questions and which acted as interpreter of the Treaties. It was not just that Communities laws had direct effect, but governments were also thought to have lost their right to decide how those laws were to be applied and interpreted. In the event of clashes between domestic law and Communities law, furthermore,

domestic courts were to give precedence to
Communities Law (in the UK according to section 2
(4) European Communities Act). In order to ensure
compliance with communities law, institutions such
as the High Authority and the Commission were given
extensive powers under the founding treaties: the
High Authority had a particularly wide range of
powers to fine firms which broke the rules of the
ECSC (see articles 65 and 66) and 'decisions of the
High Authority which impose a pecuniary obligation
shall be enforceable ... Enforcement may be
suspended only by a decision of the Court' (of the
ECSC)(article 92). The Commission could also act
directly, without the legal intervention of
national governments, in areas such as those
covered by articles 85 and 86 (EEC) on cartels.
concentrations and abuse of dominant position. It
was this unique character of the law of the
Communities, together with the powers of Community
institutions to enforce and interpret that law,
which some lawyers considered to be the most
important 'supranational' element of the
Communities.(55)

There were, however, various difficulties in
the way of evaluating implications for the
sovereignty of states of this penetration of
national legal systems by the Communities, though
the very existence of such difficulties was some
measure of the challenge to traditional ideas about
sovereignty. I discuss these difficulties in some
detail in Chapter 9. The main problem, however,
was that as governments and national assemblies at
various points in the establishment of the basic
agreements, and in the drawing up of the detailed,
day to day, decisions, agreed to be bound, they
could equally disagree to be bound – they could
take back what they had given and, the argument
ran, this did not amount to a breach of
sovereignty. The procedures were novel, the
Community legal system was indeed unique, and might
be justifiably called supranational, but it was
still an expression of the states' adjustment to
new conditions: it served them, at their
discretion. In this argument, again, the
supranational elements helped states to survive
rather than placed them in new integrated
structures.

There was, however, a contradiction between
the appearance in contemporary Western Europe that
the exclusive competence of states had been
undermined by the Communities' legal system – and

national sovereignty therefore breached - and the
various legal safeguards to which states could in
theory resort if that legal system displeased them.
One way of resolving the contradictions was
suggested by the idea of 'entrenchment'(56): The
safeguards remained as possibilities but resort to
them was thought to have become increasingly
unlikely because of the accumulation of adjustments
in national laws and habits of law-making to take
account of the Communities' legal system. The
latter was, therefore, entrenched in the national
legal system; it became increasingly difficult,
though legally perfectly possible, to revise the
mass of national legislation so that it could be
separated from Communities law. Another way of
resolving the contradictions between the appearance
of a breach of sovereignty, such as was suggested
by the penetration of national legal systems by the
legal system of the Communities, and the existence
of continuing legal safeguards for state
governments and assemblies was, as I have
suggested, the refocussing of popular loyalties
away from national governments towards
international institutions. In this situation
sovereignty could be said to have been lost by the
state, and the supranational character of the
international institution strengthened as a direct
challenge to the state's survival, by the
reluctance of citizens to obey national law and
their willingness to obey the 'law' of the
international institution. The contradiction was
thus resolved in favour of the international
institution by removing from the state an essential
element in its sovereignty: the loyalty of its
citizens. The exclusive competence of the state to
make laws for its own territory was challenged not
directly by external intervention, but from within
by a weakening of its authority.

The pattern of attitudes towards European
integration and the European institutions in the
1970s suggested that the states were not in much
danger of losing their popular support. In the
original Six, as I have pointed out, there was
consistently good support for advanced schemes for
integration, though even this declined somewhat in
the late 1970s. About 60% of citizens were
prepared to support the transfer of greater power
to the Assembly, with somewhat stronger support in
Italy, where, as Rabier showed, there was greater
discontent with local political, social and
economic circumstances(57), and in Holland, where

there was a long tradition of sympathy for a
Federal Europe. But support for specific
proposals, even rather advanced ones, did not
amount to a groundswell of pro-Europeanism: in
practice, faced with real alternatives between
national governments and the Communities, there
would inevitably be a backlash in favour of
national governments. And a 60%, even 70%, vote
for European ventures, was by no means equivalent
to the 'sentiment of unity' in favour of the centre
found in stable federations such as the USA.

It should be remembered also that the new
member states were far less enthusiastic in their
support for Europe. In the late 1970s and early
1980, in the United Kingdom, there was a majority
in favour of withdrawal from the Communities; in
Denmark too there were serious doubts about
membership.(58) In Ireland, on the other hand,
despite the lowest support anywhere, including the
UK, for greater supranational powers in European
institutions, there was an overwhelming majority in
favour of continuing membership.(59) The Irish
were a very clear illustration of support for
Europe for good, old fashioned utilitarian reasons.
A difficulty here was that it was very difficult to
discover even in the original Six the extent to
which Europe was supported because of utilitarian
advantage. Mennis and Sauvant argued that this was
a powerful factor, though Inglehart presented a
rather more sophisticated hypothesis, concerning
the greater preparedness of those whose attitudes
had been shaped since the Second World War in a
"post-acquisitive" society to support a European
ideology.(60) A rather more encouraging aspect of
attitudes in Europe in the early 1970s from the
point of view of supporters of integration,
however, was that the French and the German people
seemed to have moved some way towards the
establishment of a security community. Donald
Puchala showed in 1970 that there had been very
considerable movement through the 1960s away from
the harsh in-group-out-group distinction made by
the French about the Germans, and the Germans about
the French in the early 1950s.(61) The level of
distrust had sharply declined; there was an
increasing belief in the similarity and
compatibility of life styles; each thought the
behaviour of the other was more predictable and was
prepared to accept the other's interest as being in
part their own; and there was a degree of
confidence about the likelihood of mutual support

in the event of an attack by an outsider. Such evidence of mass attitude changes in the direction of security community was one of the more encouraging aspects of European integration although of course it had no necessary implications for the development of a higher level of political unity. As Puchala argued, it seemed to impose a certain limit upon the extent of disagreement at the political-diplomatic level, but was not necessarily indicative of any movement towards the creation of a European nation.

Mass attitudes among European peoples towards integration and towards each other showed some degree of increase in mutual sympathy and interdependence. There was, however, little evidence to suggest that there had been any movement towards a European nation; the European peoples were still very much intact and the bases of a new sovereignty had not emerged. It might safely be concluded that the dynamics of integration which had been stressed particularly in the approach of the older Functionalists, had not overwhelmed the European states. In the older states in particular attitudes probably changed sufficiently to slow down any dramatic reassertion of national autonomy, though in the new states this would find little or no oppositon in popular sentiment.

These then are the limits which have been imposed by the member states upon the dynamics of gradualist integration which were suggested by the theories and approaches discussed in Chapter 1. In each aspect there was a measure of change towards greater mutual involvement, but the state had on the whole emerged intact. The challenges to sovereignty were successfully resisted and the central institutions failed to obtain the qualities of supranationalism which I outlined. In the succeeding chapters I now turn to a closer examination of some of the aspects of the interface between the European Communities and the member states.

NOTES

1.   Max Beloff, in Carol Ann Cosgrove and Kenneth Twitchett (eds), The New International Actors, London, Macmillan, 1970, p. 95.
2.   Ibid, p. 95.
3.   See Robert Keohane and Joseph Nye, "Transgovernmental Relations and International

Organizations", World Politics, October 1974.

4.   Ernst B. Haas, "The Joys and Agonies of Pretheorising ...", in Leon N. Lindberg and Stuart A. Scheingold, (Editors), Regional Integration: Theory and Research, Harvard University Press, Cambridge, Mass. 1971. pp. 3-42.

5.   For a discussion of the notion of "Security Community" see Karl W. Deutsch et al., Political Community and the North Atlantic Area, Princeton, 1957.

6.   P.S.R.F. Mathijsen, A Guide to European Community Law, London, Sweet & Maxwell, 1972, pp. 139-140.

7.   David Coombes, Politics and Bureaucracy in the European Community, London, Allen and Unwin, Chapter 11.

8.   Robert Marjolin, Europe in Search of Identity, Council on Foreign Relations, New York, 1980, p. 68.

9.   ibid, p. 68.

10.   Ernst B. Haas, "International Integration: the European and the Universal Process", Dale Hekuis, C.G. McLintock, Arthur L. Burns (Eds), International Stability, Wiley, 1964, p. 231.

11.   See Helen Wallace, "The Impact of the European Communities on National Policy-making", Government and Oppostion, Vol. 6, No 4, Autumn 1971, pp. 520-338, especially p. 528.

12.   See Chapter 3 below.

13.   Council Decision of 21 April 1970, 70/243/ECSC/EEC/Euratom, O.J. 1970, L 94.

14.   For details see below Chapter 8.

15.   See K.C. Wheare, Federal Government, Oxford University Press, London, 1951 (2nd Edition), pp. 112-114.

16.   ibid, p. 114.

17.   For instance in 1980 there were two Supplementary Budgets.

18.   Wheare, loc. cit., p. 101.

19.   Geoffrey Denton, footnote 25,Chapter 6.

20. Wheare, loc. cit., p. 110.

21.   See Helen Wallace, Footnote,Chapter 3.

22.   Denton, loc. cit., p. 300.

23.   Robert Marjolin, loc. cit., p. 65.

24.   See footnote 24, Chapter 6.

25.   P.A. Reynolds, An Introduction to International Relations, London, Longman, 1971, p. 26.

26.   See William Diebold, The Schuman Plan: a Study in Economic Cooperation, Praeger,

New York, 1959.

27.   See Emile Noel, _How the European Community's Institutions Work_, Community Topics, Nos 11 (1963), 27 (1966), 32 (1969), and 39 (no date), European Communities Information Service, Brussels.

28.   See Uwe Kitzinger, _Diplomacy and Persuasion_, Thames and Hudson, London, 1973, p. 124.

29.   For an evaluation of the Neofunctionalist approach see R.J. Harrison, "Neofunctionalism", in Paul Taylor and A.J.R. Groom, _International Organization: a Conceptual Approach_, Frances Pinter, London, 1978, pp. 253-269.

30.   Andrew Shonfield, _Europe: Journey to an Unknown Destination_, Harmondsworth, Penguin Books, 1972, pp. 16-17.

31.   See Roy Pryce, _The Politics of the European Community_, Butterworths, London, 1973, pp. 87-91.

32.   R.J. Harrison, 1978, _loc. cit._, p. 266.

33.   William Averyt, "Eurogroups, clientela and the European Community", _International Organization_, Autumn, 1975, Vol. 29, No. 4, p. 967.

34.   _ibid_, p. 967.

35.   _ibid_, p. 967-968.

36.   The anacronym for 'quasi-autonomous non-governmental organizations' in Britain.

37.   Juliet Lodge and Valentine Herman, "The Economic and Social Committee in EEC decision making", _International Organization_, Vol. 34, No. 2, Spring 1980, p. 276.

38.   Emil J. Kirchner, "International Trade Union Collaboration and the Prospects for European Industrial Relations", _West European Politics_, Vol. 3, No. 1, January 1980, p. 133.

39.   _ibid_, p. 134.

40.   _ibid_, p. 132.

41.   Personal interviews held in Brussels, Summer 1980.

42.   See Geoffrey Pridham and Pippa Pridham, _Transnational Party Cooperation and European Integration_, London, George Allen and Unwin, 1981, Chapter 5.

43.   _ibid_, p. 284.

44.   Reported at a Seminar held at the Goethe Institute, 1979.

45.   Werner J. Feld and John K. Wildgen, "National Administration Elites and European Integration: Saboteurs at Work?", _Journal of Common

Market Studies, March, 1975, Vol. XIII,
No. 3, p. 255.
    46.   Of the 81% which said that they felt
pressure to conform with the 'norms' of their
departments only 44% favoured political union,
whilst of these 68% favoured economic union. Ibid,
p. 260.
    47.   ibid, p. 258.
    48.   ibid, p. 257.
    49.   Bernard Mennis and Karl P. Sauvant,
'Describing and Explaining Support for Regional
Integration: An Investigation of German Business
Elite Attitudes Towards the European Community',
International Organization, Autumn, 1975, Vol. 29,
No. 4, p. 984.
    50.   ibid, p. 984.
    51.   ibid, pp. 993-994.
    52.   See footnote 29 above, this chapter.
    53.   John Austin, Lectures on Jurisprudence:
the Philosophy of Positive Law, abridged and
introduced by Robert Campbell, New York, Henry
Holt, 1875.
    54.   Karl W. Deutsch et al.
footnote 5, ibid.
    55.   See J.D.B. Mitchell, 'Community
Legislation', in M.E. Bathurst, K.R. Simmonds, N.
March Hunnings and Jane Welch (eds.), Legal
Problems of the Enlarged European Community,
London, Stevens 1972, pp. 87-103, especially p. 88.
    56.   See J.D.B. Mitchell, S.A. Kuipers and
B. Gall, 'Constitutional Aspects of the Treaty and
Legislation Relating to British Membership', Common
Market Law Review, London, Stevens, May 1972, Vol.
9, No. 2, pp. 134-150, especially pp. 143 and 145.
    57.   Commission of the European Communities,
Euro-barometre, No. 9, July 1978, p. 5.
    58.   See, for example, p. 25, ibid.
    59.   ibid, see below Chapter 6.
    60.   Ronald Inglehart, "An End to European
Integration?" American Political Science Review,
Vol. 61, No 1, March 1967, pp. 91-105.
    61.   Donald J. Puchala, "Integration and
Disintegration in Franco-German Relations 1954-65".
International Organisation, vol. XXIV, Number 2,
Spring 1970.

Chapter Three

INTERGOVERNMENTALISM IN THE EUROPEAN COMMUNITIES [*]

In this chapter I begin my examination of the limits imposed upon the role of the Communities' central institutions by discussing the changes in the general character of integration in the Communities since the early 1970s. This examination is continued from different perspectives in Chapters 4 and 5.

The member states have not been absorbed into a new Euro-federation, nor have they become the vassals of a supranational Commission. Indeed most students of these matters agree that the most appropriate term to describe the broad character of relations between the Nine in the Seventies is intergovernmentalism. Some have tried to pick out the special features of this condition.(1) Mostly though, students have assumed that intergovernmentalism is intergovernmentalism is intergovernmentalism, and that relations between European states are in their fundamentals much the same as those between states elsewhere.(2) I argue here, however, that the character of intergovernmentalism in Europe in the late Seventies and early 1980s, was significantly different from that in the early Seventies and that there were indeed various shades of intergovernmentalism. The general conclusion is that the European Communities have not remained on a single plateau of intergovernmentalism through the 1970s, but that there has been a significant reinforcement of pressures opposed to integration since the middle part of the decade: these defined the limits of the central institutions' capacity for independent action.

In this discussion there are three broad themes. First is the changing character of the perceived interests of the member states in the

60

integration process as reflected in their diplomatic relations. How far were interests seen as convergent? To what extent were member governments prepared to invest economic or political resources in the integration process? Second is the changing status of the existing institutions of the European Communities. Developing intergovernmentalism obviously concerned the expansion of the role of those institutions in the Communities which were controlled by the representatives of governments, at the expense of that of the "European" institutions, in particular the Commission. The declining status of the Commission in the Communities' decision making, as compared with that of, say, the Presidency, was a central measure of increasing intergovernmentalism in the decade.(3) And third is the impact of the establishment of a number of new institutions in the Communities in the 1970s, such as those concerned with the coordination of foreign policy and the European Councils. It has been argued by some students of European affairs that the foreign policy procedures have been sufficiently successful to justify a guarded optimism about the development of "political union" among member states.(4) They are seen as a promising alternative to the Neofunctionalist strategy of economic integration: integrative effort is thought to have been switched to the level of political foreign policy questions, involving more frequently ministers and heads of government.(5) The conclusion which is ventured, however, is that the procedures for coordinating foreign policy have helped to weaken the position of the older institutions and that the new optimism about the chances of increasing integration at the political and foreign policy level should be treated with some caution.

This chapter is in three parts which deal, first, with the period from 1970 until 1973 to 74; the second deals with a transitional period in the mid 1970s, and the third examines the character of integration in the years 1975 to 1980. These dates are inevitably somewhat arbitrary; they are intended only to mark out the approximate times of the changes in the character of intergovernmentalism in the period.

The role of the institutions, and the pattern of decision-making within them, are not simply the consequence of disagreement in particular policy areas, or a response to particular problems. They

are influenced also by much longer term underlying
attitudes about, for instance, the need to preserve
national sovereignty, or to seek a common destiny,
which are themselves reflected in specific policy
areas. In this chapter I deal with these
underlying attitudes.

Diverse Potentials 1970-73

In the early years of the decade there was
evidence to encourage those who were in favour of
further integration but also, as I will show, an
increasing number of problems and associated
disagreements between governments. Indeed the
direction of change in integration was difficult to
determine: there was then in the process in Europe
a degree of teleological ambiguity. It is,
however, a mistake to suppose that an economic
challenge, such as that posed by the oil crisis in
late 1973, necessarily leads to disagreement and to
disintegration. As I show in the next section the
increasing disagreements in late 1973 and later
were as much the product of a number of underlying
changes as of the activities of OPEC, though the
latter triggered their expression. The question
which needs to be answered is that of why the
states did not seek to solve the problems caused by
the energy crisis by taking more integrative steps
rather than by stressing autonomy.
Another aspect of the teleological ambiguity
of the period was that even those who favoured
integration were divided into two groups: those who
saw intergovernmentalism as a way towards that
goal, and not a retreat from it; and those who
stressed centralisation and the more traditional
supranational approach. Dahrendorf spoke for the
first group when he argued in newspaper articles in
1972, which were developed in a book published in
1973, that it was time, in his view, to abandon the
theoretical orthodoxy of the "First Europe" (i.e.
that of an increasingly centralized set of European
institutions) which he called Functionalism, in
favour of a problem-orientated approach involving,
where necessary, intergovernmental arrangements
within the Communities or between members and
non-members.(6)
These would allow governments to get down to the
real business of striking well-founded agreements
amongst themselves. In practice, it was argued,
the decline of the First Europe was already visible
in the more intergovernmental Davignon arrangements

for attempting the coordination of foreign policy
questions among the Six (after 1973 - the Nine and
1980, the Ten) which had been initiated at the
Hague Summit of December 1969, and in the meetings
of, for example, economics Ministers and heads of
central banks, which took place outside the
Communities' framework, and under the Council of
Ministers. He called this new style the "Second
Europe". We should recognize, Dahrendorf argued,
that these developments offered the opportunity of
escaping from the bureaucratic inertia of the
Commission-focussed institutions of the First
Europe. He was asserting, in other words, that the
European Communities had indeed become more
intergovernmental in the early Seventies and that
this was to be regarded as a favourable development
which held out promise of an expansion of the range
of common problem solving. It was to be seen as
the way forward.

Dahrendorf's interpretation of the character
and the potential of the Second Europe is
significant in that it reflects the views of a
distinguished scholar formed whilst he was himself
a member of the Commission. We are alerted,
therefore, to the potential of the developments
which he had noted in the early Seventies, in
particular, those which followed from the range of
initiatives which were made at the December 1969
Summit meeting. This potential was, however, also
noticed, and welcomed, by other authorities who
continued to support the goal of a unified Europe
and the deepening and extension of what Dahrendorf
had critically dubbed the "First Europe". Altiero
Spinelli, a staunch longstanding Federalist, and
also a Commissioner from 1972 to 76, argued in 1972
that "at the end of 1969 the wind began to change
and from then until the present time (mid-1972) the
European theme was revitalized".(7) In particular
he stressed that the international monetary crisis
of 1971 had produced for the member states of the
European Communities a powerful challenge to take
common action: "if the countries of the enlarged
Community are not capable of taking common
international action - be it monetary, commercial
or political - then everything may collapse".(8)
He argued, though that the challenge could be met.
The warning was an exhortation to those who were
seen to be moving on the whole in the right
direction, though their speed and resolution might
be greater. There was a "moment of creative
tension which began to be formed in the course of

1971 and will probably extend not only into 1972, but also to a lesser extent into the first years of the existence of the enlarged community."(9) Though President Pompidou still "speaks of confederation" it is to be interpreted as one which "will evolve into a European government, to which national governments will one day transfer certain of their perogatives".(10) Walter Hallstein, the President of the Commission from 1958 until 1967, was also impressed by the range and promise of developments in the early 1970s: he wrote in 1972 that the Werner Report on European Economic and Monetary Cooperation, which had been drawn up in 1970, and approved – with some amendments – by the Council of Ministers in February 1971, was "the most important document in the history of European Integration since the Treaty of Rome".(11) There were, therefore, a number of influential students of integration in the early 1970s who were disposed from various perspectives to be optimistic about European integration.

The statesmen of the member states were, however, surprisingly slow to define the limits of their potential cooperation in this period, despite increasing disagreements between them such as those resulting from the financial crisis of the Summer of 1971. They seemed rather to be themselves caught up in the dynamic process which had begun at the Hague. Although the monetary crisis led to the abandonment of the first "snake" after the floating of the D-mark in May 1971, nevertheless the idea of Economic and Monetary Union proved suprisingly durable.(12) In March 1972, it was agreed that a new "snake" – this time in a "tunnel" – should operate from April 1972, and in October 1972 it was decided at the Summit Meeting in Paris that "the necessary decisions should be taken in the course of 1973 so as to allow the transition to the second stage of the Economic and Monetary Union in January, 1974, and with a view to its completion not later than December 1980".(13) They concluded that their relations should be "transformed into a European union" by the "end of the present decade". (Article. VII). There is a strong sense, not merely of the realisation of a coincidence of interest, but of a community, or transcendent one. The range of commitments undertaken by the member governments was associated with a degree of uncertainty about how far they were prepared to go which lent encouragement both to intergovernmentalists and to those with more federal inclinations.

Beside the relative optimism of the two schools of pro-integrationists and, indeed, of members of governments, in the early years of the decade should, however, be set the evidence of disagreement and failure to move forward into the area of more positive integration. As I have suggested elsewhere there was then a kind of oscillation between support for advanced schemes for integration and some movement in that direction and retreat into the assertion of short term interest.(14)

One reason for this was that in the early 1970s there was no equivalent of the central bargain between the key-states on which integration had been built in the 1960s. For instance, EMU, which had been supported by the French primarily for foreign policy reasons - (she wished Europe to establish her own monetary personality in oppositon to the USA) - proved to be too vulnerable to adverse movements in the international system.(15) In March 1973 the West Germans succeeded in establishing a joint float of European currencies against the dollar, which was undoubtably a success for West Germany's diplomacy, but which in the event was bought at the expense of increasing division within Europe. The weaker currencies fell out of the float: The French had to withdraw in mid 1974, the British had withdrawn earlier. Attempts to realise the new initiatives led too soon to perceptions that rewards to be gained from them would not be evenly distributed between members. The benefits and costs of particular initiatives, such as that on industrial policy, were also not easy to balance against those of other policies, such as EMU - package deals were more difficult to arrive at. This contrasted strongly with the rather elegant simplicity of the first bargain: it had provided a clear-cut programme, benefits and costs which could be matched, and which seemed to be reasonably equally distributed, and could be entrusted, because its implications were well understood by member states, to a central 'motor' in the form of the Commission. The new difficulties may be encapsulated in the judgement that the initiatives, going beyond the Treaty, were more highly political in character than those in the Treaty.

The failure of member states to develop more harmonised mechanisms for managing their economies was highlighted by the energy crisis in late 1973.

The instruments to tackle the problems posed then
simply did not exist at the Community level, and,
as I show in the next section, the chances of
developing them were weakened by other underlying
changes. The various governments failed in their
attempt to develop anything more than a fairly
basic common energy policy, could not evolve ways
of tackling the various inflationary pressures and
other economic problems generated by the
price-hikes on a collective basis, and had no
common policy in dealing with oil-producing
countries. As economic circumstance declined the
ability of the Communities to solve the problems
which were posed was also reduced.

Yet there were significant differences between
the position of the three major states. Edward
Heath was no federalist - though he later moved in
that direction - yet was unclear about how far he
would go in working for higher levels of
integration.(16) Indeed, at Paris in October 1972,
he seemed to be arguing for the reinforcement of
the institutions of the First Europe when he called
for the "strengthening and enrichment of the
dialogue between each of these and Parliament."(17)
Willy Brandt was probably prepared to go further
than Heath towards federal institutions. But
President Pompidou, despite Spinelli's judgement,
tolerated the other' enthusiasm, rather than
partook of it. Indeed, his image of the ideal
arrangement of the European institutions was
similar in many ways to that advocated by
Dahrendorf: he preferred an active,
intergovernmental Europe, a community of statesmen
involved in the solution of problems - to use De
Gaulle's language - 'on terms specific to
them',(18) and pursuing united policies in relation
to the outside world, particularly the USA.

Given this French preference and opposition to
the alternative patterns of development which were
at least implicitly supported by her partners, it
is surprising that President Pompidou did not
propose regular Summit meetings, formally
recognized as the head of the Communities
institutions, much earlier than the autumn of 1973.
He argued at a press conference on 29th September
1973 that Summit meetings should be held at regular
intervals and that they should become 'an integral
instrument in the process of European decision
making'.(19) Edward Heath was by then also
prepared to support the proposal, and argued in its
favour at the Conservative Party Conference that

Autumn. Brandt was less enthusiastic but accepted that 'we need more frequent meetings of heads of government as suggested by the French President.'(20) Pompidou called, on the 31st October, for the holding of a Summit meeting to discuss the institutional question and to prepare a European position in relation to the energy crisis: Europe was to assert herself in the face of what the French construed as an arrogant usurpation of European interests by the Americans in their relations with the new cartel of oil producing states into the Middle East. The meeting was held in Copenhagen on 14-15 December, 1973: there was no agreement on a common European policy on oil, despite considerable French pressure and bitterness about the propensity of some European states to link up with the Americans. But there was agreement on the principle of institutionalising Summit meetings: governments "decided to meet more frequently" ... "meetings will be held whenever justified by the circumstances and when it appears necessary to provide a stimulus or to lay down further guidelines for the construction of Europe" ... "it is for the country providing the President to convene those meetings and to make detailed proposals".(21)

The Summit Conference was held in December 1973 not entirely because of the French President's wish to tackle a range of policy problems at the highest level, but also because about then was the first occasion on which it had seemed appropriate to push firmly for the introduction of European Councils. The French did not wish to appear anti-European in the eyes of partners who were, however uncertainly, committed to versions of the First Europe. A strong advocacy of European councils at the Paris October 1972 Summit, for instance, could have weakened Pompidou's perceived special relationship with Heath, and could have encouraged in the latter and his colleagues a greater caution in their commitment to Europe. He was aware that their enthusiasm had produced initatives which could bring real benefits for France. Before the 1972 Summit, therefore, he 'deplored the other governments' lack of response to French calls for common policies on economics, money, industry and technology, as opposed to the prevailing obsession, as he saw it, with institutional matters'.(22) When the timing was appropriate about a year later he had no hesitation in reversing this argument and stressing such

67

institutional questions. The French also perceived
a need, simply, to wait until the intergovernmental
machinery, both in the form of the various Councils
and their dependent committees, and in that of the
political cooperation machinery, had been extended
and sufficiently well established for European
Councils to be seen as an appropriate culmination
of a successful enterprise. The old hesitations
about political coordination, particularly those of
the Benelux countries, had to be allowed to wither
away. Pierre Werner had expressed such hesitations
as late as 1970: he wondered whether the time had
come 'to reopen the dossier on political
cooperation'.(23)

At the same time, Pompidou implicitly
acknowledged that in his view the First Europe was
a continuing threat: the tender plant of political
cooperation had to be shielded from possible
contamination or invasion by the First Europe.
Hence he refused to permit the setting up of a
Political Secretariat at Brussels, and insisted
that meetings of Foreign Ministers should take
place in the framework of the political
consultation machinery: Commission Presidents
Malfatti and Mansholt had both attempted to protect
the Commission's role by allocating to individual
Commissioners responsibility for keeping in touch
with, and wherever possible, attending meetings of
the expanding range of intergovernmental
committees.(24) Ortoli's Commission showed some
signs of reflecting in itself a more vigorous
intergovernmentalism, in that its appointments were
more blatantly representative than had been
previously admitted. But even Ortoli came to
assert the interests of the Commission when he
demanded the revision of the Treaty so that the new
business which was now beyond it - largely the
Hague initiatives - could be brought within its
scope and thus made subject to the procedures of
the First Europe.(25) And until the mid 1970's the
Commission's attitude towards integration was to
seek a common Communities' system in such areas as
social policy, company law etc., rather than
harmonised national ones.(26)

Pompidou's initiative can, therefore, also be
seen as in part a retort to these continuing
pressures from the Commission in that the new
European Councils were to be at the head of
both the older Communities' institutions and their
procedures and the new intergovernmental ones. It
is also conceivable that Pompidou sensed in the

Autumn of 1973 that his own time was running out
(he died in March 1974) and that he should move to
confirm the Second Europe soon. Thus, although the
decisive trigger of the calling of the Summit was
probably the oil crisis, together with the
realisation that increasing policy differences
could appropriately be tackled at that level,
nevertheless the placing of the institutional
question near the top of the agenda was probably
the result of a number of other tendencies and
pressures. It should be recalled that Pompidou was
now disposed to dwell on such questions, although
he had ridiculed this inclination in his partners
only a year earlier. In the period from 1970 until
1973/4 there were, therefore, a number of
uncertainties and ambiguities about the pattern of
development of the European Communities. There
were those who remained optimistic about the chance
of further integration, although these included
both intergovernmentalists and supranationalists,
and some evidence to support both these views.
There were, however, a number of disagreements and
problems culminating in the energy crisis in 1973,
which were themselves ambiguous in their
implications. A Communities' approach to their
solutions was still a conceivable option until
1974. In the next section of this chapter I
examine the underlining changes which worked
against the exercise of that option then, and their
effects upon the pattern of development of the
European Institutions.

Diversity Confined

At the meeting of Heads of State and
Government in Paris in December 1974, President
Giscard d'Estaing, Pompidou's successor, was mainly
responsible for obtaining the agreement of the
governments to a broad package of institutional
changes, and initiatives. He had carefully
prepared the way for the Summit with informal
consultations of his colleagues, followed by
extensive official and ministerial discussions. At
the heart of the institutional changes were the
agreements, first, that the new European Councils
would meet three times a year in the company of
Ministers of Foreign Affairs and 'whenever
necessary in the Council of the Communities and in
the context of political cooperation'(Art. 3 27);
and secondly, that ministers of foreign affairs
'meeting in the Council of the Community, will act

as initiators and coordinators,' 'in order to
ensure consistency in Community activities and
continuity of work.'(Art. 3) Giscard also
indicated his willingness to abandon Pompidou's
policy of keeping discussion of political and
Community questions separate: it was agreed that
the Foreign Ministers "may hold political
cooperation meetings at the same time"(Art. 3) as
those to discuss Community activities. The rest of
the package included a rather brief, though
vigorous, reassertion of the commitment of members
to Economic and Monetary Union - the last mention
of this commitment in declarations of Heads of
State and Government (Art 14); and the European
Regional Fund was set up on the insistence of the
British though at 1,300 million units of account
over three years, it was very much smaller than
they had hoped.

But there were also a number of proposals
which seemed to confirm the commitment of members
to integration of a rather advanced kind: they
accepted the goal of holding direct elections to
the European Assembly by 1978 and asserted that
'the European Assembly will be associated with the
achievement of European unity'(Art 12); a working
party was to be set up to study the possibility of
'establishing a Passport Union and, in anticipation
of this, the introduction of a uniform
passport'(Art. 10); and it was agreed that the time
had come for the Nine to agree as soon as possible
on an overall concept of European union and,
consequently Mr. Tindemans, Prime Minister of
Belgium, was invited to produce a report to the
Heads of Government before the end of 1975. It
might have appeared that at the end of 1974 Giscard
d'Estaing was taking over the mantle which Brandt
had worn at the Hague in December 1969.

This evidence allows, however, both a 'soft'
judgement of Giscard's December 1974 package and
also a 'hard', rather critical one. The 'soft'
judgement is represented, for instance, by Emile
Noel: he claimed that the Paris Conference
represented Giscard's conviction that "a
significant change, without counterclaim, had to be
made in some aspects, particularly of an
institutional nature, in France's policy towards
Europe."(28) Giscard should be seen as a supporter
of integration whose policies represented a radical
departure from those of Pompidou. Wallace and
Allen also imply that Giscard's dropping of his
predecessor's policy of isolating the foreign

policy machinery from the Community institutions, was the result of his pro-Europeanism: they suggest that Giscard was now prepared to accept a role for the Commission in the coordination of foreign policy issues - such as the Euro-Arab dialogue; because by mid-late 1974 the governments had a greater sense of convergence in their foreign policy; and, also, because Giscard was prepared, unlike his predecessor, to tolerate some strengthening of the institutions of the First Europe.(29) The hard line, in contrast, interprets Giscard's policy on Europe's institutional development as being very much in the French tradition which began with De Gaulle and extended through Pompidou: Giscard is seen to have used in December 1974 an opportunity to achieve a goal which had been vigourously sought by De Gaulle in the early Sixties, and which Pompidou would have sought had he lived beyond the period of diverse potentials' - that of establishing Foreign Ministers and officials, and Heads of Government as managers of the Communities system, and as the main link between the governments and the central institutions, thereby further entrenching intergovernmentalism and stifling any further claims to power by institutions such as the Commission.(30)

The changing attitude of his partners towards integration in late 1973 and 1974 would have encouraged the French President in this strategy. In late 1973 it had been evident that the member states were increasingly disagreeing about the way forward, but it was still possible to see these problems as representing temporary difficulties. There were also, of course, a number of disagreements about foreign policy, such as that towards the USA, though, I do not deal with this at length here. (See chapter 5) By December 1974, there was, however, evidence of a considerable alteration in members' interests. They were now clearly limiting their commitment, and striving for a much shorter term balancing of their accounts with the Communities. One problem was that Willy Brandt's European enthusiasm was increasingly constrained by his Ministers' reluctance to see West Germany continue as paymaster of Europe. Leaders amongst these Ministers were Helmut Schmidt and Hans Apel.(31) West Germany was increasingly a satisfied power: the success of the Ostpolitik had removed at least one reason for their continuing investment in the Communities, namely the support

of Western Europe in East Germany.(32) At the same
time a number of younger politicians were emerging
in West Germany who had a weaker perception of
their country's need to make amends for the damage
done by Nazi Germany: they were not prepared to be
exploited by her partners, either consciously or
unconsciously, because of their feelings of
'war-guilt'. For a number of reasons, then, West
Germany's preparedness to commit herself in a
fairly open-ended way to European integration
weakened in late 1973 through 1974. When Helmut
Schmidt succeeded Brandt as Chancellor in the
Summer of 1974 the new German Government took a
much shorter term view of its European interests.
The first clear expression of this new stance was
probably the West German refusal to countenance a
large scale Regional Fund: it emerged through 1974
that she was not prepared to approach the level of
contributions which had been demanded by the
British. This was the subject of considerable
acrimonious debate in Britain and Germany through
1974. West German statesmen angrily asserted that
there was a limit to their preparedness to help the
sick economies of their partners.

These changes were matched and reinforced by
changes in the attitude of the British Government.
The new Labour Government which came to power in
February 1974 was cautious in its attitude to
Europe since the Labour Party was committed to
renegotiating the terms of Britain's accession and
was strongly polarised between supporters and
opponents of membership.(33) By the time of the
December 1974 Summit negotiations between Britain
and the rest had already started, and it was
likely, given the circumstances in the country and
the Party, that the Labour Government would take a
rather short term view of their interests. Indeed,
one of the central features of the British position
was their insistence on a _juste retour_: they sought
what they conceived to be a fair return from the
Communities which inevitably focussed attention
upon the balancing of books in the shorter term.
The settlement reached at the Dublin Conference in
March 1975, was that Britain's contributions to he
European Budget would be related to the relative
value of her GNP in the Communities; there would be
a 'claw back' if the contributions exceeded a
certain sum defined in these terms. Helen Wallace
commented that: 'The net position of member states
was included as an element in the calculation of
entitlement to benefit from the pay-back mechanism.

This in itself was a major departure from Community
orthodoxy which had hitherto prevented any allusion
in EEC legislation to even a hint of juste
retour'.(34)   In the period of renegotiation,
therefore, the British provided a powerful pressure
towards the abandonment of the traditional
principle followed by the Communities that
discussion of fair national shares in their
internal exchanges was 'non-communautaire'.(39)
      In the months before the December 1974 Summit,
however, attitudes towards foreign policy
coordination had moved in the opposite direction.
In late 1973 they had been in disarray over oil
policy and their relations with the USA.   In April,
1974, however, members had managed to work out at
the Schloss Gymnich Conference a modus vivendi in
their policies towards the USA, and after
Pompidou's death the French dropped their hard line
on the separation of 'political' from 'Community'
questions.   The Euro-Arab dialogue increasingly
involved both Commission and governmental officials
and was thought to be proceeding well.   Wallace and
Allen referred to these developments as
representing a 'change in both the atmosphere and
effectiveness of political cooperation in the nine
months between January and October 1974'(36)   They
were matched by a steady expansion and entrenchment
of the range of procedures for coordinating foreign
policy.   At the December 1974 Summit the states
reaffirmed "their determination gradually to adopt
common positions and coordinate their diplomatic
action in all areas of international affairs which
affect the interests of the European
Community."(Art.4)   I discuss the further
development of, and limits upon, the political
cooperation machinery in Chapter 5.
      The changing attitudes of his partners towards
the pattern of integration could therefore be seen
as having presented Giscard with an opportunity to
change the centre of gravity of the Communities'
institutions by the simple device of simultaneously
establishing the Foreign Ministers as coordinators
and initiators 'in Community activities', and
allowing them to consider Community business and
political questions at the same time.   These were
precisely the objectives which de Gaulle, and
Pompidou, had sought in their strategy towards the
European institutions.   The Foreign Ministers
Council was strengthened in the Communities -
though it did not follow that its members would
always be able to agree on what to do.   But the

Foreign Ministers Council became the forum within
which attempts were made to strike agreement upon a
wide range of matters, such as Britain's claim for
a budget rebate: it was the key forum. The change
also confirmed that the duties of the Presidency
would be carried out on behalf of member states
mainly by Foreign Minsters, and not, say, by
Minsters of Economics. They were encouraged to
accompany Heads of Governments at meetings of the
European Councils; they were also the only
Ministers who were asked to be involved in and link
both the foreign and the internal aspects of the
Communities' business. One welcome consequence of
this development from Giscard's point of view was
that it reinforced the position of the Quai D'Orsay
in managing relations between the French government
and the Communities compared with that of other
Ministries. The Quai was both more cautious in its
approach to the Communities and traditionally more
accessible to the President's control.

Wallace and Edwards observed that "it is the
Foreign Minister who takes on the mantle of
expectations and who generally remains the chief
focus of domestic and community attention" ... "the
initial programme provides a yardstick against
which the Presidency is judged at the end of its
term of office, when the Foreign Minster is then
held to account in subsequent press and public
commentary."(37) In 1975 the practice was
initiated by the Irish at the beginning of their
Presidency of planning the Communities business for
the coming six months with the Commission. Wallace
and Edwards concluded that "this has now become an
established practice, and it emphasises the
responsibility for communication of each Presidency
at the apex of its hierarchy."(38) The
strengthening of the Presidency in this way seemed
to reinforce the judgement that the
institutionalisation of the Councils was designed
"not so much to 'lock' high political actors from
the nation states in the supranational
decision-making process" but rather to "restrict
the efforts of Eurocrats to extend their
jurisdictional competences with spill-over into new
spheres".(39) The welcome given by some 'First
Europeans' to the European Councils was on this
evidence misjudged.

The increasing disagreements about internal
policy and the stress upon shorter-term interests
in West Germany and Britain no doubt encouraged
Giscard in his view that it was now unlikely that

the Commission could impose itself upon the
Presidency. By now it lacked any obvious potential
partners in the member states, such as those which
had been available to it in the 1960s. Although
Pompidou's fears of the First Europe had been
probably somewhat exaggerated, the earlier
uncertainties in France's partners had constituted
a reminder to him that they could conceivably move
behind the Commission, and thus challenge the
'political union'. There was now, however, a
groundswell of anti-supranationalism which tended
to dispel any doubts which Giscard had on this
score. Indeed the reservations on direct elections
entered in the Final Communique by Britain and
Denmark were themselves evidence of this - and
could therefore also be seen as having been welcome
to Giscard as part of the package. At the same
time the changes in Britain and West Germany made
it possible to offer apparent concessions to those
who still hankered after the First Europe: as I
have pointed out, Holland and Belgium had been
vigorous opponents of De Gaulle's plans to
strengthen the position of the Foreign Ministers
and it was tactful to reduce the risks of
resurrecting these fears either in present or
future governments in these countries. There were
also general advantages in having a reputation for
being pro-European. The concessions on Direct
Elections, on the European Passport, on European
Union, and so on, should in this view be seen as
merely expedient: there was not much chance that
they would be realised, or have any effect, and
they could, therefore, be safely offered.

By December 1974, therefore, the position of
the Commission in the European Communities had been
considerably downgraded compared with that of the
Presidency. Greater stress was now to be placed on
the foreign policy coordination machinery in the
business of the Communities and in policy
coordination. There was also an increasing stress
upon the short term interests of states in their
mutual relations: they insisted upon balancing
their contributions to the Communities with their
receipts in the short term. By late 1974 any
surviving potential for supranationalism seemed to
have been muzzled. The Economist hailed the
outcome: 'the grand design of Europe is mercifully
dead, and long may it remain so. In its place the
very real clubmanship of a working Europe now has a
real chance of coming alive.'(40) The Dahrendorf
model of integration seemed to have prevailed.

Intergovernmentalism Entrenched

By the mid Seventies, the Presidency and the European Council had been established as central organs in the institutions of the European Communities, and within these new elements foreign ministries - foreign ministers and their civil servants - had been placed in central guiding positons.

It was also the case, as I have shown, that by the mid-1970s member governments were increasingly cautious in their commitment to the Communities. These tendencies contributed to a number of problems concerning the institutional development of the Communities: there were failures and deficiencies in the institutions themselves, with which I am mainly concerned at this point, and there were adverse reactions of governments to their lack of success in the institutions. In the late Seventies and early Eighties it was not difficult to pick out examples of the latter: the French decision to defy the injunctions of the Communities' Court and to forbid imports of British lamb(41); the suggestion, in response to the Assembly's decision in late 1980, that the Budget should be increased, that the French and even the West Germany governments might deny their legal obligations and simply not pay their contributions(42); the threats that lay behind the British government's demands that its net contribution to the Budget should be reduced.(43) States were increasingly threatening to seek to satisfy their interests by defying the law of the Communities, and increasing the level of threat which they were prepared to use in their mutual diplomacy. During the bitter wrangles between the British and other members of the Communities in the early 1980s about Britian's budgetary contribution there were frequently very serious disagreements which raised the question of whether the Communities could survive in its existing form.(44)

There were, however, two kinds of judgement about 'the way forward'. The first held that it was necessary for Europe to concentrate on building a European Foreign Policy in the first instance, and that agreement about internal questions, including the strengthening of the institutions, would follow behind this. This was the approach which the French had traditionally advocated and which the British now seemed to support, and, as we

have seen, is inherent in Giscard's 1974 package.
The second view on the way forward stressed, in
contrast, that a common foreign policy would only
emerge from the completion of Europe's internal
arrangements. Whilst accepting that many of
Europe's problems had external dimensions it was
nevertheless practical and desirable for Europe to
move ahead on her own: foreign policy was likely to
follow from economic policy, budgetary policy, and
so on. At the moment, however, the European
Communities were inevitably merely a 'sounding
board' for national foreign policies, rather than
an effective coordinating mechanism.(45)

There were a number of difficulties in the
mid-late 1970's in the way of further internal
progress which concerned both particular measures
of cooperation and the role which the states were
prepared to allow to the regional institutions.
The main source of these difficulties was member
governments' underlying attitudes towards
integration and their expectations with regard to
the Communities, which were not simply a
consequence of the specific problems. Indeed,
these attitudes contributed towards the
difficulties in particular areas.

This is not to underestimate the great
economic difficulties facing member states in this
period, which, of course, were greatly exacerbated
by the high price of energy, but rather to suggest
that the governments response to these was not just
a matter of the essential character of the problems
- if such existed. The economic problems were
serious but they were in themselves not a
sufficient explanation of the increasing
disagreement between governments in the European
Communities. To explain these the specific
problems need to be related to the underlying
attitudes of governments towards such large issues
as national sovereignty, their sense of common
destiny, and their general expectation of
integration. The stronger the belief in being
involved together in a great enterprise, the
greater the chance of support for integrative
approaches even to the more serious problems. It
is obvious that in the late 1970's the governments
were less likely to choose integrative solutions to
the problems posed by the worsening economic
circumstances than they had been in the early
1970's. Nevertheless I am here not primarily
concerned with the economic problems, which have
been well discussed elsewhere,(46) but rather with

the underlying attitude which contributed
significantly to their response, and with the
institutional developments which were affected both
by these attitudes and by related judgements about
the ways of solving their economic problems.

By the mid-late 1970's, the view had arisen
among governments and some scholars that the
interest of states in their mutual relations could
be treated as 'pure' or as uncontaminated by dogma
or any other kind of higher principles. As I have
said, the complaint was made about the Europe of
the Sixties by Professor Dahrendorf, that the
process of reconciling the interests of states was
made more difficult because of attempts to
subordinate them to the principle of European unity
or supranationalism. He argued that interests
should be freed from such restrictions and related
problems tackled on their own terms.(47) It is,
however, hard to see how interests could be freed
from some larger principle of arrangement. In the
absence of the dogma of supranationalism the dogma
of national sovereignty took over. In their choice
of interests and in their arrangement of priorities
among interests, governments inevitably reflected
their judgement about the chances of a long term
convergence of interests and expectations of unity.
In the circumstances in the Communities in the
mid-late 1970s the undermining of mutual confidence
was followed by a rapid escalation in the level of
concern with short-term national interests. By
January 1981 the British Prime Minister could
assert with little fear of contradiction: "there is
no such thing as a separate Community interest; the
Community interest is compounded of the national
interests of the Ten member states."(48) Such an
assertion in earlier periods would have been
unacceptable.

In the European Communities member states had
developed an unusually dense pattern of
interdependent interests. In the event of these
interests' remaining unsatisfied it was therefore
more difficult for them to be refocussed upon other
member states in the international system. Some
member states in the Communities began to behave
rather like a couple in a marriage which was in
difficulties: they had done too much together for
too long to make it easy to seek satisfaction
elsewhere. At the same time an increasing mutual
resentment and bitterness was generated by the
other's apparent intransigence. The range of the
interests which were seen to be interrelated, and

the earlier intimations of unity, were likely to
encourage states to treat each other as
untrustworthy and deceitful once they began to
reassert the principle of national sovereignty.

The linked difficulty also arose that it
became more difficult for member governments to
agree upon a principle of arrangement. The more
the interests of the states were stressed the more
difficult it became to decide which interests
should be satisfied first and which should be
postponed. The fallacy of seeking unity by
identifying the various actors' interests in the
system was thus revealed: such an approach tended
to entrench pluralism and to increase the chances
that it would spill back into conflict. The chance
of creating deadlock by states seeking everything
first would be increased. The important question
in seeking and preserving unity is usually that of
which interests are actors prepared to postpone or
abandon in the common interest and not the opposing
one about which interests they required to be
satisfied. It is for this reason that the concern
of some scholars in the late nineteen-seventies and
early eighties to identify "fair national shares"
in the Communities was unlikely to be rewarding.
The attempt was likely to further enhance the
governments' determination to obtain the wide range
of their interests with the Communities in the
short term, and thereby reinforce the deadlock.

I should mention here two underlying
developments which greatly increased the
difficulties in resolving conflicts of interest
among member states. They are that the Communities
had become both relatively open to the
international system but that its members were
increasingly linked with each other. In the late
Seventies the growing divergence between the
members and the economic crisis amplified the
divisive influences upon internal policies which
derived from the external links of members.(49)
The interest of states in maintaining their ability
to defend themselves against adverse developments
in the international economy increased their
reluctance to agree, for instance , to a common
fiscal policy or to common budgetary policies. On
the other hand the external trade links of states
reinforced their determination to manage their
economies so that they could take advantage of any
general upturn in international trade even at the
expense of their partners. The difficulties in
developing more integrated European ventures in

various areas of high-technology were at least
partly due to this. A common industrial policy
would have inevitably weakened the separate states'
ability to develop particular strengths in their
economy which could be exploited in international
trade.(50) And the need to develop advantageous
trading relationships with non-members, such as the
OPEC countries, or Japan, was inevitably a barrier
in the way of the consolidation of the common
commercial policy. The pattern of trading
relationships of states with non-members also added
to the problems revolving round the Budget in the
late nineteen-seventies and early eighties. States
which imported more, either in manufactured goods
or in food, from non-members were required to make
a greater contribution to the Budget in tariffs and
levies than those which imported less. This was
one origin of Britain's grievance that its
contribution was excessive. A low, or an equal
level of trade involvement with non-members would
have removed at least this source of what was in
the judgement of some commentators, a grave
inequity in members' budgetary contributions. The
budgetary arrangements were postulated, in the
early 1970's, upon the assumption of a relatively
greater involvement of the states, particularly the
larger ones, with each other than was in fact the
case in the late 1970's and early 1980's.(51) Thus
there were a number of ways in which the relative
openness of the European Communities tended in the
late 1970's to add to the divisions among members
about the development of their internal policies.
The increasing divergence between the economic
performance of the "rich" states, and the "poor"
states, made it more likely that such divisions
would arise.
        In the early 1980s it was difficult to be
specific about the implications of these
developments for the Communities' institutions, in
particular the central dyad: the Commission and the
Council. But a number of limits emerged upon the
further development of integration, in the form
represented by the Neofunctionalist concept of
'spill-over".(52) In the late 1970's member states
became much clearer about the lines beyond which
integration could not be allowed to proceed. Of
central importance here was the financial line: the
richer states, led by West Germany, asserted that
they would not accept any increase in the
Communities' budget beyond the 1% of V.A.T. agreed
in 1971. The implication was that member states

would have themselves to make up any shortfall in
Communities' revenue, in financing, say, the Common
Agricultural Policy, when Communities' resources
ran out. There were, in other words, to be clear
limits on the scale of Common funding and of
resource transfers within the European Communities.
Less explicit limits could be traced in a number of
Council meetings when package deals seemed more
difficult to reach than they had been and diplomacy
more acrimonious. (I have already given some
examples of this.) States seemed to be stressing
their short-term interests much more vigorously:
the Spring meetings of the Agricultural Council
were occasions of gladiatorial combat; the annual
budgetary cycle was increasingly messy with
inter-institutional conflicts as well as severe
disagreements between governments. In the meetings
of the Council of Ministers the voting system
sometimes began to look less like that of consensus
building, the traditional image, and more like that
which had once been known as the liberum veto.
Each state laid stress upon its right to veto
common actions. There were occasions when they
became forums for mutual cross-sterilization, the
most striking examples - but by no means the only
ones - being the meeting in Dublin in 1979 when
Mrs. Thatcher insisted upon the discussion of
Britain's excessive budgetary contributions in the
face of the determined opposition of the others,
and the later meetings of Foreign Ministers when
the British refused to accept increases in food
prices until the Budget rebate had been agreed.
Indeed, the logic of the package deal was often
inverted: " if you give me that, I will give you
this," became more often, "if you don't give me
that, I won't give you that". Another limit, which
I mention below, was the explicit restriction upon
the transfer of further powers from national to
Communities' instititutions.
      In the late 1970s the Spierenburg Committee,
which had been set up by the Commission to
investigate its problems, complained that the
Commission had begun to compromise too soon in its
consultations with governments.(53) The
corresponding Committee set up by the Council of
Ministers, called the Committee of Three Wise Men,
also reported that the Commission "has not
developed a coherent overall vision of its own
which could help to give proportion and direction
to the large number of its proposals." The
Commission was losing its ability to stand back

long enough to define the general interest and was, as it were, being sucked at an early stage into the high pressure wheeler-dealing between governments. Helen Wallace had indeed noticed a tendency in this direction as early as 1971: she observed that the Commission's proposals to the Council then tended to be less detailed than previously and that details were later filled in within national administrations and in negotiations between them.(54)   Spierenburg concluded that the Commission should be amended internally so that its ability to define and hold general interest positions in the context of the increasing mass of intergovernmental councils and committees would be strengthened.   The Committee of Three Wise Men commented that "this general phenomenon of excessive load of business (<u>too many demands and expectations</u>) aggravated by slow and confused handling may be summed up in the French word 'lourdeur'".(55)

These difficulties were, however, not just a consequence of the Commission's internal arrangements. As the level of tension between governments in the Councils and their committees increased and the expectations of governments of getting what they wanted declined, so it became increasingly difficult and, indeed, futile for the Commission to spell out detailed European solutions. It was inevitably tempted to cut its losses and to concentrate upon getting into the ring with the governments which were prone to try to exclude it, and to get what it could from the brawl.   Indeed the more the Commission articulated an independent position the more likely it was that it would be excluded.   It was argued on the resignation of Roy Jenkins from his position as President of the Commission in January 1981, that his main achievement had been that of gaining access for the Commission to the various intergovernmental forums, especially the European Councils. He was thought to have produced rather few grand new initiatives – the one exception being that for the European Monetary System – and Jenkins was described by some commentators as having spent too much time on attempting to gain access.(56) Given the character of intergovernmentalism in the late Seventies and early Eighties, however, it is hardly surprising that the Commission President should have concentrated upon 'being there'.(57) Spierenburg's proposals for internal reform of the Commission in order to strengthen the voice of

Europe were likely in prevailing circumstances to prove unsuccessful. The problem was not just with the Commission but also with the quality of relations between governments: its role and limitations were thrust upon it.

There seemed little prospect in the early Eighties of any strengthening of the Communities' institutions, and if anything, it seemed likely that they would be further weakened: the Communities were in a period of entrenched intergovernmentalism. Governments imposed limits upon the extent to which the European Parliament could acquire new powers: the British Parliament and the French Constitutional Council, in particular, were unlikely to agree to the yielding of their powers to the European body. It also seemed most unlikely that the Council of Ministers could move towards meaningful majority voting. It had indeed been agreed that governments should allow majority voting in some areas, but how could this mean anything when states could still decide on the interests which were to be the subject of these procedures?(58) Majority voting could only exist in any meaningful sense in the context of the existing institutional arrangements if states could be outvoted and common action taken in areas about which they felt strongly. Although the British were thus outvoted in May 1982 when they tried to veto the annual farm price increase, it was unlikely that this practice would be a regular one. And the Commission's powers were unlikely to grow until the context of its work in relations between governments had significantly altered.

Was it likely that the alternative of working through the Foreign Policy coordination machinery could generate pressures which would overcome these difficulties? As I point out in Chapter 5 there was in Europe in the late Seventies and early Eighties no evidence that any mechanism was developing which could obtain coherence or consistency in foreign policy, and there was no overriding principle in terms of which European Foreign Policy could be defined, such as that which traditionally had that effect in states, namely the principle of sovereignty. If this is absent the products of the foreign policy coordination machinery can in essence never be more than the expression of a chance coincidence of interest, and would be eternally vulnerable to the logic of diversity(59): the different traditions, and patterns of the involvement of the European nation

states in international society would be liable to
continuously recreate divisions of interest. At
the 1974 Summit members had only agreed to
coordinate their "diplomatic action" in areas
"which affect the interests of the Community." (I
discuss the underlying foreign policy interests of
the member states in Chapter 5). There were,
however, a number of features of the foreign policy
coordination procedures which created special
difficulties in the way of accepting a central
authority. They increased states' reluctance to
proceed further. It is not just that there were
different interests but that the way the procedures
worked tended to lead states to stress their right
to be different. The procedures had the effect of
legitimising a <u>Gesellschaft</u> of different actors
pursuing their own interests, which were only
coincidentally convergent. They helped to entrench
further the intense pluralism which I have
discussed. Under De Gaulle the French frequently
behaved as if membership in the Communities
increased their ability to pursue their own
interests. They tended to exploit Community
membership on their own account. This form of
behaviour was increasingly evident in the late
Seventies and early Eighties in the other states.
  The essential character of the new 'club' of
foreign policy administrators and ministers, in the
Presidency, in the foreign policy coordination
machinery and in the European Councils, required a
respect for diversity. Foreign Ministers such as
Lord Carrington, argued that their countries' own
distinct interests must be respected but conceded
that they may be better obtained through membership
in the Communities. The way in which responsiblity
for the Presidency and foreign policy was
transferred from state to state tended to reinforce
this position. Medium sized and small states
acquired an importance in the world of
international diplomacy which they would not
otherwise have had: every 4 1/2 years, Luxembourg
and Dublin, Copenhagen and the Hague became, when
their countries had the Presidency, major European
capitals. These states then acquired a diplomatic
weight both in relations with other members and
also in relation to outsiders because the latter
could never be sure of the contribution of even the
smallest state to what could emerge as a unified
European position.
  The small and medium sized states hesitated
about establishing a single foreign policy

secretariat, or even the kind of permanent planning office attached to the Presidency which the British advocated. They suspected that officials from the bigger states would tend to move into positions of greater responsibility even if a peripatetic staff attached to the Presidency were established. Conversely when the big states argued in favour of centralisation or of a new planning staff they were vulnerable to the accusation that this was for them merely a way of strengthening their own control over the foreign policy coordination procedures. France saw Paris as a suitable location for a permanent secretariat; Britian saw advantages in a permanent secretariat, even one that was peripatetic. (See Chapter 5 for an examination of the specific proposals, and their problems, in this context).

These various suggestions, including the small states' preference for the rotating Presidency, were ways of obtaining or preserving a measure of independent power in the context of the 'cooperative' procedures: each state perceived the benefits of membership of the club for its own interests, but also, in the existing institutional context, was reminded of the costs of moving towards greater 'supranationalism' in the procedures for coordinating foreign policy. The stake of each member in diversity was increased by the very procedures which were intended to assist with coordination. It was indeed ironic that in accepting the form of the Communities which was sought by De Gaulle - a political union - member states were also reinforced in any propensity they may have had to act like him. The problems which had emerged in internal cooperation were, therefore, made more difficult rather than reduced by the experience of foreign policy coòrdination. In reinforcing the governments' propensity to stress their immediate separate interests within the common system, the problems of tackling 'positive' integration were increased: governments became less willing to make the kind of mutual commitment necessary in these more politically sensitive areas.

The implications of the strengthening of the position of foreign ministers, and foreign office officials, for developments in the Communities' internal policies varied somewhat from state to state. The French Foreign Ministry, which had been dominated by De Gaulle, was likely to be very careful about questions of sovereignty; the

confirmation of its position in managing French
relations with the Communities was a further
safeguard against creeping supranationalism to
which the more functional ministeries were more
vulnerable. The British Foreign Office, under
David Owen and Lord Carrington was in contrast
supportive of European cooperation though
ambivalent about its more ambitious long term
implications. It was, however, handicapped by its
tendency to favour good 'civil' relations with
other foreign offices, and with other departments
of state in Britain; by its pragmatic style, and
lack of any long term game-plan; and its resulting
vulnerability to those in the Cabinet, such as
Denis Healey, who were hostile to any attempt on
the part of the Communities' institutions to
strengthen their position. Lord Carrington's
Foreign and Commonwealth Office, though
enthusiastic about foreign policy cooperation, was
profoundly ambivalent about strengthening the
European institutions. When foreign ministries
took up the baton, therefore, it was given either
to those who were against winning the race, or who
were too cautious to do so. They enhanced a
tendency to seek to win small battles in thwarting
others, to muddle through without loss, to react to
others' pressures, to move from crisis to crisis
and to be embarrassed about any evident concern
with the principle of community building. The
increasing role of the foreign policy officers was
not by any means the only cause of these changes;
underlying economic circumstances also created
powerful pressures in this same direction. Nor did
they themselves take over the negotiations. But
their habits and prejudices were liable to
establish the norm.

Conclusions

        There were, therefore, a number of differences
between the pattern of intergovernmental
arrangements in the early Seventies and that of the
late Seventies. In the early Seventies there was
an ambiguity in the evidence about the direction of
movement, though there was a feeling that some
progress in internal questions was possible and
that there could be an increase in the level of
integration involving, possibly, more power for
central institutions such as the Commission. By
the mid-Seventies, however, uncertainties had been
resolved. Major states were imposing clearer

limits upon the level of international integration, and, although the Commission's formal status had not been changed, new institutions had been established alongside it which by implication diminished its status. Governments concentrated increasingly upon questions of foreign policy coordination though they remained unwilling to make the kind of compromise which could have sustained a European Foreign Policy.

Dahrendorf had implied a fallacy that in the event helped to weaken the drive to European integration in the Seventies, that intergovernmental cooperation in external relations through the Davignon mechanisms had exactly the same implications for integration as intergovernmental cooperation in internal questions. It was seen to be illustrative of a new approach which could also be followed in internal questions. Governments speedily discovered that the former was easier, up to a point, than the latter: and foreign policy cooperation had no necessary implications for cooperation on internal questions. The idea that governments could work out cooperative solutions to a series of loosely related specific problems also proved to be an illusion: when they tried to do this they immediately began to stress interests which were defined in the shorter term and which in many cases were mutually exclusive. Worsening economic circumstances certainly contributed to this tendency. Yet Dahrendorf had implied that interests had an essential character which had been obscured by the dogma of the First Europe, whereas it appeared that interests were also constrained and moulded by longer term expectations and larger principles. The dogma of the First Europe was merely the dogma of the times, which in any case would have been necessary. When the Community dogma went, the dogma of national sovereignty reemerged. In the circumstances – particularly economic – of the late 1970's concern with national interests speedily evolved into a sterile form of pluralism.

The member states of the European Communities were in the late 1970's and 1980's tied together in a wide range of economic and other functional interdependences, and there was a coincidence of expectations and interests on a number of questions concerning internal and external developments. But what was missing was any sense of where the Communities were going, and of how far they could go towards unity, which was increasingly reflected in the structure and methods of work of their institutions. The long term effects of the energy crisis certainly contributed towards these problems, but, as I have explained, they were also the consequence of patterns in underlying attitudes toward integration.

NOTES

* This Chapter is adapted from an article which appeared in <u>International Organization</u>, Fall, 1982.

1.   See Donald Puchala, "Of Blind Men, Elephants and International Integration", <u>Journal of Common Market Studies</u>, Volume X, No. 3, March 1972.

2.   For an explanation of intergovernmentalism see Carole Webb, "Introduction: Variations on a Theoretical Theme" in Helen Wallace, William Wallace and Carole Webb, <u>Policy Making in the European Communities</u>, John Wiley and Sons, London, pp. 1-31, esp. pp. 17-22

3.   For an account of the evolution of the Presidency see Geoffrey Edwards and Helen Wallace, <u>The Council of Ministers of the European Community and the President in Office</u>, Federal Trust for Education and Research, London 1977.

4.   See Mr. Leo Tindemans's Report to the European Council. <u>European Union</u>, Bulletin of the European Communities, Supplement 1/76, Brussels, 1976, pp. 14-19 . For a consideration of the distribution of support for Political Union see Phillip Taylor, <u>When Europe Speaks with One Voice</u>, Aldwych Press, London, 1979.

5.   For an account of the development of the political cooperation machinery see William Wallace and David Allen, "Political Cooperation: Procedure as a Substitute for Policy", in Wallace, Wallace & Webb (eds.) <u>loc. cit.</u>, pp. 227-246.

6.   'Wieland Europa', <u>Die Zeit</u>, 9 and 10 July 1972; <u>Pladoyer fur die Europaishe Union</u>, Piper Verlag, Munchen, 1973.

7.   Altiero Spinelli; <u>The European Adventure</u>, Charles knight and Co. Ltd., London 1972, p. 20.

8.   ibid, p. 20
9.   ibid, p. 21
10.   ibid, pp. 21-22
11.   Walter Hallstein, <u>Europe in the Making,</u>

Allen & Unwin, London 1972, p. 145.

12.   See Robert W. Russell 'Snakes and Sheiks: Managing Europe's Money', in Wallace, Wallace and Webb (eds.), loc.cit., pp. 29-89.

13.   Paris Summit - Final Communique, Sixth General Report on the Activities of the Communities, Brussels-Luxembourg, 1973, para. 1.

14.   Paul Taylor, "The Politics of the European Communities: the Confederal Phase", World Politics, Vol. XXVll, April 1975, pp. 336-360, esp. pp. 348-349.

15.   See V. Baratteiri and Anthony Thomas, "EEC Monetary and Economic Cooperation" International Affairs, October 1975, pp. 499-517.

16.   See Edward Heath, Old World, New Horizons: Britain, the Common Market and the Atlantic Alliance, London 1970 (Harvard University: Godkin Lectures)

17.   Quoted in Annette Morgan, From Summit to Council: Evolution in the EEC, Chatham House - P.E.P., June, 1976, pp. 15-18.

18.   Le Monde, September 11, 1965, quoted in Leon N. Lindberg, "Integration as a Source of Stress on the European Community System", International Organization, Spring 1966, pp. 233-265.

19.   Quoted in Annette Morgan, loc.cit., p.18.

20.   Bulletin of the European Communities, Vol. ii, 1973, p.13.

21.   "Declaration issued at the end of the Conference ... by the President of the Conference, Mr. Anke Jorgensen, Danish Prime Minister", quoted in Seventh General Report on the Activities of the Communities, Brussels-Luxembourg, 1974, p.487.

22.   Quoted in Annette Morgan, loc.cit., p.15.

23.   Bulletin of the European Communities, 1, 1970, p.52.

24.   See Paul Taylor, "The Politics of the European Communities: the Confederal Phase", loc.cit., p.350.

25.   See President Ortoli's Introduction to the Sixth General Report on the Activities of the Communities, Brussels-Luxembourg, 1973, p.4.

26.   See Alan Dashwood, "Hastening Slowly: the Communities' path towards Harmonization", in Wallace, Wallace and Webb (Eds.), loc.cit., pp.290-291.

27.   "Meeting of the Heads of Government of the Community, Paris, 9-10 December, 1974,

Communique," quoted in Eigth General Report on the Activities of the Communities, Brussels-Luxembourg, 1974, pp.297-304.

28.   Emile Noel, "Some Reflections on the Preparations, Development and Repercussions of the Meetings between Heads of Government (1974-1975), Government and Opposition, 1976, p.20.

29.   William Wallace and David Allen, in Wallace and Webb (eds.) loc.cit., pp. 239-241

30.   For an examination of de Gaulle's intentions in introducing "Political Union" see Susanne J. Bodenheimer, "The 'Political Union' Debate in Europe", International Organization, Vol. XXI, No. 1, Winter 1967, pp. 24-54.

31.   See Christoph Sasse, Regierungen, Parlamente, Ministerrat: Entscheidunge - prozesse in der Europaische Gemeinschaft, Europa Union Verlag, 1975, pp. 31-39.

32.   See Roger Morgan, West Germany's Foreign Policy Agenda, Centre for Strategic and International Studies, Sage Publications, Beverly Hills/London, 1978, especially pp. 48-52.

33.   See Nora Beloff "Harold's Handy Fig Leaf", The Observer, 2 March 1975, p. 4.

34.   Helen Wallace, Budgetary Politics: The Finances of the European Communities, University Association for Contemporary European Studies, and George Allen and Unwin, London 1980, p. 60.

35.   For a discussion of Britain's increasing insistence upon 'fair national shares' see Geoffrey Denton, "Reflections on Fiscal Federalism in the EEC", Journal of Common Market Studies, Vol. XVI, no. 4, pp. 283-301.

36.   Wallace and Allen, loc.cit., p. 35.

37.   Geoffrey Edwards and Helen Wallace, loc.cit., p. 35.

38.   Ibid, p. 36.

39.   Juliet Lodge, "Towards the European Political Community: EEC Summits and European Integration", Orbis, Vol. XIX, Summer, 1975, p. 646.

40.   The Economist, December 1974.

41.   See Commission of the European Communities, Thirteenth General Report on the Activities of the Communities, Brussels, February 1980, p. 280.

42.   See Financial Times, 17 January 1981. An article by Robert Mauthner reported that Gaston Thorn, new President of the Commission, would not take France to the European Court for its refusal to pay its share of an increase in the Budget

pushed through by the Assembly. West Germany and Belgium had also refused to pay their share of the Budget. In February 1981 it was reported that the Commission would indeed bring all three before the Court.

43.   See Michael Hornsby, The Times, 27 February, 1980. The British Government was reported to be considering the possibility of illegally withholding its V.A.T. contributions to the Communities Budget if her partners would not conclude a satisfactory deal.

44.   See Chapter 8.

45.   I am grateful for this point to Robert Jackson M.E.P., made at a Seminar at Oxford University, November 21st, 1980.

46.   See Michael Hodges and William Wallace, Economic Divergence in the European Community, Allen and Unwin, London 1981.

47.   Dahrendorf, loc.cit.

48.   The Times, February 3, 1981.

49.   Hodge and Wallace, loc.cit.

50.   For a discussion of current problems in the Communities' Industrial Policy see Loukas Tsoukalis and Antonio da Silva Ferreira, "Management of Industrial Surplus Capacity in the European Community", International Organization, Vol. 34, Number 3, Summer 1980, pp. 355-376.

51.   See David Coombes with Ilka Wiebecke, The Power of the Purse in the European Communities, Chatham House/P.E.P., London 1972.

52.   See Chapter 1 above.

53.   See Bulletin of the European Communities, No. 9, 1979, p. 19.

54.   Helen S. Wallace, "The Impact of the Communities on National Policy-Making", Government and Oppositon, Vol. 6, No. 4, Autumn 1971, p. 528.

55.   Report on the European Institutions, Committee. of Three, presented to the European Council October 1979 (no place of publication noted), p. 9. My insert in brackets.

56.   See Michael Hornsby, "Four Years as the Man in the Middle", The Times, London, December 31, 1980.

57.   In 1980 a film starring Peter Sellers dealt with the advantages of simply "being there", i.e. in the right place at the right time, in acquiring power and status, over those of having ability, capacity and even mature judgement!

58.   The Heads of Government considered that it was "necessary to renounce the practice which consisted of making agreement on all questions

conditional on the unanimous consent of the Member States ...", <u>Communique of the Meeting of Heads of Government of the Community</u>, Paris 9-10 December 1974.

    59.   The "logic of diversity" argument was developed by Stanley Hoffman in his article "The Fate of the Nation State", <u>Daedulus</u>, UC, Summer 1966, especially p. 864.

Chapter Four

THE COMMISSION AND DECISION-MAKING IN THE EUROPEAN
COMMUNITIES

In this chapter I consider the Communities'
decision-making system, centred upon the
Commission-Council relationship, in greater detail
than in the earlier chapter. In the next chapter I
deal with those aspects of the process which relate
more explicitly to external relations. There are
striking differences, as well as similarities,
between the response of governments to institutions
such as the International Monetary fund (IMF), or
the Organization for European Economic Cooperation
(OEEC, now OECD), on the one hand and the
institutions of the European Communities on the
other. The IMF and OEEC encouraged each government
to think of itself as the sole, legitimate, and/or
ultimate, spokesman for the state. It was the
government's interpretation of views among the
various groups in the state which mattered.
Dealing with the international institution, in
fact, reinforced the idea that there was indeed a
national interest and that the particular
government was its rightful interpreter. In
contrast, the working methods of the European
Communities tended to fragment the idea of national
interest and to weaken a government's claim to be
its spokesman. The views, and attitudes towards
integration, of groups other than governments, were
more frequently expressed, and indeed the
Commission encouraged this. A more cautious
approach by governments was, therefore, to be
expected. In addition, the appearance in the
European Communities of an extensive range of
transnational, economic, social and cultural links
encouraged in governments a more watchful attitude
towards further incursions because of the threat to
national powers which their further development
could pose.

The Commission and Decision-Making

The working method which was developed first within the European Coal and Steel Community (ECSC), and which was reflected in the design of the European Communities, involved an independent initiating agency – the Commission – in extensive, continuing consultation with nongovernmental groups within the state as well as with governments and their agents. The importance of these consultations was underlined by their relevance, under the terms of the Rome Treaty, to the taking of decisions, mainly in the Council of Ministers, on questions which could affect the whole economic, social, and ultimately political life of member states. It must be stressed that these consultations were very extensive indeed (as extensive as the range of work of the Communities), that they took place mainly as the result of initiatives taken by the Commission, and that their timing in the policy-making process was very often decided by the Commission. The effect was to make it very difficult for governments to maintain their exclusive claim on the national interest. The Commission's activities encouraged other groups within the state to articulate their positions in the European context and to present their views as an alternative and a challenge to those of the government. There were occasions on which representatives of trade unions or industrial confederations sided with Commission members against the members of the permanent delegation of their own nationality. The Commission frequently spoke of the trade unions and employers' organisations as its "social partners", a clear reference to the continuing potential for joint opposition to the views of governments. In these circumstances, the idea of national interest was fragmented, and the traditional task of governments of presenting a coherent position for the whole state was made more difficult.

It must not be concluded that the extent of the fragmentation of the idea of the national interest was a measure of the decline of national governments in the European Communities. The point is rather that the method of decision-making, by fragmenting the idea of national interest, had alerted some sections of government to the potential challenge to their autonomy from the Communities. They had lost something; compared with the general pattern of relations between governments in the 1930's and before, when <u>raison d'etat</u>, <u>Realpolitik</u>, and the zero-sum game mentality were more frequently the dominant factors of international politics, they had lost a great deal. But the process of losing this much encouraged a watchful defensiveness rather than posing a fundamental challenge to their existence.

Policy-making in the European Communities by the 1970's was not of a supranational kind, such as that which Neofunctionalists had predicted in the early Sixties, but rather had become a system of coordination which shared many common characteristics with other inter-governmental institutions such as NATO, or the OEEC - OECD. Coordination is a way of producing common policies among actors which have legal, or formal independence in the areas to which the policies refer; it involves adjustments in the initial positions of the actors in line with the agreed policy and it assumes the acceptance of the overriding importance of common objectives as reflected in a programme of action which is run over a period of time. Policies are adjusted by them in an agreed direction; and policies are fitted into a programme which is seen to be of mutual advantage.

One of the central processes in co-ordinating policy may be summarised under the heading of the confrontation of policy, a term that was coined to describe a technique which was first identified in the OEEC.(1) It refers to the close examination of the policies of each actor by other actors and by the international institution. The state which bears the examination is made to defend its departures from the proposed programme, and the international institution explains and defends it. The sense is conveyed during the confrontation process that the availability of the benefits of the programme is conditional upon successful co-ordination. In this way the policy of each participating state is confronted with the policy of every other participating state in the context of the overall view of the institution: it is a two-way juxtaposition, international institution with each state, and states with each other. The central importance of this process in the Communities system was probably immediately attributable to the confirmation of the system of taking decisions on the basis of unanimity in the Council of Ministers, the main decision-making body on which governments are represented.

In the Treaty of Rome a qualified majority voting system should have applied to an increasing

range of areas in the second and third (final)
phases of the transitional stage. The use of
majority voting would have discouraged the
appearance of several of the procedural and
institutional devices which had become familiar
features in the 1970's. It would have encouraged
the Commission, which was the main initiating body
in the Community system, to concentrate, in its
relations with the Council of Ministers, upon a
single policy, or a very closely-related cluster of
policies, and to introduce into that policy a much
stronger European element. It would have had a
lesser incentive to employ the technique of linking
a wide range of areas together in what has been
called a package deal(2), which involved the
trading-off of the interests of one state against
those of another in relation to various elements of
the package. The Commission would have been
encouraged by majority voting to try to build
coalitions of support in the Council for more
European solutions, and to risk offending a
disapproving minority. Furthermore, the need for
unity on any important issue was the foundation
upon which the very complicated system of
consultations among participating actors was
developed: the Commission had to work for consensus
among the actors by using extensive consultation
and amendment and confrontation before the decision
was taken. The stress upon these procedures led
directly to the development of an institution which
came to rival the Commission in the co-ordination
process, the Committee of Permanent Representatives
(COREPER). This was a committee of permanent
delegations based full-time in Brussels, which met
every week, and attempted to establish agreement
between delegations and between them and the
Commission.(3) Although COREPER remained the main
administration level intergovernmental committee in
Brussels, other standing committees of officers
also emerged and played a rather similar role in
more specialist areas. These included the
Agricultural Committee and the 113 committee.
     Policy-making in the European Communities
became crucially dependent upon the co-ordination
of the position of national actors through their
permanent delegations in Brussels.(4) The
importance of the issues involved for member states
was illustrated by the high status of permanent
delegations' officials, and by their number and the
range of home departments which they represented.
Heads of permanent delegations were of

ambassadorial rank and normally came from the Foreign Offices of member states. Other officials were transferred from senior positions in a wide range of national ministries. Delegations varied in size; the number of senior staff in the British delegation, in 1976, was forty-five above the level of Second Secretary. The convention emerged that the Committee of Permanent Representatives would itself take decisions on the less controversial issues after due consultation, but any more controversial political issues were forwarded for decision to the Council of Ministers. The Committee was, of course, responsible to the Council, and in a sense stood in for the Council when it was not in session. After the Hague Conference of December 1969, a further layer of decision-making, however, emerged in the Communities which also demonstrated the assertion of the separateness and sovereignty of the states in the co-ordination process in the Communities then. Increasingly, crucial decisions on Communities policy were left for Summit meetings of Heads of State or Government, christened European Councils in 1974, which after December 1974 met three times a year, once in the capital of the two states which held the Presidency, and once in Brussels. Their introduction was a further step away from the supranational model supported by pro-Europeans in the early 1960s, which had envisaged the development of the role of the Commission together with the introduction of majority voting into the Council of Ministers.

It is useful to point out here that in the European Communities there were three levels of programme with which the coordination process was concerned. There were those programmes which were associated with an _area_ of proposed activity such as Commercial Policy, the Common Agricultural Policy and Regional Policy (in this chapter I illustrate my argument mainly by reference to the Common Commercial Policy); there was the programme of programmes, the overall framework into which the particular programmes were to be fitted, which could be called the co-ordinated economic system of the European Communities; and there were the focussed programmes within the area programmes, which were intended to achieve specific objectives in the arrangements of the member states, such as the protection under stated conditions of the right of individuals to remain in the territory of another state.

The Commission and Decision-Making

The process of co-ordinating policy may be
conveniently divided into three phases. The first
phase began with the statement of general
objectives and intentions in the particular area of
policy, which may be contained in the Rome Treaty
(articles 110 to 116 on commercial policy), or in
statements made in the Communiques of Summit
Meetings, (for example, in the Final Declaration of
the Paris Summit, October 19-20 1972); on
commercial policy see paragraphs 11, 12, 13 and
14)(5), or in sessions of the Council of Ministers,
or in generally approved Grand Designs such as the
Commission's Action Programme of 1962,(6) or the
Reports of Tindemans or of Vedel. Such statements
were generally about the first level of programmes
and referred to policy areas rather than the
focussed programmes of the third level: they
referred to expectations in the area of common
commercial policy, rather than intentions to act in
specific areas of policy such as anti-dumping.
Commitment at this stage was likely to be expressed
more forcibly where the area was felt to be less
salient, and where it was less specific; the more
salient the area, and the more specific it was, the
greater the level of caution indicated at this
stage.
    The next step was the Commission's response
to the advice, requests, and initiatives of the
Ministers. An initiative was now taken at the
third level of the focussed programmes in the
appropriate Directorate-General of the Commission.
(Directorate-General One in the case of commercial
policy(7).) It is worth remembering that the
majority of programmes at level one could be split
up into a large number of focussed programmes. In
the case of the commercial policy the extent of the
range of these programmes was extremely imprecise,
but the following matters seem to follow from the
treaty or from related 'ministerial guidance':
methods for identifying the country of origin of
goods entering member countries from third
countries; the reduction of quotas on imports from
third countries and the establishment of an agreed
list of liberalised products; the setting up of
procedures for managing trade agreements with third
countries, and for abolishing bi-lateral trade
agreements; (This programme applied until the early
1970's particularly to relations between the
Communities and Eastern Europe: it was not until
1973 that trade arrangements with COMECON countries
became a Community responsibility. Later the

Commission became more concerned to limit bilateral
trade agreements between member states and Japan.);
procedures in the event of dumping and other
'unfair' trade practices by non-members; equalising
arrangements for financing exports, particularly
the export credit systems. In producing its
focussed programmes the Commission worked in one or
other of these areas. For mainly political
reasons, little progress was made in any of them
before the late 1960's.(8) Since then, however,
there has been progress on a number of specific
areas.

        In producing its draft proposal the
Commission staff consulted with representatives of
organised European interest groups, with experts,
and with the members of the permanent delegations
of member states. In the case of the commercial
policy - on a quota system for instance - it
consulted the representatives in Brussels of
various affected manufacturing industries. At this
stage it was attempting to inform itself about the
kind of arrangements which would be ideal in, for
instance, the liberalisation of imports or action
on dumping, and the kind of arrangements which
might have proved acceptable to member states. At
this point the advisers from state delegations were
not necessarily in close touch with home ministries
about the specific topics under discussion and the
chances were therefore greater of a convergence of
interest between delegations and the Commission
sustained by a shared expertise. It was not, of
course, that delegates would now support advanced
schemes for European integration, but rather that
they were more 'expert', 'rational', and individual
and less restricted by political directives. At
the conclusion of this process the draft proposal
in the form of a Commission initiative would have
emerged.

        The second phase of the co-ordination of
policy in the EEC was dominated by the
confrontation of policy between national positions
and between them and the views of the international
institution. It began when the Commission itself,
following the so-called collegiate principle,(9)
decided to accept the proposal, and sent it on to
the Council of Ministers for decision: any General
Report of the Communities contains an account of
the wide-ranging proposals which were sent by the
Commission, in its role as formulator of
Communities legislation, to the Council, the main
decision-making body and law-maker in the

Communities (it made around 300 <u>regulations</u> per annum). The Commission proposal was then forwarded to the Committee of Permanent Representatives, which now, in its formal deliberations, began the process of evaluating the acceptability of the proposal for its members. This is a second style of work of the Representatives, quite different from the first, rather more co-operative, informal style: they were now in the position of obtaining politically informed reactions from home governments, in response to the Commission's proposal. In addition delegations submitted them to their own experts and consulted relevant interest groups: they might also seek clarification and possibly modification from the Commission. In its formal meetings the Committee, and supporting sub-committees would attempt to reconcile national views on the proposal, and, if successful, the agreed draft would be approved without reference to the Council: if agreement could not be established the <u>confrontation</u>, in the presence of Commission representatives, would be transferred to a meeting of full Council. At both Committee and Council levels national ministries were fully engaged; the political element was now very evident. It reflected the co-ordinated positions of the ministries in the various national capitals. The dual role of the state delegation to Brussels, on the one hand, in providing informal and expert advice to the Commission, (and in this case sometimes acting as an ally of the Commission in their relations with home capitals); and, on the other hand, in acting as national agents in the process of the confrontation of policy, was a crucial mechanism in reconciling the international goals of the international organization and the interests of member states. One illustration of national delegations' role as an ally of the Commission was the reported screening of issues which would attract a critical public response by the British delegation at the time of the Referendum in 1975. An institution which in this sense faces both ways is an essential element in a process of coordinating the policies of sovereign states, and this is true of the wide range of international institutions which follow this method of work.

The Commission's proposals did not always enter new territory. A particular proposal might be the latest in a series of linked proposals which sought to expand co-ordination in a focussed area.

For instance, regulation (EEC) No. 1439/74 of the
Council of 4 June 1974 on common rules for imports
and dumping, referred to eleven previous
regulations (all passed since 1968) in the same
area, and each of these followed from a Commission
proposal. The Commission was therefore aware,
because of past experience and because of its
consultations at the time, of the likely response
of the states to its proposals. But, in some
areas, where the initiative broke new ground, the
proposal might be extremely contentious, as with
the proposal to transfer responsibility for trade
arrangements with East European countries to the
Communities,(10) and in this case, the
confrontation of policy might be prolonged. (Under
these circumstances it would take place at Council
level or even at a Summit Meeting.) In new areas,
in particular, the package deal technique was an
aspect of confrontation: several proposals, which
might be in different areas, were linked together
by the Commission in a total package. States were
persuaded to give concessions to other states on
some proposals contained in the package in order to
gain concessions from them on proposals from which
they expected to benefit. Package deals were,
however, invariably made at Council level.

There were two stages of confrontation - in
the Committee of Permanent Representatives, at the
administrative level, and in the Council of
Ministers, at the political level. The
construction of package deals, where links were
worked out between different issues, was more
likely to be successful at the political level:
administrators focussed on specific issues and
lacked the competence and authority to establish
trade-offs between different issues.

The third stage of co-ordination followed the
making of the regulation in the Council. An EEC
regulation has a legal status, in that it is
directly binding on members, and on individuals and
groups within the state. It required changes in
behaviour of the actors to which it was addressed
which were reinforced by the law of the
Communities: disobedience might lead to the
instigation of proceedings against the offender and
the use of legal sanctions (see Chapter 9). The
practical results of a successful act of
co-ordination were therefore very obvious. On the
other hand, there were a wide range of safeguard
procedures in the Treaty of Rome, and in
regulations, by means of which states sought to

protect their status as separate actors in the
co-ordinated system. These largely referred to
courses of action which were open to states in
emergency situations such as a severe adverse
balance of payments.(11) There were, however,
general reservations and exclusions; for instance,
all the Community's regulations which allowed
employees and self-employed persons to reside in
another member's territory, to work there, and to
receive social welfare benefits equivalent to those
received by nationals, were subject to the terms of
Article 48, paragraph 3, which allowed states to
exclude individuals on 'grounds of public policy,
public security or public health'. Article 9 of
the Council's Directive of 17 December 1974, which
greatly strengthened the rights of 'nationals of a
member state to remain in the territory of another
member state after having pursued therein an
activity in a self-employed capacity', repeated the
terms of Article 48 in stating that 'member states
may not derogate from the provisions of this
directive save on grounds of public policy, public
security or public health'.(12) Another exclusion
from the terms of the rules of the Communities
perhaps less surprisingly, were goods or
information deemed essential to national
security(13); a list of products which were judged
relevant to national security was drawn up by the
Council in 1959, as required by Article 223
(paragraph 3), but it has not been published.(14)
    A typical arrangement of safeguard procedures
may be found in the context of the commercial
policy in the regulation of 4 June 1974 on common
rules for imports.(15) In the preamble member
states were empowered, provided that their actions
were on an interim basis, to take protective
measures individually. The regulation also stated
that in the event of changes in trading patterns
which threatened 'to cause injury to Community
producers' (article 7), such as dumping, a
three-stage procedure may be instituted.(16) The
first was surveillance, which required importers to
obtain a licence from member states; second was
action by the Commission to limit the offending
imports (article 12); the third was action by
member states (article 14),(17) which might also be
taken where such measures were justified by a
protective clause contained in a bi-lateral
agreement between the member states and a third
country. (Art. 14, (b)) In the third procedure,
the Commission must be consulted after steps had

been taken at the national level, but in the second procedure the states might require the Commission to act within five days (Art. 12, para 4). The Council had the right to override any action proposed by the Commission (Art. 12, para 5). In the event of disagreement between members and Commission about the gravity of the situation the Commission was liable in practice to accept the members' view. The member states were, therefore, placed in a strong position because of their ability to trigger a Community procedure, and to challenge it through the Council if they disapproved of it, and by their right to act unilaterally if they judged it necessary without much fear of effective action by the international organisation.

It is arguable that governments constructed the institutions of Europe and defined their roles and their specific tasks within the Rome Treaty so as to make it easier for them to defend their interests as integration proceeded. At the time of the negotiations in Brussels and in Rome, the Six realised that although they could agree in detail about tariff reductions, the creation of a Common Market, and the gradualist approach, there were many questions, for instance in agricultural policy, commercial policy, regional policy, and social policy, on which they could then only agree in outline. There was indeed an expectation that future compatibilities would allow detailed agreement but there was no certainty that this would follow. It was agreed, therefore, that a mechanism would be created - namely, the Commission - which would draw up detailed proposals to which governments could respond at greater leisure.(18) The governments were in the position of being asked to agree to schemes which were put to them rather than initiating their own proposals. Their role was the responsive or defensive one of catching the ball rather than throwing it. From the beginning, it could be argued, the institutions of the Communities made it easy for national governments to adopt a defensive stand if they so wished; they were designed to allow a relatively undramatic, stonewalling approach if it happened that in practice the government's expectations of future compatibilities were unrealised. This defensive style may be seen as a characteristic and natural response of governments to the Communities rather than an unnatural departure from the intentions of the founders. This is, of course, in sharp contrast with the Neofunctionalist interpretation.

It is, however, perhaps paradoxical that the granting of unusual powers and the right of initiative to an independent body of international civil servants should be part of a deliberate strategy for making it easier for governments to reduce their level of cooperation or to resist further integration. It is not surprising though that, faced with a broadly uncooperative or defensive posture on the part of members, some governments became impatient and tried more desperate remedies. West Germany's procrastination on the arrangements for financing the Community's agricultural policy was probably one of the causes of France's partial withdrawal from the Communities in June 1965, at the onset of the crisis. The Commission's proposals of March 1965 on institutional reform would probably have received the usual undramatic, defensive cold shoulder from the French had they not been linked with an issue about which the French Government felt strongly, and had agreement on this issue not already been considerably delayed in French eyes. The same kind of impatience was shown by West Germany before the Hague meeting of 1969. The occasional crisis was more likely when states were not firmly committed to a timetable, and when the procedures themselves allowed procrastination. One may conclude that a characteristic dynamic of integration in Europe at this point was the reaching of a critical level of impatience with partners as a result of their failure to provide perceived benefits. This may also be true of the crisis over the Budget in the early 1980s.

It was probably inevitable that as integration proceeded, sections of national governments would become more aware of the need to defend themselves against its implications. Governments in the European Communities no longer presided over states whose various "functional" tiers were largely coextensive. In many respects, states had been economically, legally and politically penetrated by systems which extended throughout the area of the European Communities and, occasionally, beyond them. One result was that governments were now unable to take decisions which referred to their own territory without taking into account a range of influences, pressures, and sometimes rules which originated outside their own frontiers, and which they were unable to control. It was calculated that in West Germany, "about two-thirds of all

questions of agricultural policy ... can no longer
be made in a purely national context, but rather
must be made within the decision-making structure
of the agricultural system of the European
Communities."(19) Upwards of fifty per cent of the
external trade of members of the Communities was
with other members, and for smaller states this
proportion was even higher. Within the
Communities, according to one commentator, were to
be found about three hundred nongovernmental
international organisations, increasing at around
5% a year, including some powerful multinational
companies - by far the largest concentration in the
world.(20) It is hardly surprising that
governments, when faced with these developments,
should have become more sensitive to the
implications of "spill-over".

Writing about relations between developed
states in general, Edward Morse found that "It is
often concluded that the increases in national
cohesiveness that accompany modernization
counteract international interdependence. Actually
the reverse is true." He elaborated: "as the
levels of interdependence within a state rise, the
same order of trade has increased implications for
domestic employment, fiscal, monetary, and welfare
policies."(21) Increasing governmental involvement
in national economies, and the increasing
organisation of its sectors, led to a greater
sensitivity in national governments to adverse
developments in the international economy. But in
reacting to increasing levels of international
interdependence, governments sought to involve
themselves in larger areas of national economic and
social life. This reaction derived from their urge
to defend themselves against international
functional encroachment on their traditional
domain; it was not just another example of
governments asserting their traditional powers.

These developments can be related to certain
arguments about Functionalism: opponents of that
approach to international organization noted the
tendency for an increasing range of activities
within the state to become politicized; governments
were becoming more involved in activities within
the state, and more questions seemed subject to
political controversy. Functionalists had said
that integration would occur more easily in
non-contentious and non-political areas (which no
one would deny) and, further, that as integration
proceeded, a greater range of such non-contentious

areas would manifest itself. (David Mitrany argued that political disagreement would tend to be about different issues – welfare rather than high politics – as integration proceeded; and not that there would be no politics and no contention.)(22) It is readily accepted that governments had, indeed, become more involved in a greater range of issues within the state. But they had become involved in part because of the earlier success of the Functional approach to integration; in part because of the practical requirements of integration which frequently demanded decisions of governments about matters with which they had not been previously directly concerned (such as the manner of drawing up the accounts of railways); and in part because of factors such as modernization and the changing political culture. A much greater range of issues had international dimensions and implications for the standing of governments. It may be that governments had become increasingly sensitized to the political implications of integrative ventures. But they were so sensitized because of the past success of the Functional approach.

It is necessary to distinguish at this stage between the <u>scope</u> and the <u>level</u> of integration: scope refers to the horizontal extent of integration, the number of functional areas which were linked together in some way within the larger territory; level refers to the manner in which the areas were organized – in particular, the extent to which they were ruled from new centres which could act independently of governments. A salient feature of Europe in the 1970s was that the scope of integration was extensive (a wide range of matters had been brought within the integrated area), but the level of integration was low. It was very difficult to show that there had been any significant transfer of authority to the Brussels institutions; they could take decisions on some questions, such as the day-to-day management of the common agricultural policy, but these powers were exercised within the framework of policies agreed on by national governments and only with their approval. Another outstanding feature was that the low level of integration, the fact that national governments retained ultimate control, had to be balanced by the habits of cooperation on a significant range of questions and of using established procedures, and by the development of pressures toward agreement in cooperative arrangements. The European Communities Act, which introduced Communities law into the British legal system, was likely in the view of Mitchell, Kuipers, and Gall to lead to the entrenchment of the practice of parliamentary acceptance of Community decisions in Britain, much as the Statute of Westminster of 1931 entrenched the practice of accepting the independence of Commonwealth governments.(23) Pressures toward agreement derived from public expectations, the high level of interdependence, and the range of regional constraints. Decision-making in the European Communities was therefore decentralized but highly interdependent; members had become more sensitized to the implications of further integration, but were in practice united by entrenched practices of consultation.

Another development in the Communities decision-making in the period is that of the "managed Gesellschaft". The central features of this system were the undermining of the hierarchy of actors and interests, both at the national and the European level and, as a corollary, the legitimization of an increasing range of interests which were fed into the political arena. The development of mechanisms for the management of relations between existing actors of more or less equal status, whose interests were generally seen as having more or less equal validity, seemed to be increasingly the condition for stability. It was not that all interests were in principle equally worthy or just, and that this was part of the essential condition of society; but rather, that they had come to be accepted as such, at least in part because of the integration process. At the same time, governments were no longer able to marshal popular support or tolerance in the way that was once possible. Changes in popular attitudes had helped to undermine the authority of governments. This undermining of the hierarchy of interests, as well as the fracturing of the earlier agreement about priorities among values and attitudes within the state, had contributed to the reduction of the status of governments in the Communities' political system. There is no doubt that the deterioration in the economic situation and particularly after the international monetary crisis, and the energy crisis of 1973, greatly accelerated this process. Despite the increasing pervasiveness of government activity, the authority and status of governments seemed to be declining.

Dissatisfaction with existing conditions within a particular state was also reinforced by comparison with conditions in other states; claims – which may even have challenged the authority of governments – were legitimized. The developments of May 1968 in France, and the success of the workers there in achieving unprecedented increases in wages, certainly sharpened the appetites of trade unionists in other European states and reinforced their determination to achieve a more equitable distribution of wealth. Indeed, the events of May 1968 have been considered as the real starting point of the tendency toward higher wage claims, thought to have contributed so much to inflation in many European states in the 1970s. Expectations within the Communities, and the fact that transmission of demands was made easier by the extensive range of interdependencies and transnational links, aided the process of fracturing the national interest and helped to undermine the hierarchy of interests within the states.

If membership of the European Communities contributed to the weakening of the Gemeinschaft in the nation-state, and helped to undermine the hierarchy of values and attitudes, the declining authority of governments, and the reduction of the effectiveness of their mechanisms for control also encouraged organised groups to increase their demands on governments, and to view their own and the governments' interests as possessing an equal validity. The Community links had contributed to these developments.

There was, however, no tendency for governments to be eliminated as actors from the European Gesellschaft. (I discuss this concept in Chapter I.) In fact, their right to remain as actors was, if anything, reinforced by developments in the Communities then. The absence of a Gemeinschaft as the European level meant that there was no means of deciding whether any actor should have been eliminated from the system. As has been implied, it was accepted that satisfaction of any one interest depended upon the construction of appropriate alliances of power and influence between groups, including governments, rather than upon a government's ability to relate specific demands to a general interest. This was as true at the Communities level as at the national one. The Commission of the European Communities – the main independent, active element in the Brussels institutions - was pressed to renounce its claim to be a rival centre of authority, a putative European government. Its role had now become that of an actor, like any other in the European Gesellschaft, with the specific task of encouraging European arrangements and encouraging alliances to solve particular problems. In other words, it was no longer appropriate for it to set out to challenge national governments. In helping them to define their interests and to form alliances, it reinforced their right to exist. The total effect was an equalization of the hierarchy of actors both at the national and at the European level.

The character of the Commission and the major features of decision making in the Communities indicated the abandonment of the ambition to build at Brussels a centralized European government - a development which mirrored at the European level the changing status of governments at the national one. It can be said that before 1965, the Commission was self-consciously defining a European interest, and that it was active in initiating policies for European integration and creating the norms of European would-be polity. That was a period of greater optimism in the Commission about the building of a more centralized Europe, a mood - for it was largely a question of mood rather than actual achievement or method - sustained by the personality and ideas of Walter Hallstein. It was he who, in the beginning of 1965, told a group of American journalists that he could be seen as a kind of European Prime Minister.(24) The crisis later in 1965 marked the deflation of this optimism: the resistance to the Commission's proposals of March 1965 of expanding the powers of the institutions, and the confirmation of the powers of European governments in relation to Brussels (of which the French Government was the instrument), led to a period, between 1965 and 1969, in which the Commission's mood was subdued. During that time, the dominant features of the Commission's methods were a relatively passive involvement in the process of mediation between the governments, and the execution of agreed policies. The Commission of the European Communities had been recreated in a more traditional style of international bureaucracy.(25)

After the Hague Conference of the Heads of States and Governments of the Six, in December 1969, a third style of Commission involvement in decision making in Europe began to emerge. Its

status in the system was renewed, though its
commitment to the goal of becoming a European
government was weaker. The Commission began more
actively to seek the reaching of agreements between
governments, but it was brought to see itself more
as a partner in the system, with governments,
rather than as a supranational agent. As I show in
Chapter 3, the Commission made some attempts to
return to its earlier role, but they were resisted,
in the early 1970's. In addition, the Commission
actively sought to coordinate the work of Europe's
institutions, even those strictly outside the
framework of the Communities, and to manage the
Gesellschaft though in the late 1970s increasingly
under the Presidency. The Commission's resolve in
transcending the other actors in defining Europe
was weakened though not extinguished, but it
continued its attempts to build agreements among
them. This role of the Commission was another of
the features of decision-making in the 1970s.
     The range of proposals for further integration
which emerged from the Hague meeting was the first
fruit of a phase of integration which, because of
the German recovery, was marked by much more
intensive diplomatic activity, at a higher level,
than there had been in the Communities since 1958.
(I discuss these developments in Chapter 3.) The
German interest and activity were instrumental in
demonstrating that diplomacy and the convergence of
diplomatic objectives were now the touchstone of
success in the integration process. The Commission
was faced with a new situation in which,
paradoxically, the condition of further progress
towards integration was the reassertion of the
separate identity of the government actors and
their engagement in a higher level of diplomacy
than had hitherto been the case. The membership of
Britain in the Communities had strengthened the
idea of the informal representativeness of
individual commissioners. It is certainly not
suggested that any members of the Commission or
their staff were in receipt of specific
instructions, but member governments aimed to get
their men into positions of responsibility for
areas in which they were particularly interested.
With the advent of British membership, the notion
that European Commissioners should in some way
strive for the definition of the pure form of
European interest was weakened, though probably not
entirely dropped. It was no accident that
reponsibility for two areas in which the British

Government was particularly interested was allocated to British Commissioners: George Thomson acquired responsibility for regional questions, and Christopher Soames was placed in charge of relations between the Communities and the developed countries.

The danger that the ascendancy of governments might have led to a decline in the calibre of individual Commissioners and a mood of dull resignation, as had happened previously, was on the whole avoided for a time precisely because of the active and continuous involvement of diplomacy in questions of integration. Because of their awareness of the importance of integration to their separate interests, governments appointed men of high ability to the Commission. At the same time, it was inevitable that a phase of integration which stressed diplomacy and the rights of individual actors should have spawned institutions which did not necessarily accrue to the centre in Brussels. One response of the Commission was to attempt to continue the practice, which had been developed in relation to the Council of Ministers, of sitting in on all meetings and, as formulated when the Communities were the Six, of "acting as a seventh member". In the 1973-77 Commission Wilhelm Haferkamp (Germany) and Henri Simonet (Belgium) represented the Commission at the meetings of Ministers of Economics and Finance which were held outside the framework of the Communities; President Ortoli and the Secretary-General of the Commission, Emile Noel, acquired responsibility for maintaining links between the Commission and the member-states group for political cooperation (The Davignon Committee). As I explain in Chapter 3, however, the French Government was resistant to the Commission's strategy in the area of foreign policy coordination and in the main excluded Commission representatives from the Davignon machinery until the end of 1974. These are indications of the way in which the Commission attempted to strengthen its role as a coordinating element in a more dispersed system of decision making.

Thus, the Commission, in relation to developments at the European level, had in some ways itself changed as the role of governments had changed at the national level. It found itself unable to sustain its claim of being a putative European government which would develop its own authority and power as national governments seemed to have been weakened in these respects within the

state. Proposals were indeed made, without
success, to amend the Treaty of Rome under the
terms of Article 236, so that new areas could be
brought within the framework of the Treaty,
protecting the cohesiveness of the central
institutions.(26)   The Commission and governments
had in a way become more like each other as actors,
seeking alliances with other actors as one
condition of success, and attempting to extend
their presence in striving for proper coordination
and management. Like national governments, the
Commission also sought alliances with the so-called
"social partners", trade union federations and the
representatives of the national confederation of
industry in Brussels. It is, of course, the case
that in addition to the pressures of the European
Communities, there were influences deriving from
the processes of modernization and the development
of the welfare state, which affected governments
and the Commission alike, and which were conducive
toward the same changes in their status as actors.
Among these were the development of attitudes and
values, in national leaders and in Commissioners,
which tended to be managerial and technocratic in
style and disposed them to see the major test of
their success in material standards. The
experience and style of the European Communities
certainly reinforced these attitudes.
     It was also noticeable in the 1970s that there
was frequently an apparent contradiction between
advanced schemes for integration and retreats into
national independence in the stated intentions of
governments. I illustrate and discuss this at
various points in this volume. It is revealed, for
instance, in the holding of direct elections to a
European Assembly, and in the adoption of a common
cover for national passports, at a time when
governments were increasingly prone to disagree.
The terms of the Treaty of April 1970 on the powers
of the European Assembly over the Communities
budget after 1975 were also the subject of endless
and somewhat puzzling reinterpretation: a
maximalist interpretation, which a careful reading
of the Treaty certainly justifies,(27) was that
after 1975 the Assembly would have the final say on
the Community's budget, and that it could legally
reject the budget as a whole if it so decided.
(This right was seen as applying to the whole
budget regardless of whether parts of it had been
previously "regulated" by the Council; the Assembly
could not, however, re-allocate expenditure among

various parts of the budget in the regulated sector.) The minimalist interpretation on the other hand was that the Assembly's right to reject applied only to the administrative budget, about 12 per cent of the whole.(28) It was perhaps not surprising that the French Government, having signed the original Treaty - the wording of which was hard to misunderstand - supported the minimalist position, while the Assembly itself, with rather weak support from the smaller states in the Communities, supported the maximalist one. In the summer of 1975, however, a further treaty was signed which seemed to confirm the maximalist position: it was agreed that the Assembly could reject the whole Budget "for good reasons", and the Council was required to act positively if it were to reject the Assembly's modifications. The Budget Council was the only one in which the majority voting system as stated in the Rome Treaty, was followed. But doubts about the extent of the Assembly's budgetary powers remained: states seemed extremely uncertain about the extent to which they were prepared to go towards this limited supranationalism, although they could not restrain themselves from making apparent concessions in that direction. In other areas, too, such as that of Economic and Monetary Union, governments seemed to be responding both to practical difficulties in the way of further cooperation, such as those caused by the international monetary crisis of 1971, and also to their own doubts about making the kind of political commitment which it required. Sometimes they acted as if they possessed the necessary "political will", but then hesitated before the fateful step.

One reason for this was probably a confusion in the minds of European statesmen between questions about the level of integration and questions about the scope of integration. It was natural that, once extensive interdependence had developed, doubts about further integration should be greater if the next steps appears to involve a sacrifice of governmental control to the centre - and there were many who argued that this was indeed involved in economic and monetary union - and to increase the threat to their survival as actors. However, these pressures were only partly based on the reality of the political situation which prevailed in the European Communities. The difficulty was that statesmen became convinced that it was now virtually impossible to act in Europe without transferring greater authority to the centre — that the scope of integration could not be increased without significantly increasing its level. In this view, statesmen and the Commission were probably wrong: they were the victims partly of their own rhetoric in more euphoric moments and partly of a mistaken strategy by the Commission which had not yet been entirely abandoned. Statesmen had been taken in by their own assertion of being "one", and believed that this must mean the birth of some transcendental European entity; the Commission and integration theorists, such as the Neofunctionalists, in continuously reminding statesmen of the relevance of practical questions to political unity and in implying that a particular question was indeed political succeeded only in warning statemen of possible dangers and of frightening them into confusing questions about the level with questions about the scope of integration. In discussing this danger, Ralf Dahrendorf particularly blamed the Functionalist approach to integration and the Commission's acceptance of it. He criticized the strategy of integration which posed a necessary link between one level of integration and the next, and which maintained that governments were led inevitably from a Common Agricultural Policy to monetary union, and thence to "political union by 1980". He labelled any such gradualist strategy "Functionalist",(29) though the older style of Functionalism, that of Mitrany, would certainly have led the Commission to develop a strategy such as was recommended by Dahrendorf — of concentrating entirely on questions of scope, and of avoiding the "necessary logic" of European political integration, which involved moving to higher 'levels' of integration.

The danger was that achievements in the scope of integration would be endangered by inventing a "necessary" relationship with the level of integration. For instance the European Monetary Fund idea could have been separated from the ambitious proposals for European Union contained in the Werner Plan and seen as part of a more modest arrangement for managing currency relations among the states of Europe on the model of the International Monetary Fund. The European Monetary Fund of the late 1970s was within a much more limited currency-management system. Both Commission and governments needed then to concentrate upon the short-step, problem-solving approach and avoid crippling intimations of federalism.

These were some of the major features of decision-making in the European Communities in the 1970s, as reflected in a range of characteristic features of the actors, the system, and the behaviour of governments. Together they constitute a pattern of decision-making behaviour which is particularly revealing about the limits imposed then upon the dynamics of integration postulated by the Neofunctionalists. Europe then was a Europe of the coordination of policy, rather than of supranationalism, and of contradictions among policy preferences rather than spill-over; and of a managed Gesellschaft, or a concordance system, rather than of an emerging central authority.

NOTES

1. See M. Palmer, John Lamber, et al, European Unity: a Survey of the European Organizations, Allen and Unwin, London, 1968, pp. 88–89.

2. See Roy Pryce, The Politics of the European Community, Butterworth, London, 1973, p.67.

3. Roy Pryce, loc. cit., pp. 67–69.

4. The following section is based on interviews conducted in the Commission, and in the Office of the British Delegation, in March and April, 1976.

5. See the Declaration of the Heads of State or Government in Sixth General Report on the Activities of the European Communities, 1972, Brussels, February 1973, pp. 14–15.

6. See account of the Action Programme in Sixth General Report on the Activities of the Communities (1 May 1962–31 March 1963), Brussels, June 1963, pp. 21–26.

7. The Commissioner in charge from January 1977 was M. Ortoli.

8. See European Community Information Service, Commercial Policy of the European Community, Brussels, January 1973, p. 5.

9. See E. Noel, O.B.E., How the European Community's Institutions Work, Community Topic, 39, Brussels, 1974, pp. 7–9.

10. See Ralf Dahrendorf, 'The Foreign Policy of the EEC', The World Today, Royal Institute of International Affairs, London, 1973.

11. See Article 73, Treaty Establishing the

<u>European Economic Community</u>.

12. <u>Official Journal of the European Communities</u>, 20 January 1975, (75/34/EC), No. L, 14, p. 12.

13. Article 223.

14. According to advice given to the author by the Legal Section of the European Communities, October 1975.

15. Official Journal of the European Communities, No. L. 159, 15 June 1974.

16. <u>Ibid</u>, p. 3.

17. <u>Ibid</u>, p. 5.

18. For an account of the powers of the Commission, see Roy Pryce, <u>The Politics of the European Community</u>, Butterworth, London, 1973, pp. 55-64.

19. Karl Kaiser, 'Transnational Politics: Toward a Theory of Multinational Politics', <u>International Organization</u>, Vol. XXV, Autumn 1971, p. 799.

20. See Kjell Skjelsbaek, 'Transnational Associations and their Functions', in A.J.R. Groom and Paul Taylor (eds.), <u>Functionalism and International Relations: Theory and Practice</u>, University of London Press, London, 1975.

21. Edward L. Morse, 'The Transformation of Foreign Policies: Modernization, Interdependence, and Externalization', <u>World Politics</u>, Vol. XXII, April 1970, p. 389.

22. See Mitrany, <u>A Working Peace System</u>, reprinted with other essays, Quadrangle Books, Chicago, 1966; analysis in Paul Taylor, 'The Functionalist Approach to the Problem of International Order: a Defence', <u>Political Studies</u>, Vol. XVI, October 1968, pp. 393-409.

23. J.D.B. Mitchell, S.A. Kuipers, and B. Gall, 'Constitutional Aspects of the Treaty and Legislation Relating to British Membership', <u>Common Market Law Review</u>, IX, May 1972, 141-47.

24. <u>Common Market</u>, V (September 1965), 190.

25. David Coombes, <u>Politics and Bureaucracy in the European Community</u>, Allen and Unwin, London, 1970.

26. See President Ortoli's Introduction to the <u>Sixth General Report of the Communities</u>, Brussels, February 1973, p. 4.

27. <u>Treaty Amending Certain Budgetary Provisions</u> ... as presented to Parliament, January 1972, Cmnd. 4867, 8-9.

28. David Coombes and Ilka Wiebecke, <u>The Power of the Purse in the European Communities</u>,

PEP/Chatham House, London, 1972.

29. <u>Pladoyer fur die Europaische Union</u>, Piper Verlag, Munich, 1973. Dahrendorf does not distinguish between the older style of Functionalism of Mitrany and its derivatives, particularly Neofunctionalism, although it is not suggested that this was the intention of the Neofunctionalist theorists. The 'necessary logic' approach was the result of an uncritical adaptation for purposes of political strategy, by those involved with the European Communities, of the neofunctionalists' scholarly account of the ways in which a regional political system might be described and explained. For an analysis and critique of both approaches, see Groom and Taylor (fn. 20).

Chapter Five

THE EUROPEAN COMMUNITIES AS AN ACTOR IN
INTERNATIONAL SOCIETY

In this chapter I discuss the procedures of
the institutions of the European Communities, in
particular the Commission, and those of the
machinery for political cooperation, the Davignon
framework, in the conduct of member-states'
relations with the outside world. These should not
be seen as alternatives to those outlined in
Chapter 4; rather are they those which additionally
apply in the external context. In the wide range
of Communities' external relations there were
through the 1970s and early 1980s a number of
illustrations of what might seem to have been
actor-behavour: the Communities appeared to be
acting as a unit in international trade
negotiations (the Tokyo Round),(1) in conferences
on North-South economic relations (the Conference
on Economic International Cooperation in Paris,
1976-1979), and in East-West negotiations such as
those at Helsinki in the early mid-1970s.(2) And
member states produced joint initiatives, for
instance, in relation to the Middle East crisis, as
when they asserted in 1980 that the Palestine
Liberation Organisation should be a party to all
settlements in that area, and in response to the
crisis in Poland, in the early 1980s, and in
relation to the Falkland Islands crisis in April
1982 (see postscript to this chapter).
　　Such behaviour was not, however, the product
of a unified foreign-policy making procedure in the
Communities. The Commission was mainly responsible
for conducting negotiations in matters of trade
with third parties, and initialled the treaties
which concluded such negotiations. In more purely
political questions, such as the European response
to Soviet moves in Afghanistan or in Poland, the
Commission's role was a very minor one and it was

the Political Cooperation machinery, centred around the President-in-office, which was primarily involved.

This range of patterns of institutional involvement raises a number of questions about the Communities' role as an actor in international society. First, where were the lines drawn between the Commission's involvement in foreign policy and that of the member states and of the intergovernmental Political Cooperation machinery? Secondly, what was the role of the Commission in those areas which were in some sense its responsibility? Was there evidence to justify the view that in these areas the Commission's role could indeed be properly described as supranational? Thirdly, to the extent that the regional instruments centred upon the Commission were deficient, either in the range of their coverage of foreign policy, or in their powers in relation to it, was the decentralised inter-governmental system of the Political Cooperation machinery capable of generating effective, coordinated action? It does not necessarily follow that the European Communities could not act effectively in foreign policy if its central organs lacked the powers in that area which would be expected in a more centralised system. The decentralised inter-governmental machinery needs to be examined, however, for evidence of its ability to make good any deficiencies in that respect.

The implications of these questions is that examples of actor-behaviour may be misleading in that they do not reveal weaknesses in the regional organisation's capacity for acting in a unified way in the long term. Indications of such a capacity must be sought elsewhere.(3) One guarantee of a unified response could be the granting of an exclusive competence in all matters of foreign policy. (It will be shown that the European Communities have made some progress towards the extension of an exclusive legal competence to the centre.) Another would be a very high level of convergence of the interests amongst the sub-units of the system, together with institutions which were capable of effecting coordination and pursuing goals, in the absence of the grant of exclusive powers to the centre. (The extent of the convergence of members' interests is discussed.) The system would be expected to produce a unified response over the whole range of foreign policy –

the sub-systems would not conduct their own foreign policy - together with the capacity to learn from changes in the environment: that is, foreign policy would be comprehensive and incremental in that new policies would be adjustments of earlier ones rather than disjointed responses.

The term 'incremental' points to factors which are more likely to maintain the cohesion over time of the actor's sub-systems. These are that the central experience should always be treated as more important than, and dominant over, that of the sub-systems. New foreign policies in these circumstances, would be derived from what has gone before, in the light of new conditions, and would not be decided by a sub-unit. In the absence of this evolutionary, incremental character, the chances are high that one or more of the sub-units would depart in its external relations from the position of the others. Incrementalism points to the recognition among the sub-units, either consciously or unconsciously, of the need to maintain cohesion, and their perception that this should dominate over the perceived conflicting short term interests of the sub-units. It stresses, as I have said, the dominance over time of the central or common experience. The difficulties in capturing and expressing that common experience in a decentralised system are, of course, considerable, and I examine them in the third sector of this essay.

A few illustrations of actor-behaviour are clearly insufficient to demonstrate that the European Communities has acquired in its external relations the character of an actor, in that its foreign policy is likely to be consistent over a period of time. Rather the extent to which these features have developed is more likely to be revealed in an examination of the powers of the various institutions of the European Communities, which are, of course, in large part a product of the interest of the member states in the area of foreign policy. It is not my purpose here, however, to examine in detail the European Communities' policies in the various areas of their external involvement. The focus is upon the extent to which the various institutions have developed a role in the definition and pursuit of a common foreign policy. How far have they developed the capacity of the Communities to behave in international society as an actor in the sense which I have outlined?

****

The first question to be examined is where the lines are to be drawn between the Commission and the machinery for Political Cooperation in the management of the Communities' external relations. This may conveniently be approached from the perspective of the pattern of representation of the different institutions in the various negotiation forums which involved the Communities, or member states collectively, and the outside world. This is the subject of the first section. In the second section I will examine the pattern of participation of the various institutions and members states in the negotiations in which the Commission was regarded as the Communities' main representative. In the last section, I consider the capacity of the inter-governmental Political Cooperation machinery for producing actor-behaviour. These three perspectives allow an evaluation of the extent of the development of the responsibilities of the Communities and those of the machinery for Political Cooperation in the area of external relations through the 1970s and into the early 1980s.

The representation of the general interest of the European Communities through the Commission in negotiations with third parties was gradually extended through the 1970s. The minimum role of the Commission was defined in the Treaty of Rome but was expanded in practice because of the realisation that a Commission contribution would be useful in areas from which it had been previously excluded, and because of the softening of the position of the French in 1974, who had previously opposed an extension of Commission involvement on political grounds.(4)

The Treaty of Rome only extended a specific legal right to the Commission to represent the Communities in pursuit of the so-called Common Commercial Policy: according to Article 113, para. 3, "Where agreements with third countries need to be negotiated, the Commission shall make recommendations to the Council which shall authorise the Commission to open the necessary negotiations". The legal principle is reinforced by the practical logic requiring a single actor to represent the Communities in their external trade negotiations after the completion of the Common External Tariff at the end of the transitional period, which occurred in 1969. As Article 113 also explains in paragraph 1: "After the transition period has ended, the Common Commercial Policy shall be based on uniform principles particularly in regard to changes in tariff rates, the conclusion of tariff and trade agreements, the achievement of uniformity in measures of liberalisation, export policy and measures to protect trade such as those taken in case of dumping or subsidies". It would have been extremely difficult to apply uniform principles in negotiations with third countries by any other means than through a single negotiator such as the Commission. The best known instances of the Commission's exercising this representative function are probably the two major multilateral tariff negotiations of the 1960s and 1970s, the Kennedy Round and the Tokyo Round respectively, though the Commission also acted in a number of trade agreements with individual states.(5)

In tariff negotiations, it was the Commission which actually handled the exchanges and not the states either separately or in the Council of Ministers. (I will discuss the ways in which the latter participate in the process later in this Chapter.) The Council of Ministers reinforced the Commission's negotiating role during the Tokyo Round negotiations when it allowed, as part of the negotiating Mandate agreed in the Council in 1975, the right "to pledge the implementation of a concession at the negotiating table":(6) the Commission was in effect promised that members would not undercut its position by subsequently reneging on concessions allowed to third countries during negotiations, as long as, of course, these were within the terms of the Mandate.

It also meant that the concluding agreements would not need the subsequent ratification of member parliaments, but rather would be self-executing in the manner of Communities regulations. It was the Commission that accepted agreement an this area which then needed the unanimous approval of the Council, according to the principles of Article 228, which laid down the method by which the Communities could enter into agreements with non-members. Compared with the manner of managing foreign policy in the USA, the Commission's position in this procedure was analogous with that of the President and Administration, and the Council's with that of the Senate - which has the responsibility for ratifying treaties. The major

difference was the mandate within which the
Commission was required to negotiate and the
machinery, which I discuss later, for monitoring
the Commission's performance: it was as if the
various states in the USA had the right to
stipulate the terms on which federal foreign policy
was negotiated. During the Tokyo Round, the
Commission negotiated on questions other than
tariff barriers: convenience and commonsense
indicated this. But in November 1979, the Council
of Ministers decided that the Communities, i.e.,
the Commission, could sign all the Tokyo Round
final instruments, the content of which had been
agreed earlier in the year, except for those on
tariff reductions on European Coal and Steel
Community products, (7) on reductions in technical
barriers to trade, and on arrangements for the
aircraft industry. In the excepted areas, both
member states and the Commission were to sign.
    Whilst the member states seemed uncertain
about how far the Commission should be allowed to
extend its representative function beyond that of
pure tariff negotiations, the Court of the
Communities strongly supported its extension.(8)
Article 228 asserted that all of the national
agreements under the EEC Treaty, "shall be
negotiated by the Commission," and "concluded by
the Council ... after consulting the Assembly." In
the early 1970s, member states generally insisted
that the EEC had powers only to conclude
international agreements where the Treaty provided
expressly for this, i.e., in matters of trade. But
in July 1970, the Court argued in connection with
the conclusion of the European Road Transport
Agreement (ERTA) between the EEC and outsiders that
the Communities had the "right to conclude
agreements with outsiders in any area where the
Communities had exercised a power internally".(9)
It was not enough, however, that the Communities
had the right to exercise such a power: it must
have in fact done so. In the area of transport,
the Communities had already approved a regulation
for internal application in October 1969. In later
opinions the Court sought to extend further the
right of the Communities to conclude agreements
with outsiders and the role of the Commission in
negotiations, and initialling agreements, by
deciding that the Communities could act, "whenever
it was necessary for the attainment of one of the
objectives of the Community". (10) The legal right
of the Communities to act was only limited now by

the requirement that it applied only with reference
to internal powers granted by the Treaty for
specific objectives. The member states could still
act if the matter was within the general scope of
the Communities - but not specified - or if it was
outside that scope. This was affirmed in the case
of the Natural Rubber Agreement of 1979; the Court
then ruled that the member states of the Communities could be a party "if, and only if, it was
eventually agreed that the scheme would be financed
out of national funds."(11)

Through the 1970s there arose an increasing
number of contexts in which the member states and
the Commission, on behalf of the Communities, each
together had rights of representation and
negotiation. These were areas where the so-called
mixed procedure came to be used by which the
Commission and the member states both acted. There
were also areas where, though the Commission had no
legal right to be involved, such as those which
were within the general scope of the Treaty but
which were not specifically mentioned, it simply
seemed more convenient to involve the Commission
alongside the member states.

Between negotiations on tariff questions, in
which the Commission clearly had a lead, and those
on "pure" political questions, which were dealt
with in the Davignon machinery, were two main
variants of Communities and inter-governmental
representation, varieties of the mixed procedure.
First there were negotiations which were intended
to lead to special relationships between the
Communities and an outside state or group of
states, which could indeed include discussions
about tariff adjustments, such as might lead to the
granting of preferences, but which might also
concern more contentious arrangements such as aid
schemes like the Common Fund or Stabex or
Minex.(12) Aid or development agreements fell into
the category of matters which remained within the
jurisdiction of member states.

There were three outstanding examples of this
type of negotiation in the 1970s: those which led
to the signing of the two Lome agreements in
February 1975 and October 1979, those of the
Conference on International Economic Cooperation
(CIEC) in 1977, and those which in the late 1970s
became known as the Euro-Arab Dialogue.(13) In
these instances, the Communities were represented
by both the Commission and the representatives of
member states led by the officials of the country

which held the Presidency at that time. In the case of the CIEC negotiations, Stephen Taylor reported that "the EEC was represented at the Conference by two delegates, one from the Commission and one from the Presidency, acting 'in tandem'."(14) This was the system of representation sometimes called the "bicephalic head": it operated in the four Commissions which were the main forums of negotiation in the CIEC. Eight other states from the developed world and the nineteen developing countries present were the other negotiators. The British Government did not, however, accept the principle of tandem representation in good grace: in the preparatory meetings which preceded the CIEC, Foreign Minister Callaghan had insisted upon a separate seat in view of his country's importance as an oil producer. The principle of common representation eventually was accepted, very unwillingly, by Britain at the European Council meeting in Rome in December 1975, on the understanding that "additional points" could be made by them if necessary.(15) In the instance of the CIEC negotiations, the Commission took the lead in some areas: for instance, Commission official Wellenstein chaired the important Development and Finance Committee for the Communities. The coordination of the positions of the two parts of the tandem was, of course, a complex process which I discuss briefly below.

The negotiations which led to the signing of the Lome agreements were also conducted for the Communities by joint Commission – member state teams, although the latter seemed to have been far more organised under the leadership of the Presidency than was the case with the CIEC: individual member states claimed a more direct part in the conduct of the negotiations. Negotiations for Lome II took place in 1978-79, mainly in four contact groups, with the EEC Commission and member states, and African, Caribbean and Pacific (APC) representatives at the ministerial level, and in nine sub-committes of officials from the Commission, together with the Ambassadors of the ACP countries in Brussels, and officials from their permanent Secretariat in that city.(16) One striking difference between the form of representing Communities' and member states' interests in tandem, compared with that in which the Commission was allowed the lead, was that it was the Presidency which was involved in signing final agreements. For instance, the Lome II

Convention was signed on 31st October 1979 by
Michael O'Kennedy, then Foreign Minister of the
Irish Republic, which held the Presidency of the
Communities at the time. In addition the
Convention needed ratification according to the
procedures of the various member states, rather
than being introduced into member states by the
Article 228 procedure.

There were, however, a number of instances in
which the practice of ratification and negotiation
departed in detail from what was legally possible:
Lome II was ratified by member states, though parts
of the agreement could legally have been subject to
the Communities' procedure. In the ERTA case,
also, although the Court had decided that the
Commission had the exclusive right to act in that
particular area, it did not take over the
negotiations: they had been concluded by the
member states and to have changed the procedures at
that stage, and possibly re-opened some of the
negotiations, would have been extremely clumsy and
irritating to outsiders.(17) Despite the participation of the Commission in the negotiations, and
despite their contribution in the preparing of the
positions of the members, the main responsibility
in these negotiations was in practice in the hands
of the Council and the representatives of member
governments. This conclusion was also reached,
however, about the CIEC by one observer. The
tandem procedure was "fundamentally a Council
animal".(18)

The European Communities also participated in
the so-called Euro-Arab Dialogue through both the
Commission and the Council of Ministers, led by the
President. The Dialogue was initiated during the
Copenhagen Summit Meeting of December 1973, which
was taken somewhat by surprise by the unannounced
visit of a group of Arab foreign ministers. Later,
on 15th June 1974, the foreign ministers of the
European Communities sent an aide memoire to the
twenty members of the Arab League, which led to a
meeting between the French Foreign Minister (the
European Communities' Presidency), together with
the President of the Commission, and the President
and Secretary of the Arab League.(19) On the
European Communities' side, a Coordination Group
was established, in which both member states and
the Commission were represented, which met several
times in November 1974 to prepare for the first
meeting of the Euro-Arab General Commission,
scheduled for 26-28 November. In fact, this

meeting did not take place - it was called off by
the Arabs. The Euro-Arab Dialogue was not
inaugurated until 18th-20th May 1976. One crucial
reason for the Commission's involvement in the
practice of the negotiations was that a political
decision had been taken to stress in the Dialogue
the development of fruitful economic and technical
cooperation. As the French Foreign Minister
commented somewhat disingenuously, "We said that
the Dialogue neither bore on oil nor was concerned
with the questions of peaceful settlement in the
Middle East".(20) Discussions were confined,
therefore, to questions in which the Commission had
an immediate interest and a specialist judgement.
The member states also had an interest in
supporting Commission involvement as a way of
confirming the character of the dialogue in the
eyes of the Arabs as non-political. The French
Foreign Minister admitted, however, that the
success of the exchanges could contribute to "a
more stable balance in the Near East and the
Mediterranean". At the time (1975-77), the
Commission and the states were engaged in
constructing a global Mediterranean policy, which
led to agreements with Israel and the so-called
Maghreb and Mashreq countries.(21)
      The second variant of Community-Council
representation, between the pattern of working
mainly through the Commission and mainly through
the machinery for Political Cooperation - in which
the Commission had only a minor role - occurred
when negotiations concerned matters which were of
importance from the point of view of the internal
economic integration of the Communities, but in
relation to which the Treaty of Rome had given no
formal role in external relations to the
Commission. They were a part of the general scope
of the Treaty. Such issues could also be of great
political salience in member states. One example
of this pattern occurred during discussions between
the Communities and other developed states,
particularly the USA, in the context of the
monetary crisis of the early 1970s. The
discussions on the part of the European Communities
were conducted by the President-in-Office and the
Commission was not formally involved in them. The
Commission was, however, very active in presenting
policy proposals to the member governments, and the
Council relied a great deal upon its expertise.
For instance, in response to the dollar crisis of
March 1973, the Commission urged the adoption of a

narrower exchange band together with the strengthening of mutual support mechanisms, the coordination of monetary policies of the Nine, and tighter exchange controls. This package of proposals was essentially what was conveyed to the Group of Ten by the President-in-Office on 16th March 1973.(22) The Group was moved to recognise the modest success of the Communities in moving towards internal coordination of monetary policies and accepted that the Central Banks of the Nine would be released from their obligation to intervene in the fluctuation margins of the US dollar: currencies of the European Communities would now float against the dollar. Although the Commission was not directly involved in the negotiations it, therefore, contributed significantly to the Nine's ability to act as a unit, and to be seen to be doing so in the larger forum. As Sjostedt commented, "The EEC's capability for the performance of actor-behaviour is strongly conditioned by the internal state of structural integration within the Community".(23) When member states needed to act as a unit externally, the role of the Commission might also be strengthened to the extent that external action depended on internal coordination.

The last way in which Communities' interest might be represented was, as I have mentioned, through the foreign policy machinery of the member states themselves and particularly through that of the President-in-Office, as a part of the working of the machinery for Political Cooperation. I discuss the form of that cooperation between governments later in this chapter. Here my concern is only to point out that in questions of a more purely political nature, of which the implications for economic integration were few or not immediate, the tendency of member governments was to exclude the Commission from any role in negotiations and to work mainly but not exclusively through the President-in-Office. Through the 1970s, though, particluarly after the decline of French opposition to Commission participation in meetings of government representatives in the framework of political cooperation in 1974, the Commission was increasingly involved in discussions where it had an interest. (It should be stressed that the political cooperation machinery was not part of the Communities' framework.) After 1975, the participation of the Commission, particuarly the President, in meetings of the European Council became more frequent. And the principle of accepting involvement on a pragmatic basis was extended to the economic Summits with the Americans and the Japanese in 1977 and 1978. The Commission President was accepted by President Carter, though somewhat reluctantly by the French and the British: he was excluded from discussions on energy and the world economy but allowed in on discussions concerning the North-South dialogue and the Tokyo Round negotiations.(24) In meetings which did not concern the Communities' institutions directly, the tendency was to exclude the Commission unless there was a good reason to the contrary: some of the reasons for exclusion seemed somewhat whimsical, but no doubt reflected the national governments' sensitivity to any extension of the Commission's influence in these areas. In November 1981, the European Council accepted the London Report of 13th October, in which the Foreign Ministers held that the Commission's role in the machinery for political cooperation should be accepted and formalised.(25)

Perhaps the earliest example of governments' reluctant acceptance of Commission participation in the preparation of the Communities' positions in an area regarded as being primarily political was at the Conference on European Cooperation and Security (CSCE) at Helsinki in 1973.(26) Indeed the CSCE was a valuable forcing house for the development of the Communities' "actor" role, because it necessitated a clearer definition of the areas – or "baskets" in this particular case – in which the Commission could properly exercise a representational role, and those from which it could be excluded. The member states' representative in the negotiations was the President-in-Office. But Commission President Malfatti argued strongly that European Communities issues were also involved and this view was somewhat reluctantly accepted by the member states: a separate 'ad hoc' group was set up with Commission leadership to advise the EEC negotiators on Communities' questions. The Commission, which had been involved grudgingly, came to play a useful role in bringing the Nine together in the CSCE, particuarly in relation to the economic questions included in Basket 2.

When the members of the European Communities acted on political questions, they tended to work through the diplomatic machinery of the state which held the Presidency. But bilateral diplomacy

between the member states and a third country was
also conducted through the channels of the country
which was then in charge. For instance, in July
1974 the European Communities' Foreign Ministers
expressed concern about the Turkish invasion of
Cyprus via the French ambassadors in Athens and
Ankara. At least two demarches calling for a
ceasefire were conveyed in this way. Sjostedt
concluded that, "through these channels the EEC was
thus capable of acting in a unitary and consistent
way in a rapidly changing situation".(27) This was
also the machinery through which the Communities
made demarche in 1980 in Tehran to support the
demand for the release of American hostages taken
by the Iranians.(28) The state in charge might also
push a preferred course of action as part of an
agreed strategy: for instance, the British Foreign
Minister, Lord Carrington, pushed the Venice
initiative on the Middle East problem during the
period of the British Presidency in 1981, as part
of an agreed programme of action which included the
preceding Luxembourg and Dutch Presidencies. This
practice did not prevent, of course, other leaders
or statesmen from presenting the Communities' view.
But occupation of the position of the Presidency
presented an opportunity to members to pursue a
Communities' initiative: and its diplomatic
machinery was a natural channel for any common
action that might be agreed. After all, no other
common machinery was available!
    The preceding patterns of representation of
the European Communities' interests in negotiations
with third countries were reflected in the various
international organisations with which they dealt.
In 1976 there were 'working relations' with about
fifty other international bodies. According
to Article 116 of the Rome Treaty, members were
enjoined, after the end of the transitional period,
"in respect of all matters of particular interest
to the Common Market", to "proceed within the
framework of international organisations of an
economic character only by common action". In
practice, in 1976, according to Sjostedt, the EEC
was a full member only of GATT and of a number of
commodity organisations, such as those dealing with
lead, cocoa and tin. But it had observer status in
37 other international organisations - including
the United Nations - and had been "invited by the
Secretariat" to participate in four others.(29) In
the cases of full membership, the Commission acted
as the Communities' representative. In other

economic agencies, a more pragmatic procedure was
followed, with the Commission acting on
Communities' questions and the Presidency on
questions deemed to be outside its sphere of
competence. It was difficult to discover whether
the Commission took over from government
representatives as the range of its competence was
expanded by the Court of the Communities in the
manner I discussed earlier. In a number of the
global organisations, however, such as the UN and
the various specialised agencies, the member states
of the European Communities were organised to
facilitate regional consultation, and frequently
spoke through the representative of the
President-in-Office.(30) In 1977, for the first
time, a member of the Commission, M Cheysson,
addressed a General Assembly main committee, the
Economic and Financial Committee.(31)

In the preceding paragraphs, I have given a
somewhat impressionistic account of the division of
labour between the Commission and member states in
the representation of the European Communities'
interests in their external relations. There were
four kinds of patterns: the Commission had the lead
in one, both Council/Presidency and Commission had
a role in the second - the tandem procedure; the
President led but was heavily dependent on the
Commission in a third; and the Commission was
grudgingly allowed to participate, though very much
under the dominance of the member states and the
Presidency, which excluded it if they judged it
necessary, in a fourth. In the 1970s, there had
indeed been an expansion of the Commission's
exclusive role of representation and also an
increasing number of cases in which the Commission
acted in areas allocated to it together with the
representatives of the member states. The mixed
procedure became standard practice in negotiations
involving North-South issues.

There were, however, sometimes differences
between practice and legal possibility. The Court
had made the claim by the late '70s that the
Commission had the right to act in external
relations, and agreements should be concluded by
the Communities' procedure (Article 228) in any
area, including internal questions, which was
specifically mentioned in the Treaty as being a
Communities' responsibility. However the
application of this principle sometimes gave way to
practical, pragmatic considerations and member
states remained capable of determining the margins

of Commission competence on an ad hoc basis.
Matters which it was allowed to negotiate on in the
Tokyo Round in 1977-79 had been subject to the
'tandem' principle in the CIEC in 1977. Member
states also retained the right to decide whether
the Commission should be involved in a consultative
capacity in some forums, such as the European
Councils or the Economic Summits. Although the
extent of the Commission's competence had been
extended and the areas of certainty and uncertainty
could be located, the student of the Communities'
external relations would be ill-advised to rely
upon the legal principles as enunciated by the
Court in deciding who represented the Communities
in particular areas. Practical politics naturally
played a part.

The conclusion is hard to avoid, therefore,
that despite some movement in favour of the
Commission, the Communities were a great distance
from the grant of an exclusive competence to the
regional institutions in matters of external
relations. This is not, however, to underestimate
the role of the Commission in conducting
negotiations with outsiders in the 1970s, in those
areas where it had responsibility.

****

Having sketched the line between the
Commission's and the member states' rights and
habits of representation, I now turn to an
evaluation of the Commission's role in those areas
where it had undeniably exclusive representational
competence, namely in matters of trade. The most
important of the negotiations which focussed on
trade in the 1970s were the so-called Tokyo Round
negotiations between the signatories of the General
Agreement on Tariffs and Trage (GATT), the most
influential of which were the European Communities,
the United States and Japan. The Round was
initiated at a meeting of Ministers in Tokyo on
12th to 14th September 1972 - hence its title! -
though there had been exploratory talks before,
such as those between the United States and the
European Communities in Brussels from December 1971
until February 1972.(32) At the Tokyo meeting, the
Communities were represented by the President-in-
Office; Ministers produced a Declaration on
International Trade Relations, which was rather
vaguely worded in view of the different interests
and priorities which they held, but established a

132

Trade Negotiations Committee which began work in Geneva in late October 1972. Negotiations were eventually concluded in 1979, having been protracted by profound disagreements between members earlier on and interrupted by the energy crisis of late 1973 and the 'waiver' crisis of late 1978.(33)

These negotiations are the context in which the role of the Commission will now be examined. It should be stressed, however, that my focus is not upon the development of the negotiations themselves, but rather upon the extent to which the Commission developed its own powers in relation to the members of the European Communities in this external relations context. The underlying question concerns the limitations in this area on the Commission's exclusive competence to represent the member states of the European Communities in negotiations with outsiders. The Tokyo Round was only one of the contexts in which that question could be examined: another would be the negotiations that led to the Multifibre Agreement of 1980.(34) Issues which need to be examined are the respective roles of the Commission and the member states in the definition of the principles of the Communities in the negotiations (how did the Commission and members participate in that process?); the nature of the resources available to the Commission in its relations with member states; the nature of the influences upon the member states, which persuaded them to allow the Commission to define its own goals in the negotiations and choose within broad limits its own negotiating tactics; and finally, the nature of the long term implications of the development of the Commission's authority during the Tokyo Round. (If the Commission had shown signs of expanding its powers in relation to member states within the Tokyo Round, would it be able to keep them? Was there, in other words, an incremental quality in the process by which the Commission acquired the powers which it exercised on behalf of the European Communities in the Tokyo Round?).

The major principles which determined the relationship of the Commission with the member states during negotiations such as those of the Tokyo Round were laid down in Article 113 of the Rome Treaty, particularly in Paragraph 3. The Council of Ministers authorised the opening negotiations, and this authority was extended to the Commission by the Council in July 1973, following an instruction to the executive bodies to work out a common standpoint for the next GATT round by the time of the October 1972 Summit Meeting in Paris. The Commission was also required to act "within the framework of such directives as the Council may issue to it"; this was the basis of the Council's extension of a Mandate to the Commission in February 1975, and two supplementary Mandates in January and June 1978. In these Mandates, the Council laid down the broad objectives to be sought by the Commission during the negotiations.(35) There was to be an upper limit of 20% ad valorem duties for most products traded between GATT members; no tariff reductions where existing tariffs were less than 8%; 25%-50% reductions where the existing tariff was between 8% and 20%; and 50% reductions where the tariffs were at 25% or above; the Commission was also given instructions to pursue the goal of general adherence to the principles of Article 6 of the General Agreement on Tariffs and Trade (I go into this matter in greater detail later on); there were also a number of other elements in the Mandate. The Commission was required to "conduct these negotiations in consultation with a Special Committee appointed by the Council" which came to be called the 113 Committee. The Commission was not required to seek the approval of the 113 Committee for every move it contemplated: it needed, however, to pay it serious attention because at the end of the negotiations it was the Committee's senior partner, the Council of Ministers, which was empowered to conclude the agreements on behalf of the Communities, according to the terms of Articles 228 and also 114. The Commission could initial, however, their acceptance with the negotiating partners. The agreements obtained their assent in April 1979, only after the rejection by the Council of two earlier versions, in January and February, and the return of the Commission to the negotiating forum in Geneva, to seek adjustments in the package.(36)

The Commission, for its part, conducted the negotiations on behalf of the Communities in the Trade Negotiations Committee, and in the six groups and various sub-groups which were set up in Geneva in 1975. It was also required by the terms of Article 113, 'to submit proposals to the Council for implementing the Common Commercial Policy". In the practice of the Tokyo Round, the Commission reflected this principle when it presented a

134

package of proposals on the Communities approach in a form labelled the "Soames Memorandum", after Christopher Soames, then head of the Commission's Directorate General One, which was the main participant in the negotiations on behalf of the Commission. The Communities' "overall concept" of the negotiations, derived from this Memorandum, was accepted after an all-night Council meeting on 25th and 26th June 1973.(37)   The Commission also presented various interim reports to the Council, such as the major summary report, the "Framework of Understanding", in the summer of 1978.(38)   At the conclusion of the negotiations, as I have mentioned, the Commission was required to present the agreements to the Council for their approval.

During the negotiations, the Commission was naturally concerned to build up a coalition of support among the member states for its position, and to explain the advantages and particular gains to dissenting states. For instance, in 1978 it countered the French accusation that the "Framework of Understanding" was unbalanced as between progress on tariffs and progress on non-tariff areas by pointing out that the United States had indeed made substantial concessions in a number of areas, such as on the interpretation of the terms of Article 6 of GATT. The United States had accepted the principle that countervailing duties should be imposed only if their market showed "material injury", because of subsidies in the exporting country. They had earlier allowed coutervailing duties if it could be shown that a product had been subsidised in the country of origin, regardless of "material injury" in the USA. This reporting and explaining function of the Commission's was undoubtedly one of its more significant contributions to the production of a coordinated Communities' position during the Tokyo Round. These, then, in rather broad terms, are the main elements of the Commission's and the member states' roles in defining the Communities' position in a set of trade negotiations such as the Tokyo Round.

I now turn more specifically to an examination of the weight of the two sides in this interaction. I have said enough to suggest that the Commission was under fairly close surveillance by member states during the negotiations, but whether this amounted to control or direction remains to be seen. The Commission certainly had a number of resources available to it. The staff of DGI in particular were an invaluable source of information and analysis, and had the experience of the Kennedy Round negotiations to draw on. It should be stressed that in the conduct of its external relations in the 1970s, the Commission also had the invaluable resource of unusually gifted and influential Commissioners. As Jean Rey had been able to attract even General de Gaulle's approval for his conduct of the Kennedy Round negotiations in the 1960s, and thereby created more room for manoeuvre for the Commission, so the authority of Dahrendorf, and later Soames and Haferkamp was enhanced by attracting the confidence of governments in their abilities. Cheysson's role in the negotiations on Lome I and II was also crucial. The contribution of individuals should not be underestimated!

In providing the raw material of the negotiations, the Commission was greatly assisted by the growing number of its own missions and offices in other countries, particularly in Washington and Tokyo.(39) The Commission's advice on the American position was sought and accepted during the Council's discussion of the terms of the negotiating Mandate in February 1975, but at a number of stages Commission documents were the basis of Council decisions (for example, the "overall concept" of June 1973). Sjostedt reported that, "The Commission's Report on the exploratory talks is ... one of the main determinants of the way the Council of Ministers defines the Mandate for the EEC negotiations".(40)

There were clearly elements which were not negotiable for the Communities: for example, the Community members did not accept the early US demand that agricultural tariffs should be negotiable on equal terms with those of manufactured goods. The Commission had to backtrack from the terms of the so-called Soames-Dent compromise of October 1975, according to which the Commission had accepted that there could be some trading off of the Communities' positions on agriculture and those on other issues, although it had argued that the issues should still be considered separately. The French, in particular, protested vigorously and argued that the Commission had exceeded its mandate. Eventually the Commission added a declaration that the Soames-Dent agreement did not imply the subordination of agricultural issues to the others.(41) The member states of the Communities

would also not accept the American proposal that
reductions of tariffs should be linear, but rather
insisted on a measure of harmonisation. The
Americans wanted percentage reductions across the
board from existing tariff levels; the Communities
wanted the tariffs brought into line where they
were then at different levels. But within these
parameters, the Commission was allowed a degree of
flexibility in its approach and was able to use its
information, analytical skill and perspective, to
alter member states' appreciation of the value of
the various gains which the Commission had
obtained.

Once the principle had been accepted that the
Commission should act as the negotiator, a number
of resources accrued to it from the process of
negotiation itself. It discovered in its exchanges
with other GATT members the nature of their likely
concessions: it reported what could be got.
Conversely, once negotiations started it became an
authoritative consultant on the subject of what
would need to be given. Even the more recalcitrant
and protectionist states found its views difficult
to counter. This authority was greatly reinforced
by developments during the negotiations with accord
very closely with Keohane and Nye's conclusions
about the role of international institutions in the
context of high levels of economic interdependence:
the Commission became the centre of a number of
alliances and coalitions, and its authority was
greatly enhanced by the recognition by each side
that the international staff had a special
relationship with each other.(42) The close
relations between the Commission and the US
administration during the Carter Presidency was a
considerable resource for the Commission in its
relations with the member states. The phase of
positive negotiations in the Tokyo Round probably
began with the understanding between the American
negotiator Robert Strauss and Commissioner
Haferkamp in the summer of 1977: the Americans
made then a number of concessions including
acceptance of the so-called Swiss formula on tariff
reductions.(43) The Americans accepted the
proposal that there should be a measure of
harmonisation in the tariff reduction process. The
US team and the Commission had good relations from
then on. This gave the Commission a leverage with
the US administration which member states had to
recognise. States were also unwilling to weaken
the negotiating position of the Commission by

pushing their disagreements with it to the point of appearing disunited. Glenda Rosenthal had noticed the use of a similar weapon by the Commission during negotiations in UNCTAD I in 1964-65: member states were reluctant to refute a Commission position in public lest they embarrass their chief negotiator and significantly weaken its position.(44)

In its relations with member states, one of the more fundamental resources of the Commission derived from its ability to present itself, particularly through DGI, as a high priest of free trade. It undoubtedly strengthened resistance to protectionism, which had shown signs of becoming more attractive in some states, such as the United Kingdom and Italy, because of worsening economic circumstances, by acting as a focus for those in national administrations who favoured a liberal approach. The traditionally liberal West Germans had one good ally in their Commissioner Haferkamp: more liberal elements in the British administration pressed for and were encouraged by the appointment of Sir Roy Denman to the position of Director General in DGI in early 1977. As the alliance in favour of further liberalisation was strengthened, so it became more difficult to challenge the Commission without appearing to betray the prevailing orthodoxy. In the later years of the negotiations, this pressure became particularly powerful because of the realisation that if a new framework for trade could not be agreed, there was a real risk of increasing protectionism and economic autarchy in the 1980s.(45) The Commission was an important element in a coalition of interests, including leading elements in national governments, who believed that if these negotiations failed there would be very serious economic costs. They were, therefore, inclined to avoid as far as possible any action which might seem to weaken the position of the Commission.

A number of factors helped to make this accumulation of resources to the Commission during the Tokyo Round more palatable to member states. There were considerable technical advantages in being represented by a single actor such as the Commission; as I have pointed out, these became pressing after the completion of the Common External Tariff (CET) in 1969. From then on, any negotiations between the Communities and outsiders would need to be preceded by negotiations between the members themselves and the presentation of a

co-ordinated position. Any other approach would
have risked the destruction of what had been
achieved in the CET, and the Common Market itself.
The role of the Commission was the most practical
way of conducting the internal negotiations and of
presenting the agreed position to the outside
negotiating parties: it was functionally
necessary. At the end of the day, the member
states did, of course, retain the right to veto any
concessions of which they disapproved and through
the 113 Committee they continually monitored the
Commission's performance.

From the 1970s, the Commission's role in
protecting the Common Market was increasingly
tested by a new kind of problem: that of managing
'surplus capacity' in the EEC, in especially steel
and shipbuilding, and of persuading external
competitors particularly the Japanese, into
'gentlemen's agreements' to limit their exports to
the Community. The Commission's success in hanging
on to its external role in these matters, and in
persuading states not to make their own
arrangements was attributable in part to the
realisation that the unilateral path would quickly
lead to damaging intra-European protectionism, and
in part to the unusual ability and personality of
the Commissioner in charge, Davignon. Although in
this case too, the Commission's role was
'functionally necessary', because of the existence
of the Common Market and the Common External
tariff, there was a strong sense that the
inclination of governments to cut and run was only
just in check.

From the point of view of the GATT partners,
the Commission's role had the advantage of
simplifying the negotiations to some extent: a
part of these complex multinational negotiations
was in effect carried out between a group of
important trading countries, the EEC members,
before they came to Geneva. The whole enterprise
of the Tokyo Round was essentially multilateral,
and the internal multilateralism of the EEC was a
simplifying element in a general multilateralism
rather than a departure from it. On the other
hand, if the member states of the EEC acted
together as the largest trading bloc in the world,
they were more likely to bring effective pressure
to bear on the Americans and Japanese. There were
also probably advantages in working together
through the Commission in that the representatives
of other states developed a sense of collegiality

with the officials of the international institutions more readily than they would have done with governments' representatives. The Commission was the more attractive and acceptable face of the world's most powerful trading bloc, and was less likely to raise the hackles of other governments' representatives. Working through the Commission was therefore both practically necessary and tactically desirable. The Commission and the US developed a mutual sympathy, for instance, about the difficulty of dealing with the French.

The member states also found it possible to accept the Commission's role because it was acting externally rather than internally; as I have argued elsewhere, the development of habits or capacities in the former context had no necessary implications for the latter. The Tokyo Round did not allow the Commission to develop resources which it could use to push through internal policies, for instance, a common industrial policy, which were likely to be far more politically divisive.(46) There was no sense in which the Commission was acquiring new powers for itself, which would have touched the old national susceptibilities about losing sovereignty. And in the circumstances of the late 1970s and the early 1980s, the Commission's behaviour in its trade negotiations had no obvious immediate implications for the distribution of internal resources in the Communities. The Commission's role was not such as seemed to make it possible for it to take decisions which would make the Germans richer or the British poorer. To the extent that they had developed, the Commission's external resources were therefore less politically contentious than they would have been had they been applicable to internal policies. They were, in the terms of David Baldwin, infungible, that is non-transferable from one context to another. (47)

What were the longer term implications for the Commission's future role in external relations of the development of its resources during the Tokyo Round? Although the Commission's performance then was in many ways impressive, it is difficult to accept that its role represented a model for the future, or that it represented a long-term increment in the Commission's resources. I have already made the point that members' toleration of an expanded role at the time was in part a consequence of their confidence that an external success would have only limited implications for internal integration. But too many of the

Commission's resources were a function of immediate
circumstances and chance events in the
international environment for it to be confident of
maintaining its enhanced reputation. In other
words, they were not part of any incremental
process by which the Commission expanded its
authority and developed its role in external
relations but rather a product of special
circumstances which need not necessarily recur. A
less supportive international environment would
have challenged the Commission's status
considerably. The Strauss-Haferkamp accord, on
which so much depended in the later stages of the
negotiations, was in a sense accidental. It was to
a great extent a consequence of the coming into
office in the USA of a more accommodating President
and his wish for the appearance of success
regardless, to some extent, of its substance. An
impartial observer must, indeed, conclude that the
EEC was a rather obstinate and unyielding
negotiating partner. The United States gave way on
almost every major European Communities' claim.
They accepted the so-called Swiss formula approach
to tariff negotiations, by which there was a
measure of harmonisation in tariff levels, which
the EEC had demanded; they accepted the EEC's
demand on countervailing duties -the GATT article 6
rule - despite earlier opposition; and they
accepted the EEC insistence that the Common
Agricultural Policy and agricultural levies should
not be negotiable. Had the United States'
negotiators been less accommodating, the
inflexibility of the Commission and the EEC would
have been apparent, and had the negotiations
failed, the fragility of the Commission's resources
and their dependence upon chance circumstances,
would have been more clearly revealed. The
Commission's resources were in large part the
product of a situation, the main elements of which
could alter radically and unpredictably, and what
had been achieved in the Tokyo Round was not, with
any degree of certainty, transferable to a future
set of trade negotiations. There was no obvious
incremental element.
     That the Commission did not move towards
supranationalism, and the extension of the scale of
its role in exclusively representing the
Communities during the 1970s, was somewhat
predictable. Indeed, the Commission's area of
competence was occasionally raided by the political
cooperation side, as with the agreements made on

ASEAN in 1979 and Yugoslavia in 1980.(48)   Its
contribution was useful but essentially it was
acting as a coordinator rather than as a quasi-
federal actor in its relations with the member
states of the EEC.   In other words, the
Communities' actor behaviour during the Tokyo Round
did not represent a transfer of power in this area
of foreign policy to the Commission.   It could not
tell member states what to do, but rather defined
the attainable goals and relied upon the self-
interest of states, and the pressure upon them to
compromise or risk losing a great deal, to build an
agreed negotiating position.   Various processes,
which I have discussed, helped the attaining of the
agreement.   But in judging the Commission's
performance in the Tokyo Round, it is hard to
escape from the paradox that its apparent authority
was the consequence of the government's ability to
decide what they wanted at the end of the day
rather than a challenge to that ability: the
Commission was allowed a longer leash for technical
and tactical reasons, and the threat of unilateral
action by member states was a key incentive towards
collective action.   The Commission's right to
represent the Communities in these negotiations
was, therefore, rather different from what would
normally be meant by the grant of exclusive
competence in an area of foreign policy to a
central institution.   Despite its possession of
exclusive competence, the Commission was in
practice an agent of the member states, liable to
control by them, though allowed to act on their
behalf.   The condition of the Commission's ability
to act as an agent was the member states' ability
to go their own way.   This was why they did not
quarrel with the legal right of the Commission to
act on the Communities' behalf in questions such as
trade.
        Christopher Soames commented on the community
method as revealed in this context after the
agreement on the 'overall concept' in June 1973:
"It has been for me an instructive exercise in the
Communities' methods.   The methods obviously are
not perfect ... but the experience has made me
believe more profoundly than ever that this is a
method of reaching agreement which can and will
work in a number of other problems besides those of
trade".(49)   Though he had clearly recognised the
use of a complex form of policy co-ordination in
the circumstances of a considerable degree of
commitment by member governments to success, he was

wrong in supposing that such techniques were in some sense an asset which once acquired could be put to various uses. The 1970s showed that they were not transferable to internal problems and there were reasons for supposing they were not necessarily transferrable to future trade negotiations. The thinness of the ice on which the Communities were skating was not apparent, largely because it had not fallen through.

****

I now turn to a discussion of the Communities' 'actor-behaviour' in the areas of external relations in which the Commission did not have an exclusive right to represent the Communities. What were the limit is of the member states' ability to define common foreign policies and to pursue them in a united way in the late 1970s and early 1980s? I am looking here at the achievements and problems of what is essentially a decentralised system: the member states of the European Communities did not work through the Commission but rather through inter-governmental mechanisms, particularly the machinery for political cooperation.

I have already pointed out that the Commission and member governments were involved with each other in various ways outside the area of trade negotiations. At the CIEC, for instance, the principle of tandem representation was used and this was backed up by the coordination of Communities' positions through a complex process known as Kleberisation, named after the Kleber building in Paris where the CIEC negotiations were held. At the core of these processes were a Commission team centered in DGI, and four working groups under COREPER B in which national officials and experts, together with three or four officials from the Commission, met.(50) Position papers originating in the Commission were considered in these groups, and agreed by the 'tandem' representatives. In Paris, Commission and national representatives covered each of the main sets of negotiations together and continuously evolved common positions: if disagreements emerged during negotiations, either between national representatives or some of them and the Commission, they were simply stopped while the Communities' representatives went into a huddle to sort out their differences. Undoubtedly one result of this complex and rather cumbersome process was the development of a strong sense of collegiality between the national and Commission officials involved, and at the time it was thought that the Kleber procedures would become a model for the future conduct of negotiations between the European Communities and the outside world. Whilst it is true that national-Commission interactions became easier in the various international negotiating forums in the late 1970s, cases of tandem representation were very few. Indeed, observers of Kleberisation came to the depressing conclusion that its methods of coordination were forgotten rather quickly.

Other negotiations such as those of Lome II involved both Commission and national representatives but the lead was more clearly with the national governments. The method of coordination was broadly along the lines of those laid down in Article 113. Indeed, the Kleber experience should probably be seen as marking a stage in the emergence of the inter-governmental political cooperation machinery: it represented the most forceful expression of the Commission's claims to represent the Communities' interest in areas other than those that were specifically mentioned in the Treaty of Rome. Through the 1970s, the claims of the states to represent the Communities in the inter-governmental Davignon framework were, however, steadily emerging. By the late 1970s and early 1980s, the fundamental problems of achieving actor-behaviour in areas other than those handled by the Commission were in those which were essentially inter-governmental. For this reason, I now concentrate upon the foreign policy cooperation machinery (POCO) in order to local the problems produced in the context of inter-governmental cooperation in foreign policy in the late 1970s and early 1980s. Was foreign policy cooperation in this context likely to be incremental in the sense which I have described?

The POCO machinery was outlined in the report of the Davignon Committee which was accepted by the Council of Ministers in October 1970.(51) The Committee had been set up by the Meeting Heads of State and Government at the Hague in December 1969. Through the 1970s, the procedures established as the result of the Committee's report were used with increasing frequency. There were quarterly meetings of foreign ministers and frequent meetings of senior foreign office officials and even more frequent meetings of junior ones. In addition, a

telex system, COREU, was introduced which linked
foreign offices in member states directly; and a
system of correspondents was set up by which an
official was appointed in the foreign ministry of
each member state, with special responsibility for
dealing with the partners, thus short-circuiting
the embassy system to some extent. One consequence
of these developments was that in the late 1970s it
was noticed that embassies sometimes learned the
positions of their own foreign ministry through
officials in the foreign ministry of the state to
which they were attached.(52)

The responsibility for the administration of
the POCO machinery was given to the foreign
ministry of the country which held the Presidency
at that time. This meant that POCO had no
permanent secretariat but rather a succession of
secretariats each acting for the six months' period
of a particular country's Presidency. The foreign
minister of the country holding the Presidency
acquired a position of particular importance in the
POCO machinery. He was the Communities' main
diplomatic representative and in addition became
responsible for coordinating the Communities'
foreign policy role and, in some cases, for
coordinating the affairs of the institutions of the
European Communities proper.

The process of internal consultation about the
Communities' foreign policies was matched by a
process of consultation externally. The Helsinki
Conference initiated increased consultation between
the ambassadors of the member states in third party
capitals, such as Washington and Moscow. During
the Helsinki negotiations it had seemed convenient
to help to coordinate positions through the
permanent ambassadors of the member states in that
city. And Communities' representaives acted
together in the UN, in the International Monetary
Fund and elsewhere; they assured the appointment of
Gaston Thorn as President of the UN General
Assembly in 1976.(53) It should be stressed,
though, that this machinery, both internal and
external, was essentially inter-governmental.
There was no legal obligation on members to consult
and decision were taken on the basis of consensus:
officials remained answerable only to their own
governments. Indeed, the Luxembourg Report of the
Davignon Committee had presented no policy
objectives, but rather expressed a concern to
"promote harmonisation of views, coordination of
positions and, where possible or desirable, common

actions". What had emerged by the late 1970s and
early 1980s was a system in which there was a
'coordination reflex': members got the habit of
consulting each other on matters of external
relations.

Out of the POCO system emerged a number of
coordinated responses among members of the European
Communities, though this is not the place for a
comprehensive account. The Europeans reinforced
the United States' sanctions against the Soviet
Union after the invasion of Afghanistan and mounted
a number of joint demarches in Tehran in support of
the release of the American hostages. In February
1980, they proposed the neutralisation of
Afghanistan, and they launched a European
initiative on the Middle East at the Venice Summit
of June 1980.

Undoubtedly the Europeans were brought
together in the early 1980s by the deterioration in
relations between the two super-powers. As
Christopher Hill put it: "In feeling threatened on
both geographical flanks from different kinds of
superpower insouciance, as well as by the unhappy
deterioration of their hard-won detente and
stability the West European states have not been
too inclined to parade their foreign policy
differences".(54)

Although it would be wrong to underestimate
the achievements of the POCO machinery it is
probably true that most of its commentators tend to
be concerned with what has been achieved, and the
direction of movement, rather than with the
difficulties and dangers that remain. In this
section, my primary concern is with the latter.
How far was POCO short of a common foreign policy?
A number of difficulties are indicated by its
character as a decentralised inter-governmental
system. The states were in the paradoxical
situation that there were inevitably occasions when
they needed to trust each other enough to work
through one of their number, whilst at the same
time not trusting each other enough to establish a
centralised system. They were poised on the horns
of a dilemma between idealism and realism: the
idealism of moving towards a single European
foreign policy, such as was advocated by the West
German Foreign Minister, Genscher, in a speech at
Stuttgart on 6th January 1981, in which he called
for a Treaty to establish a common European foreign
policy;(55) and the realism of only coordinating
policy to the extent that seemed necessary from the

point of view of each state's own perception of its interests. Hill posed the dilemma in 1981 in these terms: "They will have to decide whether or not to go for, as a matter of principle, a common European position at the outset of any international issue, or whether to take each as it comes, 'a la carte', so that alignments are dictated more by the merits of the problem than by the demands of any particular solidarity".(56) For the time being, at least, there is little doubt that this dilemma will be resolved by following the realist route. Hence there were somewhat low-key reactions to the Genscher speech and a subsequent West German comment to the effect that it had been largely an exercise in kite-flying.

A number of problems lie at this frontier between decentralisation and centralisation. A centralised system would involve an <u>obligation</u> to consult on foreign policy which, in the early 1980s, did not exist: it would also probably have required members to place all their foreign policy interests into the European domain. There was no clear method of distinguishing between those policies which referred to European questions, and which were therefore suitable for treatment in the POCO machinery, and those which were outside it. Although there appeared to be a happy consensus that all questions for all states were of concern to European partners, the absence of any clear indication that this was indeed so always left open the possibility that a particular state could assert that something was of no concern to the other members. A centralised system would also entail a central staff in place of the present system of relying upon the foreign ministry of the state which held the Presidency, together with effective machinery for responding to crises. Although the London Report of November 1981 did lead to the acceptance of the principle of a small-scale permanent secretariat, its form and functions remained to be seen, and its contribution was likely to be minimal. The medium-sized and small-sized states in particular had reservations. The report also proposed that any three countries should be empowered to call an emergency meeting of foreign ministers at 48 hours' notice. Only the last of these proposals had been accepted in its full form by the end of 1981, and its effectiveness in an actual crisis remained to be seen.

The absence of a clear institutional centre of POCO machinery, a permanent secretariat of significant size, inevitably increased the difficulties of developing a coherent European response. There was no memory bank of past behaviour and no mechanism by which future behaviour could be related to what had gone before. There was, in other words, no accumulation of experience in this sense, and again, no incrementalism in approach or resources. A decentralised system inevitably had no way of evolving a general policy or an 'ideal' approach, such as could generally be produced for the Communities' internal policies, and which was even evident in the case of the Tokyo Round, where the Commission could put to the member states its views of the best that could be got. The POCO machinery was in fact not a coordination system in any meaningful sense, but rather a way of harmonising the positions of the various member states.(57) The system relied upon the convergence of the interests of the various members, as defined by them; the pressures upon members to fit into a common programme produced in an institutional framework, such as are found in a coordination process, were rather slight. The lack of central institutions also made the socialisation process involving the various national officials somewhat unreliable. There was no body of officials who were involved on a full-time basis with European foreign policy making. Commentators on the political cooperation machinery tended, at the end of the day, to see the guarantee of European foreign policy in terms of this socialisation process and in terms of the convergence of national interests.(58) The socialisation process, as it had developed by the early 1980s, probably depended, however, too strongly on the chance juxtaposition of particular politicians and administrators who found each other, sometimes to their mutual surprise, congenial. A changing political scene, and the retirement of key officials, could rapidly undermine what measure of socialisation had been achieved. A central organisation with its own staff and perceptions of appropriate attitudes and behaviour would have helped to overcome the weaknesses inherent in a socialisation process which depended so much on chance coalitions.

It seemed unlikely that there would be moves towards a more centralised system in the early 1980s. I mention the implications of their absence here in order to highlight the nature of the

difficulties of a decentralised system. In the
early 1980s, the achievement of harmonised European
positions depended upon a convergence of
perceptions of national interests: it was
circumstantial and conditional rather than a
product of any sense of the overriding importance
of unified action. I mentioned the pressure
towards harmonisation that derived from changes in
the superpower context. Yet it was easy to see
that harmonisation had its limits when based upon
such pressures. For instance, the POCO machinery
had not (usually) dealt with questions of defence
because of the involve-ment of some member states
in NATO on the one hand, and the neutral stance of
the Irish Republic on the other. Discussions on
questions of security, which included an assortment
of issues, such as arms control and intra-member
arrangements, were however acceptable. In the
early 1980s, there was a move to hold discussions
in the POCO machinery on defence questions, no
doubt because of the worsening international
situation. But any move in that direction could
run into the difficulty fairly soon of seeming to
threaten the links in NATO between the European
states and the USA. If that happened, the British
and the Benelux countries would probably hesitate
about their European ties and restress those with
North America. Other members -in 1982 West
Germany seemed to be one of them - might wish to
take greater risks in European-US relations, (59)
though this had not been the cease earlier.
Similarly, in the event of a new energy crisis, the
different inclinations of the European states would
speedily be exposed. After all, the French were
not in the International Energy Authority, and it
would not be surprising if they stepped out of line
with their colleagues in dealing with the oil
producing states. The French and the other members
had disagreed sharply about their relations with
the USA about energy, since the onset of OPEC in
1973.
     Differences between the policies of member
states were derived in part from the underlying
structure of their interests in relation to the
outside world. This varied from state to state and
was a continuing potential source of policy
difference. The interests of all states and,
indeed, of any economically active unit, may be
divided into four types: there are <u>traditional</u>
interests, which include those which derive from
social and cultural, or longstanding political,

links and which follow from and sustain a sense of
obligation; there are <u>essential</u> interests, which
relate to supplies of indispensable raw materials,
such as energy, water and food; there are
commercial interests, including the maintenance and
extension of markets, which may be linked with the
granting of aid; and there are <u>pastoral</u> interests
which may include the achievement and protection of
less tangible welfare benefits, the protection of
citizens and representatives abroad, the
maintenance of safety standards in the air and at
sea, and health, and also of course, security.
Members of the European Communities satisfied these
interests in part through relations of various
kinds among themselves, but they were also sought
externally. In the external context, however,
individual members naturally stressed relations
with particular outside countries, and sought to
exclude partners from involvement with that
country: sometimes they competed for scarce
resources in relations with the same outside state.
The variety of patterns of external linkage itself
implies competition which could escalate to
conflict: this is one reason for the determination
of member states to maintain, and even extend, the
number of national embassies in third countries
through the 1970s, despite the extension of
multilateral and Communities' representation, and
for the wide variation in the number of foreign
missions resident in their capitals.(60) Member
states still felt that they had good reason to
pursue their own interests through their own
bilateral channels.
        It would be useful to illustrate this argument
in rather broad terms. The British and the French
had a traditional interest in relations with their
ex-colonies; there were of course cultural and
social links which underpinned this, and in both
cases there was a movement towards a 'Commonwealth'
relationship after the independence of the new
states. Britain's relations with her commonwealth
countries came to centre around an extensive
network of non-governmental organisations, and the
biennial meetings of Heads of Government.(61) One
measure of the continuing importance of the latter
for the British was that the briefings prepared for
the Prime Minister before the meetings took place
were the largest single briefings prepared for her
by the Foreign and Commonwealth Office.(62)
Harrison pointed out that in the French case,
relations with former colonies were conducted by a

Secretariat for African and Malagazy Affairs since
1974, which was responsible to the President, and
that the head of the agency had been Jacques
Foccart, who was also the President's chief advisor
on secret service questions. "It would be
difficult to exaggerate this single influence on
African politics and on the French position in
Africa." "He was the trusted confidant of a dozen
African presidents, many of whom owed more to him
than they did to their electorates ... (and) many
key ambassadors posts in black Africa were held by
non-career diplomats, many of them Foccart's
colleagues and leading Gaullists."(63) Although
links between France and her ex-colonies, and
Britain and hers, were loosened and diversified in
the 1970s, these traditional relationships, which
reflected an obligation as well as an economic and
political interest, survived. In the case of West
Germany, of course, the equivalent relationship was
with East Germany.

In their pursuit of what I have called
essential interests, it is striking that members of
the European Communities related to the outside
world in somewhat different ways. All states
obtained a significant proportion of their oil
imports from Saudi Arabia (31% for France, 20% for
West Germany, 25% for Britain); but Britain
imported a larger proportion of her oil from Kuwait
and, before the revolution, from Iran. (Kuwait
13%, Iran 22%), whereas France imported more from
Iraq, and West Germany imported more, perhaps
rather surprisingly, from Algeria -11% and 12%
respectively.(64)) Iraq supplied most of its oil
to Italy and France, whilst West Germany was
Algeria's most important customer. Libya also
exported mainly to Germany and Italy, and very
little Libyan oil went to France or Britain. This
rather crude data is sufficient to illustrate the
differences in the pattern of member states'
dependence on various oil suppliers. Maull pointed
out that the oil crises in 1973-74, and in 1979,
had both led to member states "rushing to conclude
bilateral deals with oil producers, often including
arms transfers on a large scale". In 1979, "the
bilateral attempts to secure oil supplies through
government-to-government contracts reappeared in
force. As a result, the structure of the
international oil market seemed about to change
once more substantially - this time reducing the
importance of the established oil companies."(65)
States had tended to "isolate themselves against an

energy crisis", and any check upon this process, such as working through the oil companies, or through a Communities-level system, was resisted. Britain's ability to isolate herself was, of course, enhanced by the fact that she was herself a significant producer of oil. The implications of the oil glut in 1981 and 1982 for these developments were unclear, at the time of writing, though in March 1982 OPEC members took steps to recover their power by cutting production. It seemed likely that states' efforts to make their own arrangements would continue.

The different pattern of imports by oil producing countries from the member states of the European Communities illustrates the variations in the commercial interests of the latter during the 1970s. Twenty-five percent of Libya's imports came from Italy (10.4% from the next most important source, France); 33% of Algeria's imports came from France (12% from the next most important importer, West Germany); whilst 23% of Nigeria's imports came from the United Kingdom (15.1% from the next most important source, West Germany).(66) In addition, Britain tended to export more to the more developed dominion countries than did the other states, and France exported significantly to her ex-colonies, although the most important of them, Algeria, had succeeded in diversifying its export markets. McKinlay and Little have shown that the percentage of French trade with low income countries was increasingly conducted with states which were not ex-colonies.(67) Member states seemed well aware of the possibilities for using aid policy for political and economic purposes and one indication of this was that a rather smaller portion of their total aid effort was channelled through the European Communities, or other multinational organisations. In 1979, 72% of British aid was distributed on a bilateral basis, whilst 83% of French aid was distributed in this way, and 65% of German. Of the Big Four, only Italy, which gave a derisory .08% of GNP, distributed more through the Communities (59%) than bilaterally (.8%). (68) It was reported in 1981 that the percentage of British aid going through the European Communities was likely to increase but this was only because of the overall reduction in Britain's aid and the fact that her contributions to the European Development Fund were fixed at a given level.(69) Again, the implications of this information on trade, as on aid, is that the member states tended to be involved with the outside world in different ways: the ways in which this could lead to competition, and possibly conflict, were sometimes fairly apparent but the potential for such a development was always implicit.

This conclusion also applies to the fourth set of interests which I have called <u>pastoral</u>. A brief examination of the main item under this heading - security - brings out the point. Although Britain, since 1967, concentrated more on the European theatre and withdrew her forces from east of Suez, it nevertheless still had more security interests outside Europe than the other member states. Britain still had the third largest navy in the world in the early 1980s, and the British government remained firmly attached to NATO and to working with the USA in the maintenance of global security wherever possible. Britain also had a continuing commitment to help with the preservation of security in the Commonwealth. A Declaration at the Singapore meeting of Commonwealth Heads of Government in 1971 recognised, "that the security of each member state from external aggression is a matter of concern to all members".(70) The implications of this is that Britain could be involved both in the maintenance of security among members, and in their defence against non-members. The Commonwealth had not been active in this regard, though a Commonwealth peace-keeping force was involved in the transition from Rhodesia to Zimbabwe, but it was an indication of interest and inclination on the part of the British. France, in contrast, was traditionally inclined to adopt a mediating role between East and West, and despite periods of working with other members of NATO and of attempting to improve relations with the USA, had partially withdrawn from the organisation and budgetary sides of NATO in 1966; and France was also much more actively involved than Britain in helping her ex-colonies in matters of security. In 1981, she had helped Chad to resist Libyan incursions and had also been involved in the Central African Republic. There were six French military bases in Africa: Dakar, Djibouti, Reunion, Mayotte, Abidjan (Ivory Coast) and Libreville (Gabon), containing, in 1978, 14,-15,000 troops. France also had a stronger concern with the maintenance of security in the Mediterranean than, say, Britain or West Germany. The latter had always been drawn between maintaining her security by stressing links with the USA on the one hand,

and seeking ensure security by making her own
arrangements with East Europe, particularly the
Soviet Union and East Germany, on the other.
Through most of the 1950s, West Germany's
dependence upon the USA was stressed, but in the
early 1960s a clash appeared when de Gaulle created
the option for Chancellor Adenauer of working for a
Europe which was more independent of the USA, and
capable of its own initiatives towards Eastern
Europe.(71)   In the late 1970s and early 1980s,
West Germany showed some signs of being tempted
towards neutrality in the emerging East-West
conflict: Chancellor Schmidt was critical of the
increasingly hawkish quality of American policy
towards the USSR - much more so than Britain or
even Mitterand's France - and wished to avoid
undermining detente and the developing trade and
other links, with Eastern Europe.   Again the point
emerges that there were important differences
between the ways in which the problems of how to
maintain security were posed in the various member
states.
    These differences between the structure of
members' interests in relation to outsiders is one
reason for the failure to establish a centralised
machinery in POCO.   Yet, as long as the POCO
machinery was decentralised, there was the
continuing danger that some states would cut and
run in times of crisis.   In view of the different
patterns of their involvement with third countries,
there seemed to be no reason to be optimistic about
the chances of their holding together.   Yet crisis
behaviour could not be entrusted to a centralised
system - there wasn't one - nor to a small group of
leaders - they could not trust each other enough
for that.   Although the acceptance of the British
proposal on a crisis procedure was undoubtedly a
step in the right direction, and could avoid such
problems as the three week delay in the European
response after the Soviet Union's invasion of
Afghanistan, it was just as likely to become a
mechanism for the early identification of
differences among the European states as one for a
speedy coordination of response.
    These then were the limits upon the
identification of a common European foreign policy
in the early 1980s.   My focus has been upon the
difficulties concerning institutions and procedures
rather than upon the policy differences between
states.   I believe, however, that the question of
the convergence or divergence of policies is of

secondary importance. These are relatively shifting sands unless reinforced by a more solid bedrock in terms of socialisation, institutional centralisation, a transfer of legal competences, and a supportive structure of interests. The failures in institutional arrangements were themselves a clear indication of the governments' lack of confidence in the long-term convergence of their interests. Though the member states had been brought, in the early 1980s, to consider some aspects of centralisation, there was little to suggest that the decentralised system would be capable of producing a unified foreign policy in the long term. The Genscher proposal, though it was backed by the Italians in late 1981, would amount to a sacrifice of sovereignty which it seemed unlikely that most governments would accept.

****

In this Chapter, I have covered the broad spectrum of the external relations of the European Communities. The conclusion must be that there is little evidence to support the view that the Communities had reached the point at which they might be expected to produce actor-behaviour in the long term. In trade negotiations, and in political cooperation, the incremental effects seemed to be rather slender. The Commission could represent the Communities, but not as an actor with exclusive competence in the field of foreign policy, but rather as a participant in a rather complex system of coordination with the member states, any one of which could have stopped it from acting, or opting out of the system. The undoubted resources posessed by the Commission were almost totally nonfungible and too much the product of the late 1970s and early 1980s.

On the other hand, the decentralised system of political cooperation was a somewhat unreliable coordinator: it is more accurately viewed as a system for harmonising foreign policies of member states, rather than as a framework for producing European policy. The limits and problems found in it suggested that it was not capable of making good the deficiencies found in central institutions with respect to the making of a common foreign policy in Europe. Too frequently progress was in terms of a circumstantial coincidence of interest, rather than of a strengthening resolve to go for something like a European foreign ministry as a symbol of member

states' commitment to solidarity.
    Europe is capable of producing occasional
examples of actor behaviour. But it seems unlikely
that these would become typical, incremental and
exclusive in the manner which might be expected of
a common foreign policy. Rather, they were the
products of a diverse, decentralised entity, which
was occasionally capable of achieving sufficient
internal coordination, and harmonisation as to
project an image of unity.

****

POSTSCRIPT The Communities gave solid backing to
the British in early 1982 when Argentina invaded
the Falkland Islands, until then a British
dependency. Member states agreed to suspend all
imports from the Argentine for an initial period of
one month. It was at the time of writing unclear
as to whether the Communities' trade ban would hold
if Argentina, or Latin American countries together,
retaliated by excluding imports from Europe, or by
acting against European firms there. West Germany
and Italy, in particular, had extensive economic
interests in the area. This development, though
remarkable as an example of harmonised action by
the Europeans, did not therefore fundamentally
challenge the points made in the concluding
paragraph of this Chapter: the potential for
disagreement remained, and the lack of a reliable
unity in the foreign policy of the member states,
in this context, was evident.

NOTES
    1. See Mario Kakabadse, The Negotiating Role
of the Commission of the European Community in the
GATT Tokyo Round 1973-79, unpublished Ph.D. thesis,
University of London, November 1980.
    2. For an account of the Communities' role
in the Helsinki discussions - The Conference on
Security and Cooperation in Europe - see Philippe
de Schoutheette, La Cooperation Politique
Europeene, Fernand Nathan, Burssels, 1980
(L'edition labor). See also Gotz von Groll, "The
Nine at the CSCE Conference", in David Allen,
Wolfgang Wessells et al, The Political Cooperation
Machinery in Europe, Butterworth, London,
forthcomin
    3. For a useful account of the emergence of
the European Communities as an actor in
international society, see Gunnar Sjostedt, The

External Role of the European Community, Saxon House, Farnborough, 1977

4.   See Dorothy Pickles, "The Decline of Gaullist Foreign Policy", *International Affairs*, Vol. 51, No. 2, April 1975, pp. 220-235, esp. p.233.

5.   See Werner J Feld, *The European Community in World Affairs*, Alfred, 1976, passim.

6.   Reported by Kakabadse, *loc. cit.*, p.133.

7.   The powers of the Commission in external relations were less extensive under the *Treaty of Paris* than under the *Treaty of Rome*. See in particular the rather limited power extended to the High Authority under Articles 71 and 73, *Treaty of Paris*, and the absence of any procedure for concluding agreements between the ECSE and third parties.

8.   See the valuable discussion of the Court's role in this extension in Trevor Hartley, *The Foundations of European Community Law*, Clarendon Press, Oxford, 1981, esp. pp. 145-188.

9.   *Ibid*, p.155.

10.   (1977) ECR at 744; *Official Journal*, 1977, C107/4.

11.   Hartley, *loc. cit.*, p. 164.

12.   See Carol Cosgrove Twitchett, *A Framework for Development: The EEC and ACP*, George Allen and Unwin, London, 1981.

13.   See David Allen, 'The Euro-Arab Dialogue', *Journal of Common Market Studies*, Vol. XVI, No. 4, June 1978, V. 323 and V. 342; and Jacques Bourriner (Ed.), *Le Dialogue Euro-Arabe*, Economica, Paris, 1979.

14.   Stephen Taylor, "EEC Coordination for the North-South Conference', *The World Today*, November 1977, p. 433.

15.   See Robert A Black Jnr., 'Plus ca change plus c'est la meme chose: Nine Governments in Search of a Common Energy Policy', in Helen Wallace, William Wallace, Carole Webb (Eds), *Policy-making in the European Communities*, Wiley, London, pp. 190-191.

16.   Carol Cosgrove Twitchett, *loc. cit.*, p.156.

17.   See Trevor Hartley, *loc. cit.*, p. 156.

18.   Observation of an official, quoted in Stephen Taylor, *loc. cit.*, p. 43-44.

19.   Gunnar Sjostedt, *loc. cit.*, p. 43-44.

20.   Quoted in *Bulletin of the European Communities*, EC 10- 1974, p. 92.

21.   A Shlaim and J U Yannopoulos (Eds), *The*

EEC and the Mediterranean Countries, Cambridge
University Press, Cambridge, 1976.
22.   Gunnar Sjostedt, loc. cit., p. 56.
23.   Ibid, p. 58.
24.   Kakabadse, loc. cit., p. 114.
25.   See Supplement 3/81 - Bulletin EC; and
*Fifteenth General Report on the Activities of the
European Communities in 1981*, Brussels, Luxembourg,
1982, p. 286.
26.   Discussed in William Wallace and David
Allen, 'Political Cooperation ...', in Wallace,
Wallace and Webb (Eds), loc. cit., p. 234-235.
27.   Gunnar Sjostedt, loc. cit., p. 45.
28.   Reported *Bulletin of European
Communities*, 1980/5, 1.5.
29.   Gunnar Sjostedt, loc. cit., p. 49.
30.   See Leon Hurwitz, 'The EEC in the United
Nations: the Voting Behaviour of Eight Countries,
1948-1973', *Journal of Common Market Studies*, Vol.
XIII, No. 3, March 1975, pp. 224-243.
31.   *Eleventh General Report on the Activities
of the European Communities*, Brussels, 1978, p.
238.
32.   Sjostedt, loc. cit., p. 52.
33.   The waiver crisis occurred when the US
failed, in October, 1978, to extend the waiver of
legislation which required countervailing duties on
imports, which had attracted subsidies in their
country of origin. See Mario Kakabadse, loc. cit.,
p. 185-86.
34.   See Chris Farrands, 'Textile Diplomacy:
The Making and Implementation of European Textile
Policy 1974-78', *Journal of Common Market Studies*,
Vol. XVIII, No. 1, Sept. 1979.
35.   See Kakabadse, loc. cit., p. 133.
36.   Ibid, p. 189-192.
37.   Kakabadse, loc. cit., p. 165.
38.   Kakabadse, p. 181.
39.   See Christopher Hill and William Wallace,
'Diplomatic Trends in the European Community',
International Affairs, Vol. 55, No. 1, January
1979, pp. 50-51.
40.   Sjostedt, loc. cit., p. 88.
41.   Kakabadse, loc. cit., p. 171-172.
42.   See Robert Keohane and Joeph Nye,
'Transgovernmental Relations and International
Organisation', *World Politics*, October 1974.
43.   Kakabadse, loc. cit., p. 173 et seq.
44.   Glenda Goldstone Rosenthal, *The Men
Behind the Decisions*, D. C. Heath, Lexington, 1975,
p. 45.

45. See David Watt, 'The European Initiative', Foreign Affairs, Vol. 57/3, 1979.
46. See William Wallace, 'A Common European Foreign Policy: Mirage or Reality?' in Bernard Burrows et al (Eds), Federal Solutions to European Issues, The Macmillan Press, London, 1978, pp. 174-186, esp. p. 185.
47. David Baldwin, 'Power Analysis and World Politics: New Trends versus Old Tendencies', World Politics, 31, 2, January 1979, pp. 161-194.
48. Christopher Hill, 'Changing Gear in Political Cooperation', The Political Quarterly, Vol. 53, No. 1, January-March 1982, p. 55.
49. European Parliament, Debates, July 1973, p. 91.
50. Stephen Taylor, loc. cit., p. 436.
51. See Wallace and Allen, loc. cit.
52. Ibid, p. 237.
53. Wallace, in Burrows et al (Eds.), loc. cit., p. 182.
54. Christopher Hill, loc. cit., p. 52.
55. Ibid, p. 51.
56. Ibid, p. 57-58.
57. For a discussion of the technical differences between harmonisation and coordination, see Paul Taylor, 'A Conceptual Typology of International Organisation', in Paul Taylor and A J R Groom, International Organisations: A Conceptual Approach, Frances Pinter, London, 1978.
58. For instance, see William Wallace, in Burrows et al, loc. cit., at p. 181.
59. See J Vincour, "The German Malaise', The New York Times Magazine, 15 November 1981.
60. See data in Christopher Hill and William Wallace, 'Diplomatic Trends in the European Community', International Affairs, Vol. 55, No. 1, January 1979 at pp. 58 and 61.
61. For an account of the Commonwealth as an international organisation, see A J R Groom and Paul Taylor (Eds), The Continuing Commonwealth: An Unusual Interdependence, Macmillan, London, forthcoming 1983.
62. Discussed in Paul Taylor, 'The Commonwealth in the 1980s: Challenges and Opportunities', in Groom and Taylor, ibid
63. R J Harrison, 'French Relations with Former Colonies', in Groom and Taylor (Eds), ibid., at pp. 13-14 of his manuscript.
64. 1975 figures. Eurostat.
65. Hanns Maull, Europe and World Energy, Butterworths, London, 1980, p. 266.

66.   Figures quoted, _ibid_, pp. 104-105, from IMF _Directions of Trade_.

67.   R D McKinlay and R Little, 'The French Aid Relationship', _Development and Change_, Vo. 9, 1978, pp. 465-466.

68.   Source: OECD _Development Cooperation_, 1980 Review: H M Treasury.

69.   Statement by Lord Carrington, 20 February 1980, _House of Lords Weekly Hansard_, No. 1097.

70.   Annexed to Groom and Taylor, _loc. cit_.

71.   See Alfred Grosser, _The Western Alliance: European-American Relations Since 1945_, The Macmillan Press, London, 1980, pp. 101-128.

Chapter Six

INTERDEPENDENCE AND AUTONOMY IN ECONOMIC AFFAIRS

In the next three chapters I concentrate more
explicitly on the limits of integration among the
member states of the European Communities as
reflected in their politics in three selected
areas.   The discussion is about the character of
the limitations upon the choice of more cooperativ
policies and is not intended as a review of
Communities policies.   The particular policy areas
were selected because of my interest in them and
because they seemed to be areas in which the
character of the limitations could be effectively
revealed.
In this chapter the main empirical reference,
which is the concern of the second section, is the
negotiations which led up to the agreement to set
up a European Monetary System in December 1978.   I
the first section, however, recent contributions t
interdependence theory are discussed and some
additional considerations are presented.   The
theoretical introduction provides the framework fo
the subsequent discussion, and illuminates the
pressures upon the less prosperous states in the
Communities in the 1970s which led them to resist
further measures of intergovernmental cooperation,
except under certain specified conditions, but als
on the other hand, to resist demands for greater
autonomy.
It should be stressed at the outset, though,
that these pressures are not seen as determining
policy.   They affected the choice of policy throug
the normal political processes in the member state
in the setting of those economic and political
circumstances which existed in the mid to late
1970s.   Perhaps the most important aspect of these
circumstances, in the context of the problem
discussed here, is the increasing divergence

between the economies of the richer and the poorer
states.(1)   This development is considered in more
detail in Chapter 8.   In the third section the
pressures which restrained the search for autonomy
are briefly discussed.

1.   Aspects of the Theory of Interdependence.

     There are, as will be expected, several points
of disagreement between scholars about the
essential features of interdependence.   Rosecrance
et al. argue that "by interdependence (is) meant
the direct and positive linkage of the interests of
states such that when the position of one state
changes, the position of others is affected, and in
the same direction.(2)   "In formal economic terms
two economies can be considered integrated (very
highly interdependent) when there is an
equalisation of factor prices."   Rosecrance et al.
stress the positive response of one national system
to flows into it from another.   Keohane and Nye, in
contrast, are more concerned with the question of
"costs", or "constraints", which are imposed on one
actor, usually the government, by changes in the
behaviour of a second actor.   They argue that
interdependence exists where "there are reciprocal
(although not necessarily symmetrical) costly
effects of transactions"(4): actors which are
interdependent are able to impose costs upon other
actors involved in mutual transactions, but, in so
doing, they would also incur costs themselves.   The
authors further distinguish between "sensitivity"
and "vulnerability": "sensitivity involves degrees
of responsiveness within a policy framework - how
quickly do changes in one country bring costly
changes in another, and how great are the costly
effects?"(5) Vulnerability decreases with the
increasing speed and effectiveness with which one
state can alter its policies so that a substitute
for the benefits of the lost transaction can be
found.   Western Europe is more vulnerable than the
USA to a severence of oil supplies from the Middle
East, but both are highly sensitive to such a
development.   The authors also place
interdependence in the context of international
regimes, and place great stress on the
understanding of changes in patterns of
interdependence within regimes.
     Richard Cooper points to a particular problem
caused for national governments by the increasing

economic flows across their frontiers(6): he refers
to a probable impact upon economic transactions
between two or more states of economic developments
within one of them. Whereas Rosecrance et al.
stress the convergence of factor prices, Cooper
focuses upon the international implications of
variations in such prices which may sometimes be
brought about by governments in order to help them
with their economies. "As nations become
increasingly interdependent, as capital and skilled
labour become less exclusively national in their
orientation, countries desiring to pursue tax or
regulatory policies that deviate widely from those
policies in other countries will find themselves
stimulating large inflows or outflows of funds,
firms or persons: these induced movements will in
turn weaken the intended effects of the policies,
or make them more costly."(7) It follows that "a
second kind of growing economic interdependence,
institutional rather than structural, can be
discerned among industrial nations. This
institutional interdependence occurs when these
countries must, by prior agreement, confer, and
even reach joint decisions, on matters of economic
policy."(8)
     In an earlier article Keohane and Nye also
pointed to some of the consequences for the state
of increasing interdependence in this sense(9).
The increasing range of mutual transactions is seen
to make it increasingly difficult for governments
to control independently their national economies:
what is seen as increasing societal interdependence
across national frontiers encourages increasing
policy interdependence, as governments are pushed
to cooperate more with the other government in
order to control their own affairs. As pointed out
by Waltz, this kind of interdependence is not
universal: it does not apply to E-W relations, or
in some respects to N-S relations; and his point
that economic interdependence may be a consequence
of systemic factors, such as the military dominance
of one state, is worth noting.(10) However the
broad features of economic interdependence which I
have outlined do seem to apply in the European
Communities, and it is not necessary here to
consider how far interdependence within the
Communities has been brought about by the strategic
dominance of an external actor, the USA.(11)
     It is useful at this stage to examine more
closely some assumptions which seem to lie behind
this kind of interdependence theory. Keohane and

Nye's approach illustrates a more general tendency in the theory of interdependence to accept the _Gesellschaft_ model of society rather than the _Gemeinschaft_ one. They seem to be more interested in _procedures_ for obtaining interests which are thought to be separately defined by actors who are essentially competitive, rather than the question of whether interests are compatible, or reflect a consensus, which would be central in the alternative _Gemeinshaft_ approach.(12) In some ways, indeed, some interdependence theorists are the most recent intellectual heirs of Thomas Hobbes. The modern equivalent of the Leviathan, however, is not a superior international power which compels the citizens in their own interest to refrain from war, but rather a procedural device such as the "regime". Subjects are seen to accept the rules of the regime because it is only by doing this that they can obtain their separate interests, as Hobbes' citizens accepted the Leviathan, so that they could establish order which was otherwise unobtainable. Keohane and Nye illustrate these Hobbesian, pluralist assumptions most clearly in their argument that interdependence is to be tested in the opportunities it creates to exert power by exploiting the "sensitivity" or "vulnerability" of partners. Canada and the USA are said to be more interdependent because of "Canada's ability to subtly hint at possible retaliation", whilst Australia and the USA were less interdependent "because Australia was less able to play on American sensitivity".(13) It might be thought paradoxical that interdependence should be illustrated mainly by the partners' ability to exert power against each other: it is as if the strength of a marriage were to be tested by reference to one partner's vulnerability to the other's threats. The reader is reminded of the possibility of linking the power-politics paradigm with the cob-web image of international society: it is not necessarily associated only with the billiard ball view. A tentative amendment offered here is that considerations of _Gemeinshaft_ may enter even into inter-state relations, but that most interdependence literature hitherto tends to ignore this possibility. Keohane and Nye's approach to interdependence is, indeed, not a challenge to power politics, but rather a redefinition of that approach.

The alternative assumption of _Gemeinschaft_ as the model of stable society is seen less clearly in the interdependence literature, though in some ways it is reflected - among the theories considered here - in the prescriptions of Richard Cooper.(14) His arguments may be taken as illustrative of this alternative approach. Higher levels of interconnectedness between states are seen to have created problems which <u>should</u> lead governments towards a recognition of their common interests. On the basis of this recognition it should be possible to make supranational arrangements to tackle common problems. In other words, the realization that interests are mutual is expected to precede the procedural or constitutional arrangements, and interdependence is seen to involve a learning process by which decision-makers are brought to recognise common interests. These views stress structural amendment and the transcending of the state system, whereas the alternative pluralist, <u>Gesellschaft</u> view points towards the maintenance of existing structures, and the satisfaction of competing interests, defined within these, in the new framework. The new procedures provide new opportunities for satisfying the distinctive separate interests of the various sub-groups.

One problem in this kind of interdependence theory, as it has developed hitherto, is therefore that it tends to ignore the relationship between <u>Gemeinschaft</u> and <u>Gesellschaft</u> which is to be found in any political process. The form which this relationship usually takes is the modification of perceptions of self-interest by such factors as emotional ties, preferences, 'we feeling', or identification of mutual values. In this sense the dominance of the <u>Gesellschaft</u> model in the literature is probably a closer reflection of reality than would have been the case if <u>Gemeinschaft</u> had dominated. The dominant <u>Gesellschaft</u> model stresses interest at the expense of relationships, and implies that the question of "what is got?" is more important than that of "from or with whom?". The question of with which partner cooperation takes place becomes one of secondary importance. The <u>Gemeinschaft</u> model, on the other hand, points to the possibility that the calculation of advantage from cooperation in relation to particular interests may be secondary to a preference for cooperation with a particular partner or partners, and that interests may be hierarchically organised in the light of such preferences. The stress is upon solidarity rather

than obtaining immediate interest satisfaction.
The preference suggested by Gemeinschaft may lead
to a clustering of cooperative ventures – regimes –
and outsiders may need to pay what could be called
an interconnectedness premium in order to persuade
a potential partner to give up cooperation with an
insider. It is apparent that the size of the
interconnectedness premium will vary both with the
scale of the rewards to be obtained (self-interest
– Gesellschaft) and with the extent of the
preference for arrangements with insiders
(consensus, community or Gemeinschaft). In broad
terms, however, it would be expected that a
stronger Gemeinschaft would require outsiders to
pay a larger interconnectedness premium.

A second underlying difficulty in
interdependence theory is the relationship between
interdependence and international integration. The
form of interdependence is likely to be affected by
the level of integration reached between the states
which are involved. One critical question is why a
particular pattern of interdependence, as reflected
in the existence of a given number of regimes, or
other cooperative ventures, does not contribute
towards the accumulation of further cooperative
ventures, or regimes. The hypothesis which is
tentatively suggested here is that in circumstances
of economic divergence there often appears a
tension between pressures towards further
integration, on the one hand, and pressures towards
autonomy, on the other, and that this tension tends
to fix the relations between actors at a particular
level of integration. The point where integration
is fixed probably lies most frequently between
successful negative integration and – unsuccessful
– positive integration.(15) (Negative integration
concerns the removal of barriers between economies;
positive integration concerns the establishment of
common ways of intervening in economies.)(16)

In the context of economic relations between
members of the European Communities in the 1970s
the primary question which is suggested by this
characteristic of interdependence is the nature of
the relationship between, on the one hand,
pressures towards the strengthening of the
cooperative arrangements among members in such
areas as monetary policy, industrial policy,
regional policy and the harmonisation of European
company law, and on the other hand, the pressures
towards protecting national independence in the
sense of preserving the autonomy of national

decision-making systems in these areas and stressing nationally-created benefits. A further question which arises is whether the particular type of interdependence might actually _increase_ a propensity to retain autonomy. One possibility, for instance, is that interdependence might be associated with a "trap" which is rather like the "poverty trap" created by the inter-related effects of the tax system and social security systems in Britain: at low levels of wages any increase in income can lead to a net decline in receipts from wages and welfare together because welfare support is lost faster than wages increase after tax. Similarly, the interdependence "trap" suggests that there are circumstances in which actors might be expected to resist increases in coordination from a particular level because it is seen as generating a net loss of values at an accelerating rate. One central difficulty is that the strengthening of systems of common rules, or regimes, may tend in a system in which factors of production can move freely to be to the advantage of more developed areas or countries and to the disadvantage of backward areas or countries.

Three ways of overcoming this problem are conceivable, though in the current state of national attitudes in the European Communities the first is likely to be impracticable. One is to seek a solution which transcends existing differences among the actors involved, which stresses the _community_ of interests, and a massive accretion of resources to the centre and the use of some form of supranational institution to redistribute them. It starts with a mutual assertion of community and proceeds to an optimal arrangement of resources based upon a notion of the general interest.(17) Another is to use what have been called in the larger international arena _sidepayments_, which starts by stressing the differences between the interests of states, though these might be later modified by _Gemeinschaft_ sentiments.(18) This approach, in effect, involves a payment by the richer states for the participation of the poorer ones in the coordinated system. One difficulty with the latter approach, however, is that there is at present uncertainty about whether such a redistributive effort would need to be permanent, which is hard to accept for the donor countries (in the European Communities, in particular West Germany), or whether it could be regarded as a temporary aid to development. The

suspicion among some economists and in the
wealthier countries that a system of large
side-payments may turn out to be a permanent
arrangement is, however, a serious disincentive to
their introduction. A further difficulty is that
pressures inevitably build up in the Communities,
as in the North-South, developing-developed state
relationship, for greater control by the donor
country over the way the redistributed funds were
spent by the recipient country, though this control
may be exercised through an international
institution. In any event the question of the
sovereignty of states, and their resistance to
intervention from outside, becomes a sensitive one.
The problem also appears of just how big the
side-payments to the backward areas have to be, and
how they are to be measured by donor states against
the benefits of common rules.

One alternative to the _Gemeinschaft_ solution,
or to higher side-payments, is an insistence on
autonomy. States may choose to resist, for
instance, the growth of common rules which detract
from the state's ability to manipulate the costs of
production so that new investment can be attracted
into itself in competition with other states. Or
they may seek to prevent the movement of factors of
production to the heartland. At the same time,
however, in some forms of interdependence, such as
that in the Communities, states may also be faced
with pressures which provide powerful disincentives
to any increase of autonomy. These pressures
suggest to policy makers that it is not just
further integration which brings a rapid increase
in the scale of costs in relation to benefits, but
that this argument also applies to disintegration.
Hence such states seem to be trapped at a
particular stage of integration in relation to
their partners. In general these seem to be the
states that are the less prosperous members of the
group.

A second alternative is for government to
accept the fact of economic divergence, and to
participate in positive integration without
realising, or accepting, that the richer states are
likely to be further enriched by such a move. The
problems of choosing between autonomy or
integration policies are only sensitive for
governments which are actively seeking to improve
their relative economic position. The Conservative
government of Mrs. Thatcher was less likely to be
troubled by the dangers of positive integration in

the form of the E.M.S., after it became more
concerned with exchange rate stability in
1981-1982, because it had itself stressed the
control of inflation above industrial expansion.
It in effect renounced the attempt, in the short
term, to increase the size of the British economy
in relation to that of the other states in order to
focus upon a problem which it considered more
pressing, namely, controlling inflation.

The calculation by governments of the benefits
which might accrue to them from particular
cooperative ventures are therefore modified by the
preferences which derive from community. If there
are clear benefits of cooperation with insiders, an
outsider will have to pay an interconnectedness
premium which is enough to overcome the preference
for cooperation with an insider. One good
indication of increasing solidarity would be an
increased interconnectedness premium for outsiders;
an indication that this was weak would be a
propensity on the part of members to strike deals
with outsiders without an undue cost for the
latter. The greater the preference, the higher the
premium. If benefits are nil, the Gemeinschaft
factor might still lead an actor to prefer an
arrangement with an insider over beneficial
cooperation with an outsider. Conversely, however,
where greater cooperation brings costs, the
side-payment necessary to overcome reluctance to
cooperate will be smaller at higher levels of
Gemeinschaft and greater where community preference
is low. Side-payments may be seen, therefore, as a
mirror image of the interconnectednes premium when
further acts of cooperation with insiders bring
costs rather than benefits.

The nature of the balance between autonomy and
integration which is characteristic of
interdependence is therefore critically dependent
on the relationship between Gemeinschaft and
Gesellschaft at a particular level of integration.
It seems likely, however, that where there are
wider differences between levels of prosperity and
lesser feelings of community the tension between
autonomy and integration will be most deeply
entrenched. Where differences are small, and
Gemeinschaft high, it may be easier to resolve
tensions by providing adequate side-payments and
thereby moving to a higher level of integration.
It should be pointed out that the consequences of
Gemeinschaft and its relationship with Gesellschaft
are not confined to the European Communties. The

Commonwealth, for instance, also has some elements of Gemeinschaft, and there are other inter-state relationships that have this quality.

2. The European Monetary System Negotiations

The arguments of the previous section are now illustrated and extended with reference to the discussions about the proposed European Monetary System (EMS) in the period 1977-79. It is not intended here to examine the economic arguments for or against EMS, but rather to consider the policy position of the two major groups of governments which were involved(19): on the one side were the group of more prosperous countries, led by West Germany, and including the other Community members of the "snake", namely Belgium, Holland, and Denmark, and also, sometimes, a "non-snake" member, France; on the other side were the less prosperous contries, led by the United Kingdom, and including also Ireland and Italy. It is also not proposed to consider the history of the "snake", but rather to take its evolution up until 1977 as a given (20) and to concentrate on responses to the Commission's initiative in 1977, particularly Roy Jenkins' speech at Florence in October of that year. The very important background factor of the increasing divergence between levels of economic performance in member states is also not considered, though it is readily accepted that such a divergence is a sine qua non of the arguments developed here.

Several features of the interdependence trap may be illustrated in the context of the EMS. It was widely thought that the proposed system would in itself be more in the interest of the heartland countries than of the periphery and that this advantage had to be offset by a significant transfer of resources from the richer to the poorer.(21) West Germany would establish a more stable currency regime in Western Europe and would thus lay the basis for a further expansion of trade with her more important trading partners: she would, in effect, "internalize" the market by eliminating the exchange rate risk; she would avoid the problem faced through the 1960s of either importing inflation from "weaker" partners, or of revaluing the D-mark and thus weakening the competitive position of her products; she would reduce the chances that the declining dollar would increase pressure unequally upon the various European currencies, tending to push the stronger

currencies upwards in relation to the weaker; and
she would increase pressures upon the governments
of the poorer countries to pursue stability-
inducing policies, rather than risking more
inflationary "growth" policies, and this in turn
would tend to help the stronger industries of the
heartland by discouraging policies to regenerate
industry in the periphery. The weaker countries,
in contrast, would lose the weapon of devaluation
traditionally used to improve the competitive
position of their products. It was to offset these
advantages, which threatened to
accelerate the transfer of wealth from the weaker
to the stronger countries, thus exacerbating
existing inequalities, that it was argued there was
a need for redistributive measures(22), and for
"the needs of the weaker areas to be tackled much
more vigorously than at the present"(23). Much of
the negotiation about EMS concerned the scale of
these "side-payments", with West Germany, Holland
and Belgium, generally attempting to scale them
down, and the UK, Ireland and Italy attempting to
increase them. There were, however, those who
argued from the start that it was unlikely that the
heartland could be persuaded to increase
side-payments to the point at which the
disadvantages for the weaker countries inherent in
the system could be offset(24). It was more
important, therefore, to follow policies which
would lead to a convergence in economic performance
and thus in effect reduce the need for
side-payments as a condition for the introduction
of the system(25).

The negotiations about side-payments were in
connection with a rather scaled-down version of the
original EMS proposal made by the Commission in the
autumn of 1977 and winter 1977-78. There is in a
number of proposals in this period, however, the
outline of what could be called a 'community
approach' to monetary stability and economic
integration among the Nine, but which failed to
receive the support either of the British or of
West Germany because it seemed to involve the
transfer of too much power to the Brussels
institutions, and was too big a step for them to
stomach. This approach, had it been accepted,
would have taken the Communities in this particular
sector a good way towards the stage of centralized
direction, a leap over the interdependence trap,
which, as is suggested in my earlier argument, may
be seen as an alternative to side-payments.

The original Jenkins proposals reflected an attempt to locate and build upon the general interest, in neofunctional terms to upgrade the common interest, rather than to arrange a deal between conflicting interests, which is the essential character of "side-payments". He argued on the 18th of January, 1978, in a speech to the European Parliament, that the EMS "must be combined with moves to promote better regional distribution of work and wealth in Europe through measures to accelerate the flow of public finance." There was need for "a more redistributive Community Budget" which should be increased to "about five to seven percent of Gross Domestic Product from the present level of under one percent"; and there was a need for "a limited but significant transfer of power from member governments to the Community"; "both the exchange rates and the monetary supply should be controlled at the European level by a European Monetary Authority."(26)

There is in the Jenkins proposals a strong reflection of the MacDougall report on financial arrangements in the Community which was widely discussed in the summer of 1977. It was pointed out in this report that the redistributive effects of the Community Budget were in the late 1970s around one percent compared with the forty percent reduction in income differentials produced by national public spending and taxation in a group of five federations and three unitary states which the committee had studied. Conclusions were that "a huge shift of fiscal authority from national governments to the EC is necessary to obtain full economic and monetary union"; that the EC Budget should be increased to around two to two and one-half percent of Gross Domenstic Product by increasing contributions to the EC raised through Value Added tax, by a payroll tax on companies investing in richer areas ("to balance subsidies offered to investors in poorer areas"), and by a "levy on oil imports designed to protect a minimum safeguard price in the Communities."(27) The Report also pointed out that differences in per capita income in the Communities could be reduced by forty percent by an annual expenditure of less than four percent of members' Gross National Product, and that, in any case, some increase in the Community Budget would be required because the limits of present financial resources could be reached by 1980 if the then current levels of spending were maintained.

172

Both the MacDougall proposals, which have been described as "fiscal federalism",(28) and the Jenkins proposals on the EMS, would have involved a considerable expansion of the role of the Community institutions in relation to the control of Community resources, together with a dramatic increase in the scale of those resources. Both proposals also supported the movement of these resources from rich to poor, though as Christopher Tugendhat has pointed out, this would be necessary "not just to help the weak, but also to ensure that the strong are not held back by the inadequacies of the weak."(29) The Commission's broad stance on redistribution may be generally described as strongly in favour; it saw an increased role for itself as a way of making such redistribution more likely. Neither the MacDougall report or the Jenkins proposals received the support of the leading EC governments, however, despite the fact that they would have brought considerable economic advantages to the less prosperous states, though at some risk, however hard to evaluate, to national sovereignty.

The MacDougall report and the Jenkins proposals are not the only elements in a conceivable Community approach to monetary and economic integration in this period. In June 1977, for instance, Commissioner Ortoli announced a plan to raise about six hundred and fifty million pounds in the New York Stock Exchange and asked the states to "approve the principle of guaranteeing a line of credit".(30) He wished to capitalize upon the Community's excellent "Triple A" credit rating in New York, and to create by these means additional finance to help economic development. It was pointed out that the burden of agricultural support left little over for such assistance in the present budget. The reaction of both the West Germans and the British governments to this proposal was rather cautious in that they did not wish the money, if raised, to be in the hands of the Commission.(31) When the loan was eventually arranged in January and February of 1978 at 1.23 billion dollars it was agreed - particularly because of pressure from West Germany, but with the support of the British - that it should be raised in tranches with the approval of the Council of Ministers and placed under the control of the European Investment Bank, whose board was made up of national finance ministers.(32) The British Chancellor of the Exchequer was reported to have said to be seeking

clarification on relations between the Commission
and the European Investment Bank in connection with
the loan.(34)   The British government seems to have
conspired with the stronger governments, led in
this case by the West Germans, to prevent an
accretion of financial independence to the
Commission, despite the fact that such a
development would probably have been more in
accordance with Britain's economic interests.   The
Commission seemed in this, as in other instances,
to be a potential ally of the British in that it
was more likely to favour the transfer of funds to
problem areas, in contrast with the European
Investment Bank, which was more vulnerable to the
cautious approach on industrial policy of the West
Germans.   The British determination to protect
sovereignty, and to prevent a jump to the Community
approach, even at the expense of her economic
interests, was also reflected in her opposition to
the European Parliament's attempt to increase the
size of the Regional Fund in December 1978, and
January 1979, even to the point of risking legal
action against herself for not paying her share of
the budget.(35)   Britain would have been one of the
major beneficiaries of the larger fund.   The
British government also opposed the proposal that
the proportion of the fund which the Commission
could itself administer should be increased,
although the Commission would probably have been
well disposed towards Britain's problems.(36)
These are again instances of Britain's rather
foolish policy of attempting to shackle a potential
ally, and of her broad opposition, together with
other member states, to a Community approach to
monetary and economic integration.
    It is not suggested that British support for a
Community approach would have ensured its success,
though this possibility should not be excluded, but
rather that British policy in these matters helped
to ensure that the Community approach in its
various aspects was rejected, despite the
possibility that this could have brought
considerable economic benefits, and that Britain
also weakened the position of a potential ally, the
Commission.   The British government seemed to lack
the ability to combine vigorous pursuit of national
interests with the appearance of support for
Community procedures and customs, a skill which the
West Germans, in particular, now have in very
considerable measure.   Even if Britain had remained
unprepared to accept the loss of sovereignty

implicit in the original Jenkins proposals and the
MacDougall report, the advantages of dealing with
the Commission more sensitively and of attempting
to strengthen the position of a known sympathizer
would have been an asset in the discussion about
side-payments which began after the Bremen
proposals on EMS in early July 1978.

A scaled-down intergovernmental version of the
EMS was formally initiated then by the West Germans
and the French, though this had been discussed
tentatively at the Council meeting in Copenhagen in
April 1978. It was reported that Helmut Schmidt,
the West German Chancellor, was "unexpectedly
active" in encouraging his colleagues to re-examine
the factors underlying the current currency
malaise, and that President Giscard d'Estaing of
France spoke about the problem of "internal
exchange rate turbulence" and the need for a
"currency zone".(37) On 17th May the Monetary
Committee of the EC, on which member governments
are represented, began discussion of the EMS,
though the various discussions between the
governments were kept under strict security. It
was suggested, however, that the main cause for the
timing of the German-French initiative was the
continuing weakness of the dollar and the resulting
uneven pressures upon the European currencies. The
stronger currencies of the D-mark zone, the old
snake, were being pushed up away from the weaker
currencies of the United Kingdom, Ireland and
Italy. It was reported, also, that by August 1977
the D-mark had accrued by 18.9% against sixteen
major currencies since 1976, a factor which
probably contributed to the withdrawal of the
Swedish Krone from the snake on August 28.(38) In
December 1977 the Belgian franc, Dutch Guilder and
Norwegian Krone also came under pressure.

The EMS proposal revealed at the Bremen
meeting looked rather like a modified version of
the old snake.(39) Although there were several
points of disagreement and ambiguity - which will
be discussed below - the broad principles were,
that there would be a fixing of the exchange rates
of member currencies against each other, though the
margin for weaker currencies could be wider than
those for the stronger members of the existing
snake. (Changes in central rates could still take
place but only after discussions with other
members, and there would be a coordination of
activities in relation to non-member countries like
the dollar); it had been reported that the

activities of currencies under pressure in the
snake in selling dollars, had actually increased
the pressure upon the D-mark because the "freed"
dollars were used to purchase the stronger
currency. It was also agreed that intervention in
the market would be in the currencies of member
countries, and that there would be a new currency
unit, called the European Currency Unit (ECU),
which would be created initially against the
transfer of 20% of the gold and dollar reserves of
members and valued against a basket of the
currencies of member states. Although the ECU
would for the time being be used as the numeraire
and as the means of settlement between EEC monetary
authorities, it would not be used to trigger
interventions. Apparently the existing very short,
short and medium term monetary support mechanisms
would remain as the primary channels through which
states would borrow to protect their
currencies.(40) It should be pointed out further
that though "fixed" the currencies were
nevertheless alterable after consultation with EMS
partners and that this immediately raised the
question of whether the various support mechanisms
were adequate if a currency were under pressure.
There was no Community control over exchange rates,
and no European monetary authority. At Bremen,
furthermore, there was no indication of the level
of side-payments . The United Kingdom government
pointed out that it was only "committed to study
the scheme" and the clear implication of this was
that the level of side-payments would be
decisive.(41) It was agreed that a final decision
on EMS would be made at the next meeting of the
European Council at Brussels on the 3rd to the 5th
of December 1978. The scheme which emerged then,
and which the British, Irish and Italians declined
to join, though the Irish and Italians subsequently
changed their minds, was in most important aspects
identical to that outlined at Bremen.
    Negotiations about the details of the scheme
and about the scale of side-payments continued
between the two meetings of the European Council at
Bremen and at Brussels, and dominated the latter.
It seemed generally accepted by the richer states
led by West Germany that the poorer should benefit
by some form of resource transfers, though donor
countries and the recipients found it very
difficult to agree on their scale. The
disagreements seemed to be about three broad types
of issues: first, there were disagreements about

the arrangements of the system itself; second,
there were disagreements about the scale of the
grants and aid for the less prosperous countries;
and thirdly, there were a range of background
disagreements which were perceived by the potential
recipient countries in particular to be related to
the EMS question and which were seen by them to
indicate the broad attitude of the donor countries
towards their problems. It is important to
consider the EMS in the context of issues which
were perceived to be related to it, and, as with
consideration of other policy areas, to place it in
the context of the broader political and economic
expectations of member states. When these three
levels of disagreement and their context are taken
into account it is surprising to the present writer
that a satisfactory EMS arrangement linking all the
less prosperous with the richer member states could
ever have been thought possible. It should perhaps
be stressed again that the calculation of interests
in relation to the EMS should be seen against a
broader backcloth of political and economic
expectations and that amongst the latter elements
the role of the Gemeinschaft factor is of
considerable importance. It was probably decisive
in the Italian decision to join. The three levels
of disagreement will now be explored in greater
detail.

As regards the detailed operation of the EMS
the view taken by the West German government, with
the backing of the Dutch, Belgians and Danes, was
that there should be an obligation on the national
authorities to intervene in the market only when
their currencies went beyond the permitted margin
as defined by the parity-grid system. This was the
system which was introduced when the snake began
its joint float against the dollar in March 1973
and involved the fixing of a "matrix" of cross
rates which related a particular currency to each
of the others. It was argued by the British, with
the strong support of the Italians, that such a
system inevitably placed added pressures upon the
weaker currencies, because any move upwards by a
stronger currency also imposed a burden of
adjustment on the weaker: they were continually
having to keep up with the currency at the top of
the snake.(42) The British and their allies
preferred rather that intervention should be
obligatory at a margin defined in terms of a basket
of member currencies, which would also be used to
define the value of the European currency unit.

Such a system would mean that a particular currency would require market intervention only if it moved to the margin defined in relation to the average value of other currencies; a movement upwards by the strongest currency need in this system have no implications for interventions by the authorities of weaker currencies. Indeed, in this eventuality the onus would be upon the stronger currency to bring itself back into line. In the event, however, the supporters of the basket system failed to convince the governments with stronger currencies: it was only possible to persuade them to accept a "presumption to intervene" if currencies moved to the margin defined in terms of the basket. There would be an obligation to intervene only at a 2.25% margin defined in terms of the parity-grid.(43) It is obvious that this apparent victory for the stronger currencies made it seem even more important to the weaker states that they should get adequate sources of credit if they needed to protect their currencies.

In relation to the latter questions factors concerning broader preferences and expectations were probably as important as calculations about tangible costs and benefits. The British governments found it hard to believe that the stronger countries, particularly the West Germans, would not attempt to put pressure upon them in the EMS to adopt deflationary, stabilizing policies in the event of pressure on sterling, rather than providing stronger lines of support to allow policies which would be more conducive towards growth. The precise size of the sums provided to support currencies was a question of secondary importance because in advance of the crisis there was no way of knowing how much support would be enough: it was of course apparent that it would be a fraction of the funds that could have been available to the monetary authority in the Jenkins scheme. The Germans showed every sign of preferring a fund which would be the smallest they could get their colleagues to accept and which would be used as far as possible under agreed conditions to produce monetary stability.

On 21st November 1978, it was reported that the West Germans and the British had disagreed at a meeting of the nine finance ministers about the maximum amount of credit which was to be available to defend exchange rates. West Germany wanted the sum of sixteen thousand million ECU's, whilst the British demanded twenty-five thousand million

ECU's. In the event the West Germans conceded the point about the size of available credit, but differences remained about its division between short-term and medium-term credits.(44) Conditions could be imposed upon the medium-term credits and to reduce those which would be available on a short-term basis. Although at Bonn the British joined with their partners in contributing to the European Monetary Cooperation Fund (EMCF) by depositing 20% of their gold and dollar reserves, uncertainty about the scale of short-term support remained. The doubts of the British government about West German intentions could not have been eased by a lecture given in early December 1978 by a leading West German academic economist, Professor Roland Vaubel, who said that the support mechanisms of the EMS were inflationary because they would lead to less stress on the responsibility of governments to take those monetary measures which might be necessary to control exchange rates.(45) The British government could perhaps be excused for fearing that the Germans would do what they could in the EMS to keep the British economy small but stable and to confirm existing levels of economic divergence rather than encourage convergence.

The second level of disagreement about EMS concerned more specifically the scale of side-payments or resource transfers from the richer to the poorer states: the detailed arrangements of the system seemed to make it even more important for the poorer states to get what they could. The British prime minister stressed this point when he said, after the announcement of his government's decision not to join, that the durability (of EMS) would depend upon the EEC's success in dealing with the problem of resource transfers. The nature of the side-payments sought varied, however, from state to state, and tended to reflect not only economic expectations but also the political ambitions of the governments in relation to the Communities. The broad position of the British was to seek the reduction of burdens particularly in the form of what they considered to be disproportionately large contributions to the budget which had resulted from the method of financing the Communities "own resources" through transers of agricultural levies, customs duties, and a percentage of V.A.T.. The British government also sought more specifically to reduce their burden by amending the common agricultural policy.(46) They seemed in 1978 to place rather

less stress on increasing the scale of·the Regional
Fund or the Investment Bank from which they were
significant beneficiaries. They were pleased to
accept such contributions as were available but
these were generally seen to be rather marginal.
(The UK was to get about 28% of the £200 million
available through the Regional Fund over three
years, as agreed at the December 1977 Summit, but
it was calculated that after allowing for
contributions and other costs Britian's <u>net</u> gain
was between £30 and £35 million per annum.(47)
This was compared with a total expenditure on
Regional Development grants in the UK of about £400
million a year.)
     The political doubts of the Labour government
about the European Communities and their
institutions caused her to view with some
scepticism the Commission's arguments as put, for
instance, by Christopher Tugendhat (Commissioner in
charge of the Budget) that the best way for Britain
to balance her accounts with the EC was to work to
greatly increase the relative size in the EC Budget
of the special funds particularly the Regional
Fund, the Social Fund, and the European Investment
Bank. At present, it was argued, too much of the
total budget was being spent on agricultural
support which did not benefit Britain because of
the method of financing the CAP which tended to
penalize net importers of food; the scale of
returns to Britain would be rapidly increased as
the total Budget was increased and more of it used
for purposes other than agricultural support.
     This argument was rejected by the British
government. They seemed unwilling to make this
kind of commitment to the Communities. It would
have involved deciding to pay much more in order to
get considerably more out, and it would probably
increase the status of the Communities'
institutions. Instead they preferred the rather
short-term and unimaginative approach of paying
less in the first place.
     The British request for this form of
side-payment was not accepted by her Communities
partners in the negotiations preceding or during
the European Council meeting at Bonn: there were no
concessions either on the Budget or on the
operation of the Common Agricultural Policy. The
partners were not prepared to accept at this stage
that Britain's contributions to the Budget were
unreasonable, in the light of the availability of
the Common Market to British industry, and in the

light of the renegotiations which had taken place
before the referendum in 1975. There was some
feeling that the other states were being asked to
pay because of Britain's consistent failure to take
advantage of the opportunities which had been
offered to her as a result of her accession to the
Communities. And there was doubt about the
accuracy of the figures which the British
government had submitted as the basis of her claim
for a reduced commitment. The Danish government
went to the length of publishing a memorandum on
the British figures which indicated that some items
had been included as a debit to Britain which could
equally be counted as a credit.(48) The Monetary
Compensation Amounts, for instance, were counted as
a credit to producers of food in the richer states
in the UK figures; they could equally be counted as
a subsidy to consumers in the poorer food-importing
countries, and if this calculation were accepted,
Britain's net contribution was considerably
reduced. One calculation indicated that Britain
was getting around £1 million a day in subsidy
through the Monetary Compensation Amounts.
Furthermore, British figures included tariffs on
imports of manufactured goods as a net EEC
contribution, without allowance for the fact that a
significant proportion of imports were resold to
other EEC countries at a profit to the United
Kingdom. British complaints about her contribution
to the EC Budget also assumed that she could return
to the world market for food and buy more cheaply
there: no allowance was made for the effects of
such a step in pushing up world food prices. The
Danish government's amendments to the British
calculations had the effect of demonstrating that
Britain had received a net inflow in 1977, and that
the actual outflow to be expected in 1980 was about
one-third of the £880 million claimed by the
British. British claims were therefore felt by
some governments to be based upon rather dubious
calculations and, when this is added to the other
doubts, it is perhaps not surprising that they were
rejected. These arguments became involved in the
quarrel about the scale of Britain's contribution
to the Communities' Budget, which I discuss in
Chapter 8.

For these various reasons Britain was unable
to obtain adequate side-payments in return for her
membership of this, intergovernmental, EMS, and
accordingly declined the invitation to join in
December 1978. The British government was also not

disposed to accept any more "supranational" approach to her economic problems and it might be suggested here that British diplomacy would have been altogether more formidable had she followed the example set by the Dutch and the Belgians in the 1960s and inclined more towards Community-centred solutions. She would have gained some additional leverage in the conduct of her economic diplomacy by seeking to ally herself with the Commission against the richer states, rather than continuously challenging any attempt at greater independence on the part of the Communities institutions.

The two other states which were eligible for side-payments were Italy and Ireland. In both cases the governments sought to increase greatly the scale of resource transfers in the positive sense in return for membership in the EMS. It was reported before the Brussels Summit that Italy was requesting a net increase over existing payments of £1,000 million per annum over five years (49) whilst the Irish government wanted £650 million per annum over the same period. (50) It is at this stage difficult to discover exactly what principles were used at Brussels in deciding upon the scale of the offer to be made to the two countries, but in the event both were offered funds very much below the level requested. France was reported to have followed a particularly hard line in relation to the Regional Fund: President Giscard d'Estaing blocked a proposed increase of 60% in the size of the fund which apparently the Germans were prepared to countenance. In the event the total offered to Ireland and Italy together was 1000 mill E.U.A. to be allocated at a rate of 200 mill. E.U.A. per annum to offset interest charges. This amounted to around £3.5 billion in total, and of this Ireland was offered £1.125 billion (225 million pounds per annum) plus a further £45 million per annum to set against interest charges; Italy obtained around twice the sum allocated to Ireland at around £450 million per annum plus interest rebate payments. Both countries therefore received sums very much less than those which they had sought. Their first reaction was to side with Britain in declining to join the EMS. A week after the conclusion of the Summit, however, the Italian government changed its mind and said that subject to parliamentary approval in Italy it would after all be joining. A senior German official was reported to have stressed that no further concessions had been made to Italy, but that further discussions would take place. On 13 December the Italian Parliament voted for membership. On the 15th December the Irish coalition government under Jack Lynch announced that it too would be joining: they had been offered an additional £50 million over five years in bilateral arrangements with West Germany, the Netherlands and Denmark. (51)

The immediate motivations for the change of mind in Italy and Ireland are probably but the most visible and readily accessible of a much larger, more complicated range of calculations and preferences. Despite a larger transfer of resources to Italy than Ireland, reflecting a conscious decision by the richer states to allocate in Italy's favour on a 2 : 1 basis, it is striking that Ireland's per capita receipts were very much greater than those of Italy. The former, with a population of around 3 million, was to receive around £375 per person whilst the latter's per capita share, with a population of around 55 million was around £43. Ireland's receipts per capita were therefore moving towards ten times those of Italy, and when these figures are placed in the context of the pattern of resource allocations already agreed the discrepancy becomes even more striking. In 1975 Ireland received 16.8 E.U.A. per capita, excluding monies payed as a result of the operation of the Common Agricultural Policy, (72.3 E.U.A. if these are included), whilst Italy received 6.6 E.U A. per capita (18.7 E.U.A.). (52) On the other hand, the Irish could fairly argue that they were entitled to a larger share of available grants and aid on the grounds that their economy was according to several indicators somewhat weaker than that of Italy. In 1977, for instance, Gross Domestic Product per capita was the lowest in the EEC at 47.6% of the EEC average (at current prices and exchange rates), whereas that of Italy was the second lowest at 56.7%. (53) However, even when this greater entitlement is taken into account, Ireland still obtained a considerably larger share of those side-payments which were offered than she seemed to deserve.

The allocations seem to have been affected, perhaps unconsciously, by the view that attitudes towards the Community in Italy were such that any shortfall would be unlikely to attract serious public hostility, and that a significant number of politicians would be prepared to put their attachment to the Communities ahead of their judgement based on the careful analysis of tangible short-term costs and benefits. The Italians were strong supporters of European integration and the most inclined towards supranationalism; they were also founder members of the Communities. They were therefore more likely to "upgrade the common interest". Figures published in 1978, for instance, suggested that 65% of the Italians thought that their country's membership in the Communities was a "good thing": this was a rather higher level of support than in Belgium (58%), West Germany (58%), or France (54%), but lower than in Luxembourg (73%) or Holland (78%). But 57% of Italians were prepared to support the idea of a directly elected European Parliament with a government which "would have the final say in some important areas"; only 29% said that the individual governments should have the final say. This was easily the strongest "supranational" support in the Communities; the next strongest was in France at 45%. Germany was at 40%, Belgium at 36% and Holland at 41%. (54) The Irish, on the other hand, were rather restrained in their allegiance to the Communities despite the tangible rewards that their more recent membership has certainly produced. Not surprisingly, 63% of the Irish leaders and 52% of non-leaders thought that membership was "a good thing". But only 18% supported the supranational concept of integration, and 68% agreed that national governments should keep the final say. (55) Amongst the three new member states Ireland was on these figures the staunchest defender of national sovereignty. It seems safe to conclude that the emotional attachment of the Irish to the Communities was rather weak, and that a part of the explanation of the high level of per capita side-payments to the Irish was that they balanced the rather weaker pull of the Gemeinschaft factors between Ireland and the Communities.

The third set of disagreements which affected the chances of involving all members of the European Communities in the EMS were not immediately concerned with that system, but nevertheless affected perceptions of how it would be managed. The British in particular disagreed with the West Germans about the adoption of an economic strategy to stimulate growth. They argued, as had several other states in the wider international context, such as the U.S.A., that West Germany and the other stronger economies should take a lead in reflating their economies and thereby attempting to stimulate the economies of her major trading partners. (56)   In May 1978 the Commission produced a paper under the responsibilty of M. Ortoli which backed this proposal.   It was suggested that this was the way to boost growth in that year to above a target of 2.5%.   But Bonn was reported to be very cautious on the prospect of reaching this growth target at a meeting of Finance Ministers on 22nd of May: she was the one voice of dissent.   And in June at a meeting of Finance Ministers in Luxembourg the West German government was reported to have killed the growth plan. (57) They were reluctant to risk increasing the level if inflation in Germany despite the fact that it was the lowest in Europe.   Again the poorer countries were faced with a West German determination to put monetary stability ahead of growth, a lesson which certainly had implications for their view of the EMS.   The same general impression must have been conveyed by West Germany's attitude towards the proposal to increase quotas in the International Monetary Fund (IMF) which was discussed in September 1977.   All the EC countries supported the principle that there should be an increase, but the West German Finance Minister, Herr Apel, backed by the Belgian government, pushed for the arrangement of the tranches so that discipline on states in difficulties could be used sooner: the West Germans argued that the first tranche should be increased by 20% only.   The British supported equal tranches. (58) Again the lesson seemed to be that the richer countries would push for monetary discipline and that this would also follow in the EMS.   They would put pressure upon the poorer states to avoid policies which risked monetary instability or increasing inflation, even at the cost of economic growth.

The outcome of negotiations on the EMS, which focused upon three levels of disagreement, was therefore that Britain found it impossible to obtain adequate side-payments and declined to join whereas Italy and Ireland eventually found that they had been offered enough.   The behaviour of the French government which delayed the introduction of EMS in the first months of 1979 is not considered here.

For the first year or so of the 'monetarist' government of Mrs Thatcher in Britain, the possibility of joining the EMS was ruled out by the decision not to manage the exchange rate.   In mid-1981, however, the government decided to

intervene more actively in fixing the value of
sterling, and the question of whether Britain
should join the EMS once again arose. This is not
the place for a detailed analysis of the case for
and against membership but it did appear that the
lack of expansionist policies made membership a
more acceptable option. As Yao-su Hu has pointed
out,(59) a higher level of inflation did not
necessarily preclude membership, as exchange rate
stability could even in these circumstances be
maintained by introducing higher interest rates.
Nevertheless, such a course would again tend to
discourage economic expansion. The argument that
expansion would involve the choice of policies
which would create pressure which in turn would
detract from the benefit of membership in the EMS
seemed still valid; and when expansion began in
Britain it was likely that the case for joining
would once again seem less convincing in the
absence of significant side-payments.
Variables which seemed to be particularly
important in affecting the outcomes I have
discussed seemed to be, first, the unwillingness of
governments to accept a move to solutions of a
Community or supranational type, involving a
measure of central control and planning based on a
view of the general interest; second, the extent to
which the economies of states diverged from each
other in terms of such indicators as per capita
income, levels of productivity, and rates of
growth; thirdly, the extent of the advantages which
might be expected to accrue to the more prosperous
states from the adoption of the proposed
inter-governmental arrangements, and, fourth, the
degree to which Gemeinschaft factors were present
which might modify views about the adequacy of
particular levels of side-payments. There are, of
course, various uncertainties in these
considerations: they are difficult to calculate in
precise terms and several of them might be subject
to a threshold. For instance, it is conceivable
that side-payments only become sensitive in
negotiations beyond a particular level of economic
divergence. But in broad terms it seems safe to
conclude that side-payments would be increased
where the scale of economic divergence is greater,
where benefits accruing to the more prosperous are
higher, and where Gemeinschaft is weaker. The
levels of aid and grants to less-developed areas in
the Communities over the last ten years do not,
however, seem to be consistently inversely

correlated to levels of <u>Gemeinschaft</u> between member
states. There are other chancier mechanisms which
sometimes affect the way in which decisions about
redistribution are made. As has been stressed
earlier, we are not arguing that decision-making
outcomes will be determined by the pressures which
have been considered in this discussion.
Nevertheless, the considerations mentioned provide
useful additional tools for the understanding of
the outcome of the EMS negotiations, and the
diffificulties in the way of Britain's membership
in the 1980s.

3. The limits on autonomy in the European Communities

In the previous section the nature of the
problems in the way of further integration between
less prosperous and more prosperous countries was
examined in the particular context of the EMS. In
this section the other side of the interdependence
trap is briefly explored with reference mainly to
the experience of the United Kingdom. What factors
seem to impose limits upon the preparedness of
governments to choose disintegration and to extract
themselves from cooperative ventures, arrangements
or regimes into which they had entered? The
argument here represents but a starting point for
analysis, and lays rather less stress upon the
experience of Italy and Ireland.

Policies which have three different kinds of
effects are likely to be closely examined by less
prosperous countries for evidence to support claims
for side-payments against their rather richer
partners: those which make it more difficult for
them to control the costs of production, by
providing, for instance, inducements or special
aids, or by adopting growth policies which increase
the risk of monetary instability; which make it
easier for factors of production to move to more
prosperous areas in the heartland; and which reduce
the states' ability to amend the terms of trade in
its favour, by, for instance, devaluation. These
policies make up the major part of what has been
traditionally called "positive integration" in the
Communities. On the other hand, the policies which
have been placed under the heading of "negative
integration", which had the effect of easing
restrictions on trade, in particular, of course, of
removing quotas and tariffs on trade between member
states, have been welcomed. Indeed, it seems to be
the case that the less prosperous states have in

general made a firm stand on the principle of not
introducing new restrictions on trade with other
members of the Communities, and thereby increasing
their autonomy. (There are some minor exceptions
to this, particularly in the area of textiles.)
They have eschewed a return to protectionism
despite such costs as are evidenced in the comment
on higher import penetration in the United Kingdom
in the second half of 1977 made by Sir Douglas
Wass, British Permanent Under-secretary at the
Treasury: "There is only a limited amount that
policy makers can do to influence the future in an
economy as open as Britain's." (60) Hesitations
about increasing autonomy in this area may be
explained at this stage of the argument in these
terms: in the circumstances of economic divergence
in the 1970s, the success of negative integration
has become the essential condition of the effective
use of those levers of policy which governments
have tried to retain for themselves by refusing
positive integration. Negative integration has, in
other words, helped to _prevent_ positive integration
between less prosperous and more prosperous states.
Paradoxically - and tantalizingly - the acquis
communitaire has become a vital precondition of
national autonomy.
     This is not to argue that a return to
significantly higher levels of protectionism in the
United Kingdom, and in other member countries of
the European Communities, is inconceivable or
impossible, but rather that there would be risks
and costs involved in such a course which were
perceived by policy-makers in the 1970s and early
1980s. There were, however, those on the left of
the British political spectrum who have advocated
the creation of a "siege economy" as a way of
responding to current economic problems. There
were also a group of economists, which included a
number at Cambridge University who advocated the
more selective use of import controls. In June
1978, indeed, it was reported that two British
Ministers, Healey and Dell, had been loath to give
the West Germans binding commitments in the
Organisation for Economic Cooperation and
Development against protectionism "unless the
stronger countries well make possible faster rates
of growth." (61) It was unlikely however that the
idea of a siege economy would gain significant
support, and the Healey/Dell threat to return to
protectionism should be seen very much as a
negotiating gambit, to get the Germans to accept

the risk of reflating their economy, which was
lacking credibility in current circumstances. The
weight of opinion amongst officials and economists
was that the actual use of the weapon would have
caused considerable damage to the United Kingdom;
it may have been useful to threaten this as a
reminder to the West Germans that they gained
considerable advantage from the acceptance of the
Common Market by the less prosperous countries.

One reason for their reluctance to erect new
barriers to trade is that access to the Common
Market is an important resource which they have to
offer to business enterprises, either to keep them
in their territory, or to persuade them into it.
Governments are able to lower the cost of
production in their area by offering various kinds
of incentives: these may include concessions on tax
payments (which are very difficult to discover and
evaluate), low interest or zero interest investment
loans, employment subsidies and grants. They are
seen as being necessary to offset the benefits that
accrue to business enterprises which establish
themselves in the more prosperous heartland areas,
in particular, of course, the Benelux countries,
West Germany or Denmark, in contrast with the more
peripheral regions of England or Scotland, Ireland
or Italy. These benefits include such
considerations as the easier supply of necessary
components, lower transport costs, a more effective
infrastructure in communications and transport
network, a more attractive environment for
management, and a larger supply of skilled workers.
Research conducted by Young and Hood suggested that
American firms in the United Kingdom were subject
to some pull to more central areas, particularly
from the more remote parts, such as Scotland. (62)
It is to overcome such centripetal tendencies that
the various forms of incentive are used, very
frequently in conscious competition with other
member states of the Communities in an effort to
attract companies, in particular, of course, the
multinationals. Such incentives would have to be
increased as levels of protectionism were
increased: it is probably fair to conclude that
they are economically viable for the "donor"
country only because they are linked with an offer
of access to the Common Market, which is ensured at
whatever point in the EEC the business is
established. As protectionism increased the scale
of the incentives necessary to overcome the
penalties of the isolation of the market for the

enterprise would very quickly reach a level at which they would by an impossible drain on the economy of the donor state.

Another reason for resisting a return to protectionism on the part of the less prosperous states was that it would affect them in the same way that it would affect all other members, including the more prosperous ones, by reducing the general level of economic activity. The judgement is that the reintroduction of tariffs or quotas on trade with partners in the EEC would quickly lead to retaliatory action and that no permanent advantage would be obtained. It is important to remember in this context that all states in the Communities have greatly increased the proportion of their total trade which they conduct with each other since the setting up of the European Communities. 35.78% of the exports of the United Kingdom were to other members of the Communities in 1976, compared with 19.64% in 1958; for some of the smaller countries this share is much higher. (Notice though that the figures for Ireland are affected by her special trading relationship with the UK).

But it should also be stressed that the value of trade in relation to Gross Domestic Product has also significantly increased. The percentage share of imports in G.D.P. in the UK has increased from 16.2% in 1958 to 27% in 1978; in the case of Belgium and Luxembourg the increase is from 29.1% in 1958 to 47.7% in 1978. This evidence supports the view that any interference with intra-Community trade would lead to a decline in the general level of economic activity and unless equivalent trading access in other contexts, such as EFTA, was obtained there would be the risk of higher levels of unemployment, and lower real wages, particularly in more backward regions, which governments would generally find unacceptable. The argument of the Cambridge economists in favour of selective tarriffs to protect British industry in key areas has therefore not seemed persuasive either to the government or to the majority of their colleagues in other British universities. I discuss some of the background of these arguments in the pattern of British trade with the EEC in the 1970s in Chapter 8.

There was, however, another cost of higher protectionism which would be experienced mainly in the less prosperous areas. The larger companies in particular would experience increased costs if the

market were isolated, because of the loss of
economies of scale, and their management would be
faced with pressures to reduce these costs by
concentrating their activities in the richer areas,
and in reducing their investments in the poorer.
It should be pointed out that where there is access
to the Common Market the scale of investment need
have no necessary relationship with the size of the
national market: consumers can be reached elsewhere
in the Common Market. But the erection of barriers
to trade gives companies an incentive to adjust the
scale of the enterprise more closely to the size of
the local market, and, of course, a poorer market
will get less investment. Some companies which had
previously manufactured components in various
countries would also conceivably be faced with
pressures to site the whole enterprise at a single
point, where their production costs were lowest,
and the best market accessible. This vicious cycle
is likely to detract considerably from the
effectiveness of the various aids and incentives.
     At the present level of divergence it seems
that the less prosperous countries are generally
able to offset the pull to the centre created by
membership in the Communities by the manipulation
of the costs of production. But it is not
surprising that countries like the United Kingdom
have been slow to liberalize their controls over
capital movements: it was not until early 1978 that
they eventually agreed in the face of pressure from
their partners to ease investment flows. The
Conservative government further relaxed these
controls in 1979. And it is also not suprising
that Community institutions have found it difficult
to obtain any clear view of the scale of special
incentives to business in member states, though
there is now a notional ceiling on incentives to
multinational companies. The latter are indeed a
particularly important prize to be won - or lost.
It has been pointed out that in 1973 24% of
Britain's exports and 30% of Belgium's were
generated by "alien" multinational companies. (63)
A significant number of jobs have also been created
by such companies and in the United Kingdom the
government went to considerable lengths to keep
such companies as Chrysler, - and, later de Lorean
- though their efforts in these particular cases
were eventually unsuccessful. At one stage the
British government agreed to pay half of the losses
incurred by Chrysler in the UK up to a maximum of
£20 million per annum. Incentives were also

offered to Japanese companies such as Sony and Datsun to expand their operations in Britain.

The conclusion, therefore, is that economic divergence has placed limits upon autonomy, as it has created difficulties in the way of further integration. On the one side the less prosperous states seek to find some way of balancing the great advantages to the centre of such schemes as the EMS, and parallel arguments probably apply in most other areas of positive integration. If such a balance cannot be established by side-payments, integration is resisted. On the other hand, the less prosperous states also face powerful disincentives to increasing autonomy. Negative integration brings advantages in present economic circumstances in particular by adding to the effectiveness of their unilateral, competitive efforts to attract and hold business enterprise. Access to the Common Market is itself an important resource. The interdependence trap has indeed seemed to produce an ideal environment for multinational business in the Communities: one in which governments are anxious to do what they can to facilitate international trade but, on the other hand, to resist the kind of positive integration which would detract from their ability to offer inducements. The policy of the larger business enterprises therefore tends to coincide with that of national governments in keeping them within the interdependence trap, caught between pressures towards autonomy on the one hand and integration on the other. By resisting positive integration governments are also in effect committed to resist the introduction of stronger rules in Western Europe, by which the activities of big business could be controlled.

NOTES

1. Michael Hodges and William Wallace, (Editors), _Economic Divergence in the European Community_, Allen and Unwin, London 1981.
2. R. Rosecrance, A. Alexandroff, W. Koehler, J. Kroll, S. Layne and J. Stocker, "Wither Interdependence", _International Organization_, Vol. 31, No. 3 (Summer 1977), p. 427.
3. _Ibid._, p. 427.
4. Robert O. Keohane & Joseph S. Nye, _Power and Interdependence_, Little Brown & Co., 1977, p.9.
5. _Ibid._, p. 12.

6. Richard N. Cooper, "Economic Interdependence and Foreign Policy in the Seventies:, _World Politics_, Vol. XXlV (January 1977), No. 2.

7. _Ibid_., p. 166.

8. _Ibid_., p. 136.

9. Robert Keohane and J. Nye, "Interdependence and International Organization", _World Politics_. October 1974.

10. See Kenneth N. Waltz, "The myth of National Interdependence", in Charles P. Kindleberger, _The International Corporation, a Symposium,_ The M.I.T. Press, Cambridge, Massachusetts, 1970, pp 205 - 226.

11. See a discussion of this dimension in R.J. Harrison, _Europe in Question,_ Allen and Unwin, London, 1974, pp 152-183.

12. See the highly sophisticated discussion and application of these concepts of _Gemeinschaft_ and _Gesellschaft_ in Ronn D. Kaiser, "Toward the Copernican Phase of Regional Integration Theory", _Journal of Common Market Studies_, Oxford, March 1972, pp. 207-232. See also Chapter 1 above.

13. _Power and Interdependence_, _loc. cit._, p. 205.

14. Richard Cooper, _loc. cit._; See also, as evidence of this approach, George W. Ball (Editor), _Global Companies: The Political Economy of World Business_, Englewood Cliffs, Prentice-Hall, 1978, in particular Ball's contribution to Chapter 10, "The Need for International Arrangements", pp. 167-173.

15. For an examination of the various forms of integration theory see Paul Taylor and A.J.R. Groom (Editors), _International Organization: A Conceptual Approach_, London, Frances Pinter, 1978.

16. For a discussion of negative and positive integration see John Pinder, "Problems of European Integration" in Geoffrey Denton (Ed.) _Economic Integration in Europe_, Weidenfeld and Nicolson, 1969.

17. For a discussion of aspects of this approach see Paul Taylor, "The Concept of Community and the European Integration Problem" _Journal of Common Market Studies_, December 1968.

18. See discussion of sidepayments in Fred Hirsch and Michael W. Doyle, "Politicization in the World Economy: Necessary Conditions for an International Economic Order" in Fred Hirsch, Michael Doyle and Edward L. Morse, _Alternatives to Monetary Disorder_, New York, 1980 Project/Council on Foreign Relations, McGraw-Hill, 1977, pp. 11-49

19. See paper in Geoffrey Denton (Editor) _Economic and Monetary Union in Europe_, Croom Helm, for the Federal Trust, 1974.

20. See Loukas Tsoukalis, _The Politics and Economics of European Monetary Integration_, George Allen Unwin, London, 1977.

21. See Loukas Tsoukalis, "Is the Re-launching of Economic and Monetary Union a Feasible Proposal?" _Journal of Common Market Studies_, Vol. XV No. 4, June, 1977, pp. 231-247.

22. See Christopher Tugenhat, _The Guardian_, 13 March 1978.

23. Roy Jenkins, quoted in _The Guardian_, 28 October, 1977.

24. e.g. Peter Jenkins, _The Guardian_, 10 July 1978.

25. See Leading article in _The Times_ 11 July 1978. Also see article in _Neue Zurche Zeitung_, 31 August, 1977: "die Functions fahigkeit eines Fix kurzsystems an eine hinreichende stabilitats politische Konvergenz seiner Teilhaber gebunden ist."

26. Reported in _Financial Times_, 19 January 1978.

27. Quoted in _Financial Times_, 9 June 1977.

28. See also Commission of the European Communities Report of the Study Group (MacDougall Report) _The Role of Public Finance in European Integration_, U.K. 1 and 11, Brussels, April 1977, _Journal of Common Market Studies_, Vol. XVI, No. 4. June 1978.

29. _The Guardian_, 13 March 1978.

30. _Financial Times_, June 16, 1977.

31. See _Frankfurter Angemeine Zeitung_, 20 June 1977.

32. _Financial Times_, 27 January 1978.

33. Reported in _Financial Times_, 21 February 1978.

34. _Neue Zurche Zeitung_, 22 February 1978.

35. _Financial Times_, February 9, 1979.

36. _Daily Telegraph_, 28 March, 1978.

37. _Financial Times_, 13 April, 1978.

38. _Financial Times_, 30 August, 1977.

39. For an analysis of the Bremen proposal see Geoffrey Denton, "European Monetary Cooperation: the Bremen Proposal," _The World Today_, The Royal Institute of International Affairs, London, Vol. 34, No. 11, November 1978.

40. For an account of these mechanisms see V. Barattieri and Anthony Thomas, "EEC Monetary and Economic Cooperation" _International Affairs_,

October 1975.

41. See Financial Times, 8 July 1978.

42. See The Times, 21 November 1978.

43. Financial Times, 6 December 1978.

44. The Times, 21 November 1978.

45. Reported in Financial Times, 7 December 1978.

46. Reported in Financial Times, 6 December 1978.

47. See Daily Telegraph, 28 March 1978.

48. Report on Advantages and Disadvantages for the United Kingdom and for Denmark in connection with the EC Budget, Royal Danish Embassy, London, December 1978.

49. Reported Financial Times, 15 December 1978.

50. Reported Financial Times, 15 December 1978.

51. Financial Times, 15 December 1978.

52. See figures in MacDougall Report, op cit, p455.

53. Eurostat.

54. Figures from Commission of the European Communities, Euro-barometre: public opinion in the European Community, No. 9, July 1978, Brussels, pp. 30-31.

55. Ibid.

56. See, for example, report in Financial Times, 22 May 1978.

57. See The Guardian, 19 June 1978.

58. Financial Times, 20 September 1977.

59. See Yao-Su Hu, Europe Under Stress, Butterworth, London, 1981, p. 82.

60. Reported in Daily Telegraph, 21 February 1978.

61. Reported in The Guardian, 19 June 1978.

62. S. Young and N. Hood, "The Geographical Expansion of US Firms in Western Europe: Some Survey Evidence," Journal of Common Market Studies, Oxford, Vol. XIV No. 3, March 1976, pp. 235-236.

63. Walter Goldstein, "The Multinational Corporation and World Trade: the case of the Developed Economies," in David E. Apter and Louis Wolf Goodman (Editors) The Multinational Corporation and Social Change, New York, Praeger, 1976, p. 136.

Chapter Seven

SOCIAL POLICIES AND THE LIMITS OF INTEGRATION

In this chapter the nature of the difficulties in the way of the expansion of the European Communities' role in the management of welfare provision, defined in a rather broad sense, in the 1970s in member states is considered. Social policy is another of the policy contexts in which the processes through which states resisted the claims for more centralised management by the regional institutions in the period may be usefully illustrated, and the limits which states set upon transfers of competence to them examined. But it is a particularly interesting context because of the great importance of the task of providing welfare among the range of tasks performed by the modern state, and because the transfer of responsibility for welfare from the extended family to the state - a development which probably took off in Western Europe in the late nineteenth and early twentieth centuries - is one of the critical stages in the consolidation of the framework of the modern state.(1) It might be supposed, therefore, that any signs of a transfer of responsibility for welfare to the regional level would be a particularly important indicator of the development of the authority of the larger unit. Indeed, as I pointed out in Chapter I, one approach to international integration, Functionalism, stressed the role of welfare provision by international institutions in diverting loyalties away from the nation state and towards the new international authorities, and thereby creating a new base of sovereignty.(2)

Another reason for examining the Communities' role in welfare provision, however, is that little has been written about the nature of the resistance by the states to the expansion of the Communities'

social and welfare policies: which policies have
been more successful and which less so? In this
chapter a rather broad definition of the items
which fall under the heading of "social welfare" is
used; the Communities' Social Action Programme,
accepted by the Council in January 1974, included
reference to environmental questions and consumer
protection as well as more conventional "employment
and social questions". The dividing line between
social questions and others was rather arbitary. I
have, however, included policies with which the
Communities have been concerned which sought to
mitigate the undesirable consequences for
individuals of the malfunctioning of the economic
system. There is in every society a prevailing
notion of those minimum standards, or that
essential quality of life, which should be sought
for every individual member of society regardless
of income: social policies are intended to achieve
such standards even if the economic system tends to
undermine them and in this sense malfunctions.
There are also, of course, occasions when attempts
are made to increase the level of provision above
the minimum, though this might be economically
difficult or politically contentious. Social
policies defined in this rather broad sense are,
therefore, distinguishable from those policies
which are focussed on the management or development
of the economy. They include environmental policy
when development has led to unacceptable pollution;
the provision of adequate social security and
welfare within states to cope, for instance, with
unemployment; and the protection of consumers
against exploitation by manufacturers, or against
exposure to health or safety risks from products.
I am concerned with the extent to which the
Communities have sought to help member states in
these areas, or have sought to replace state
mechanisms with their own. I am, of course, aware
that they might be intended to serve a number of
different ultimate goals: for example, the
maintenance of public order, or the stability of
the political system; the promotion of the
integration of the Communities as part of a public
relations campaign; or the improvement of the
economic system.
     The limitations on the Communities'
involvement with social policies arose partly
because of economic pressures. There is, however,
some evidence to suggest that governments, and
other national actors, resisted greater development

of the Communities' involvement with some social
policies even when there were few economic costs,
because such a development was seen to threaten the
authority of the states or weakened their sense of
being masters of their own destiny. The pattern of
governments' resistance is revealed in the
variations in their attitudes towards the various
sectors of the Communities' social policy: for
instance, they were broadly tolerant of the
Communities' active role in environmental policy
but were cautious in extending the "civil rights"
of migrant workers. (4) I should stress that I am
not approaching the Communities' social policy from
the point of view of its effectiveness in solving
specific social problems: this is not an exercise
in impact assessment. Rather the focus is upon the
role allowed to the Communities in various areas of
social policy as one indicator of the empirical
limits of sovereignty in the late 1970s and early
1980s.

There were probably four different roles which
the Communities played in relation to social
policy.

First the Communities acted as surrogate for
member states, in that they performed functions
which would have been necessary in any case because
of an overwhelming consensus among experts, or
because of the development of irresistable public
pressures, and which would have arisen regardless
of membership in the Communities, e.g. control of
environmental pollution; also in this categroy were
a number of decisions to eliminate so-called
non-tariff barriers on trade - particularly
important after the establishment of the internal
common market and the common external tariff in
1969 - which became aspects of social policy in a
broader sense when they concerned questions of
consumer safety or health.

Secondly, the Communities were required by the
terms of the Treaty of Rome to ease the movement
between member states of workers and the
self-employed and to adjust security systems to
make this possible: problems arose as a result of
moving towards an economic community , such as
those involving migrant labour, which were more
conveniently approached, and, sometimes, could only
be approached at a higher level.

Thirdly, there were social policy proposals
which represented the Communities' attempt to
define an ideal standard in present circumstances,
or an ideal solution to emerging problems such as

employment, e.g. proposals for work-sharing, or for raising the level of social provision. In attempting this role the Communities moved much closer towards issues which were "sensitive" in relation to sovereignty.

Fourthly were those goals which were sought by the Communities in order to develop a more positive role for themselves as providers of welfare or as managers of the system, either by putting themselves in charge of the distribution of significant welfare resources, or by seeking to regulate increased national provision or a common, "supranational" framework, e.g. a Communities system for paying employment benefit, or a Passport Union. In these cases the Communities were clearly moving even closer to issues which were likely to be "sensitive", in that they threatened exclusive national control in areas judged to be within the sovereign territory of states, and, as might have been expected, though claims were made, they achieved only modest success under this heading.

These four types of role, and the member states' response in each case in the late 1970s, will be examined in the third section of this chapter; their implications for the limits placed upon the expansion of social policy will be discussed. In the second section the economic bases of the limitations are explored. These apply mainly to the Social Fund and its operation. (Other areas of the Communities' social policies do not have significant implications for the Communities' budget.) In the next section, however, a sketch of the development of the Communities' social policy is attempted; without such an account the nature of the limitations - and on what(?) - cannot be understood. No attempt is made, however, to provide a detailed history, which can be readily found elsewhere.

****

1. The pattern of involvement of the European Communities' in social policies

The history of the Communities' involvement in social policies may be divided into three main periods. The first runs from the establishment of the EEC in 1958 until the late 1960s; the second extends from 1970 until 1975; and the third runs from 1976 until 1979-1980. The three phases may be labelled respectively, the period of "low key convergence"(5); the period of accelerating

199

ambitions; and the period of disillusionment about, and limitations upon , the Communities' involvement. The three phases reflect developments in other policy areas in the Communities: the first corresponds with the establishment of the Customs Union which was formerly declared to have been established in 1969; the second was introduced in association with the decision to "enlarge, deepen and extend" the Communities taken at the Hague Summit in 1969(6); the third reflects the problems associated with the growing divergence in the economic performance of member states which were becoming very evident in the late 1970's, together with an increasing insistence upon the forms of national sovereignty.(7)

In the first period the character of the Communities' social policy was related fairly closely to the intentions of the founders of the European Economic Community as reflected in the Rome Treaty. Articles 117 to 122 reflected three rather modest proposals which represented a minimum necessary adjustment in the area of social policy to the process of introducing the Customs Union . The founders wished, first, to facilitate the movement of workers within the Communities. Accordingly in Article 121 the Council was to ask the Commission to take steps "in connection with the implementation of the common measures", in particular as regards social security for Communities' migrant workers. In this they were specifying the procedures which were required to apply Articles 48 and 51, which asserted respectively the principles of free movement of labour in the Communities and that of the aggregation of social security benefits of migrant workers and their transfer between member states. Secondly the founders agreed to specific equalisation measures; in Article 119 the principle of equal pay for men and women for equal work was ennunciated, and in Article 120 member states agreed to maintain existing equivalents between paid holiday schemes. These measures were introduced as a response - if somewhat inadequate - to the insistence of the French Government. They wished to reduce what was believed to be an additional burden upon French industry which had resulted from the more liberal welfare policies in France, compared with her partners, and the greater proportion of their cost which was paid by employers, rather than by employees or by government. Under Article 118, though the scope of

the policies mentioned is wide, members indicated
their hesitation about pushing too hard for upwards
harmonisation. They merely asked the Commission to
promote close co-operation between member states in
the social field in a number of specified areas.
Again, however, the stress was upon areas which
were related to employment, and the implication was
that equalisation was to be sought in order to
prevent industry in one country from having a
competitive advantage over that of another. The
third intention was a rather negative one: it was
reflected, for instance, in Article 117 which
implied that the member states could expect to see
upwards harmonisation resulting more from the
success of the Common Market than from the
deliberate introduction of agreed measures:
"improved working conditions ... and an improved
standard of living for workers ... will ensure not
only from the functioning of the Common Market,
which would favour the harmonisation of social
systems, but also from the procedures provided for
in this Treaty". When read in conjunction with
other parts of the Treaty the conclusions seem
inescapable that a "social policy based on the
priorities of the Treaty would be bound of focus
around two principles: the free movement of labour
and the equalistion of competitive conditions among
enterprises".(7) These points were emphasised by
the placing of the discussion of social policy
under the heading of "Towards Economic Union" in
the General Report of 1969; in later Reports it has
found a place under more general titles, such as
"common policies" or "community policies", or under
a number of separate headings.
   The main achievements of the Communities in
the area of social policy in the 1960's were
accordingly the progressive easing of restrictions
on the movement of labour between member states,
and the equalisation of the social security rights
of migrants with those of local workers. Under
Council Regulation 15 of 1961, which operated
between September 1961 and May 1964, the movement
of labour required the issue of a permit by the
state of destination, and there were various
measures of discrimination against the employment
of immigrants in favour of nationals for four
years. In July 1968, however, the principle of
national priority was abandoned: work permits were
no longer required and Communities workers had the
same access to jobs as nationals. Arrangements for
the transfer of social security benefits earned in

one country to others were also progressively improved so that "the position today is that the social security rights of the migrants are virtually in all respects equal to those of local workers".(8)   The rights of migrant workers in relation to participation in the activities and arrangements of Trade Unions were also progressively improved, though there remained some discrimnation which I discuss in Secion 3 below.

The founders of the Communities also established a Social Fund which in the context of the Treaty should also be seen as an instrument for facilitating adjustments to the Customs Union in particular to help workers with re-training and re-settlement when they had become unemployed because of economic integration.   Unlike the Regional Fund, the Social Fund was required under the Treaty of Rome.   Article 123 said that the Fund "shall have the task of rendering the employment of workers easier and of increasing their geographical and occupational mobility within the Community".   The fund does not, however, seem to have been intended to form part of a strategy for coping with unemployment in general, however, caused.   It was to be concerned with unemployment brought about as a result of membership in the Communities which could be remedied by the physical movement of workers.   This work is reflected in Petaccio's conclusion that "most projects completed resulted in worker migration".(9)   Italian workers tended to use the Fund to find work outside, in France or Germany, and in the years 1961 to 1968 Italy received from the fund 11.2 million dollars more than she contributed whilst France and Germany contributed 9 million dollars more than they received.(10)   But the scale of the fund was small: during the whole decade only 421 million dollars were spent in Community approved schemes involving some 1.43 million workers.   According to Petaccio the fund supported only 15% of the unemployed population. (11)   In practice, also, the Fund's operation was handicapped by the lack of any clear directing strategy: the pace was sluggish, and there were no "co-ordinating linkages between randomly conceived manpower projects and regional employment planning."(12)   Despite the intentions of the founders, therefore, the Fund did not succeed in acting effectively to assist workers to adjust to the EEC: it was too small, too slow, and lacking in a coherent strategy.   (Payments were 50% of the total required for projects but were only

made after a worker had been retrained and
resettled and had been re-employed). As Petaccio
has pointed out, the whole approach to social
policy in the 1960s was rather low key. One
indication of this was that between 1964 and 1967
there was no meeting of the Council to discuss
social policy.(13)

In the second period, on the other hand, there
was a conscious attempt to follow a much more
active social policy over a much wider range of
concerns. In the Final Communique of the
Conference of Heads of States and Government at the
Hague in December, 1969, "the desirability of
reforming the Social Fund within the framework of a
closely concerted social policy" was asserted. The
European Parliament had earlier urged the leaders
"to promote a common social policy and in
particular to reform the European Social Fund,
which should become a genuine common tool for a
policy of full employment and for raising living
standards in the Community."(14) Accordingly in
1971 the Social Fund was altered with effect from
1972: it was to be used more actively to help
maintain employment in industries and regions
effected by difficulties stemming from Communities
processes, such as might result for instance, from
the introduction of the Mansholt Plan for the
reform of agriculture. Workers could also be
adapted whilst still in employment. In other words
the Fund's original purpose was reasserted and the
instruments improved to increase effectiveness. In
addition, however, the Fund could be used in cases
of "hard core" or "structural" unemployment and
provide training for special groups such as the
handicapped, the aged, women and the young. (Funds
were made available for young people under 25 by a
Council decision of 1975). As with the first Fund,
there were to be no national quotas within the
framework of guidelines discussed below, and, the
Commission could make decisions on the merits of
each case submitted to it by national authorities
again providing funds on a 50/50 basis. The Fund
was also to be financed from the Communities' "Own
Resources".

In addition to the reformed Fund, described by
Petaccio as "a programme more attuned to
centralised efforts"'(15) member states at the
Summit Conference in Paris in October 1972 also
restated the traditional goals of the Communities'
social policy (e.g. employment and vocational
training, improving working conditions), and

asserted their attachment "to vigorous action in the social field". They decided upon a number of new principles: they desired a co-ordinated employment policy, they wished to improve "conditions of life", to strengthen and co-ordinate measures for consumer protection, and to "closely involve workers in the progress of firms." (Para. 6). These new goals, together with the traditional ones, were considered by the Commission and formed the basis of the Social Action Programme which was accepted by the Council in January 1974 with considerable fanfare. The new programme also further justified the Communities' incursions into the area of environmental policy. The Social Action Programme represented the Communities' commitment to an expanded and more active role in the organisation of social policy in the Communities.

One indication of the widening of the scope of the social policy was that about one half of the new proposals would require the consent of the Council: they had now moved beyond what seemed to be allowed by a fundamentalist interpretation of the Treaty. In the early 1970s, therefore, there seemed to be some evidence to support the optimism of those who had earlier thought that "the Social Fund should become one of the chief instruments in the reconversion of the European economies and help to smooth the process of integration." (16) As has already been pointed out enthusiasm for a more active and - in the words of President Ortoli, "broad-based" - social policy should be seen in the context of the decision to move towards economic and monetary union by 1980 which was asserted at the Paris Summit in 1972.(17) For a short while, around the time of Britain's accession, there was considerable optimism about progress towards greater unity in Europe, and the expansion of the Communities' social concerns reflected this optimism.

This is not the place for a detailed evaluation of this phase of the Communities' social policy - an assessment of the limits placed upon it in the late 1970s is in the next section. Some indications of the scale and range is however appropriate. The Social Fund's budget expanded by nearly 500% in the period 1972 to 1976, and in 1976 it took up the largest proportion of the total budget of the Communities, after agriculture, at 5.95% (regional sector spending followed closely behind at 5.61%).(18) The principle of equality in

the employment of women was pursued with vigour:
the Council adopted a Directive in 1975 which added
teeth to Article 119 in that it was now necessary
for states to provide legal remedy for those who
believed the principles had been infringed. A
start was also made on the problem of improving
safety and health standards at work, stimulated by
another Action Programme on health at work approved
by the Council in June 1974. There were also a
number of Directives on the question of
environmental pollution, the screening of the
population for evidence of lead contamination,
improved definitions of asbestosis and
mesotheliomis. Great stress was also placed upon
the expansion of the consultative procedures
related to social questions centring around
Brussels, of which perhaps the most important
element was the establishment of the Tripartite
Committee of Labour, Government and Management
representatives and of the Standing Committee on
Employment. The trade unions initially boycotted
the meetings of the Tripartite Committee but
accepted their involvement in 1975.(19) The
Commission was able to strengthen its ability to
evaluate the developing social picture in the
Communities - and to strengthen its position in
the consultative machinery - by collecting
considerable quantities of information on a
comparative basis about social spending in member
states under the so-called Social Budget
procedures. (20) After 1975 there were also
regular meetings of the heads of social services in
the nine members countries and one product of these
meetings was a list drawn up by the Commission of
areas of social protection which seemed to lend
themselves to a "Community approach". There was
also progress towards the improvement of conditions
in mines, in the provision of housing, particularly
for European Coal and Steel Community workers, and
for the control of radiation under the terms of
Euratom.
      There is, therefore, ample evidence to
illustrate the point that the range of Communities'
concern with social policy had been considerably
expanded in this phase beyond the terms of the
Treaty. In the early 1970s, indeed, there was
evidence of the Communities' concern to harmonize
national systems, and to create a European system
with the commission at its centre. A number of
Commissioners saw in this more active social policy
an opportunity for improving the Communities' image

among the citizens of the European Communities by
projecting what was called the "human face" of the
Communities. This view was expressed by
Commissioner George Thomson and Commissioner
Patrick Hillery in 1975: the more obvious
involvement of the Communities in the social
protection of workers was believed to be an
essential step towards gaining their support. It
could help to form a European society, and could
form the basis of a European political system. The
Economic and Social Committee in July 1974 stressed
the need to involve and inform the public as this
was the "only means capable of awakening the
European consciousness". A more active social
policy, presumably leading towards upward
harmonization, therefore, became a part of the
political strategy of the Communities'
institutions. This development in the economic
circumstances of the late 1970s and early 1980s, in
that it alerted governments to the potential of the
Communities' role in welfare policies, probably
reinforced the governments' determination to impose
limits upon that involvement. I discuss this
reaction in the next sections.

2. Limits on the Communities' expenditure on
Social Policies
     Intimations of the governments' doubts about
the continuing expansion of the social policy of
the European Communities could be found, however,
in the mid-1970s. Michael Shanks reported that "by
the end of 1975 the Social Action Programme as a
whole was running up to schedule, and it looked as
if the whole programme would be completed on time
by the end of 1976"; but that "there was a growing
tendency to emasculate policies which, like the
poverty programme, involved the expenditure of
Community money, or which like the 40 hour week and
four weeks holiday could be costly to industry."
And "the debacle of the Social Action Programme
came in its third year. Progress on the remaining
parts of the programme ... slowed to a
trickle."(21) There were, indeed, already signs by
1976 of a determination to return to the earlier
narrow conception of the social policy, and to
"query the desirability of any Community policy
which did not flow inescapably from the Rome Treaty
provisions."(22) Many of the Communities'
proposals on social policy, which the Council had
often accepted in principle, or a guidelines, were
questioned and postponed. These included not only

206

the 40 hour working week and four weeks holiday
proposal, but also the Poverty Programme of 1975,
and the draft Directive for the harmonisation of
certain categories of social protection, which had
been on the stocks at the end of 1976.

Increasingly the policy found itself squeezed
between two opposing forces: on the other hand
declining economic performance in some states
tended to lead to a concentration upon problems
caused by unemployment; but, on the other hand, as
the need for effective measures to counter
unemployment increased, the richer states became
increasingly reluctant to commit themselves to the
provision of adequate resources. As Juliet Lodge
argues, the simple logic that "the declining
ability of states to satisfy needs may lead
supranational actors to see supranational action as
timely" proved unsustainable in the circumstances
of the Communities in the late 1970s and early
1980s.(23) The more appropriate maxim seemed to
be: "the greater the need the less the capacity."

The social policy should indeed be seen not
only as one amongst a number of victims of the
growing scarcity of resources at the Communities
level in relation to allocated tasks, but also as
an area of Community policy which was peculiarly
vulnerable to these difficulties. There were
limitations which were inherent in the method by
which the Communities' "own resources" were
provided.(24) (The Social Fund had been a charge
on "own resources" since 1971.) But as economic
circumstances deteriorated, which might have been
expected to strengthen the case for centralised
welfare provision, the states interest in
redistribution through Communities' mechanisms also
declined. This is one measure of the extent to
which the European Communities fell short of the
ideal of a "free world" federal system, and
conformed more to the model of confederalism or
leagues of states. In federal systems the tendency
had often been for the federal budget to increase
in times of crisis and for spending on welfare from
the union to be correspondingly expanded.

In the late 1970s the size of the Social Fund
in monetary terms had, indeed, continued to
increase. In the 1979 Budget 804 million European
Units of Account (EUAs) were allocated to the Fund;
in 1980 899 million EUAs (909 million EUAs after
two Supplementary Budgets), and in 1981, 963
million EUAs.(25) In the Report on the activities
of the Fund, June 1979, it was pointed out that the

Budget for 1979 'shows a rise of 35% over the previous year which represents a significant real increase in resources taking inflation into account.'(26)   It was striking, though, that the Budgets which were eventually agreed by the Council of Ministers and the Assembly in these years always reduced the proportionate value of the Fund, compared with other components of the Budget, from the level suggested by the Commission in the Preliminary Draft.   In 1979 the Social Fund was to be 5.93% of the total Budget according to the Preliminary Draft: that proportion was reduced on the Council's insistence to 5.52%; in 1981 the Council reduced the Social Fund's share from 4.62% to 4.56%.(27)   These figures clearly demonstrate the declining importance of the Social Fund in the overall Budget, and also the general inclination on the part of the Council to oppose any increase in the Fund which could be at the expense of other components which they rated more highly.   In particular, the Budgetary procedures generally had the effect of increasing the proportionate value of the agricultural commitments.   (From 63.53% of the total to 64.55.% in 1981; 65.98% to 70.27% in 1980).   The proportionate value of the Regional Fund was also generally reduced during the budgetary process.   A similar reduction was also evident on the payments side.   The Commission concluded in its 1979 Report that "the main cuts in the total appropriations for payments are in the social sector";(28) in 1980 the Commission's complaint was that " appropriations for payments adopted by the Council for the Social Fund were 25% lower than proposed by the Commission, and appropriations for the Regional Fund were cut by 35%." These cuts were all the more significant "as the appropriations had already been reduced considerably by the Commission in its Preliminary Draft Budget because of Budgetary constraints, and the amount proposed, particularly for the Funds, were thus regarded as absolute minima."(29)

The constraints upon the Social Fund should be seen in the context of the considerable expansion in the scale of the problems with which it was required to deal in the late 1970s and the early 1980s.   The Fund was intended to deal with problems of unemployment by promoting various kinds of retraining and resettlement assistance, though, of course, the extent of its contribution was governed by the funds made available to it and not by the scale of the task.   Between 1973 and 1978 the total number of unemployed in the Communities increased from 2,596,000 to 5,969,000 and the number continued to increase.(39); an average of 5.6% of the working population was unemployed in 1978 with much higher rates in Ireland (8.9%), Belgium (8.4%), and the worse off regions - such as Northern Ireland. Among some sections of the population the rate was also much higher than the average: in the United Kingdom 41.5% of the unemployed were young people under the age of 25; in Germany 25.6% and in Italy 44%.(31) One of the consequences of this increase in demands upon the Fund was that applications for support outstripped available resources, in 1977 by 62.3% and in 1978 by 93%.(32) The Fund was compelled to adopt more stringent conditions for the allocation of support and concentrated upon groups and areas which were particularly badly hit. Accordingly, in 1978 the two largest items on the Social Fund's Budget by quite a long way were support for ventures to assist unemployed among young people at 179.28 million EUAs and for ventures in the worst off regions as designated by the European Regional Development Fund (ERDF) at 263 EUAs. (According to a Council Decision of 1971 at least 50% of the total appropriations of the Fund had to be allocated to actions carried out in the ERDF regions under so-called Article 5 expenditure.)(33) In the United Kingdom in 1980 the Fund provided around 30% of the total cost of the support given to young people under 25, most of which was carried out by the Manpower Services Commission, although the British government gave no public acknowledgement of this help. Despite a substantial level of support in this particular area, only around 500,000 unemployed could receive support from the Social Fund in the Communities as a whole in each of the years 1979 and 1980, around 8% of the total unemployed. Indeed the scale of the Fund's level of involvemnt in relation to the size of the problem seemed to have declined compared with that in the 1960s.(34)

The conclusion is inescapable that the Social Fund was marginal in its contribution of resources to the task of overcoming the problems of unemployment: the member states' contributions were overwhelmingly dominant. But the Fund was also marginal in that it was rather lacking in its ability to generate policies for coping with the problem. As one official pointed out "we get brought in when there is a serious problem: when it

is too late to do anything about it."(35)   The Fund
tended to respond to the claims made upon it from
agencies within the states, and allocated resources
in the light of predetermined priorities, together
with a judgement about the particular scheme's
viability.   But it did not take the initiative in
developing a policy on the kind of activities and
industries which should be developed.   In this
respect, of course, it was in a similar position to
some of the member governments which had themselves
not developed coherent industrial policies.
(States were extremely slow in 1980 to take up 20
million EUAs in the Social Fund which had been
allocated for retraining in new technologies such
as microelectronics.)   One reason for this policy
weakness was that the Fund was rather understaffed:
increases in its staff had not matched increases in
resources.   Another was that there was little
coordination between the various sections of
Directorate General 5: the administration of the
Fund, was, therefore, not informed by any policy
perspective on unemployment problems which could
have been developed at more senior levels in the
Directorate. A further reason was that the
governments had been careful in their mandate to
the Fund when it was reformed in 1971 to impose
upon it certain controls: action under Article 5,
which mainly concerned schemes in the predetermined
development regions (French Overseas Department,
the mezzo giorno in Italy, Northern Ireland and
Greenland), did not require approval in each
category by the Council of Ministers; but action
under Article 4 (mainly young people, but also
workers leaving farming or the textile industry)
did require Council approval for each category of
action (though not for each item).(36)   Article 4
activities were more likely to have implications
for industrial policy, for the development and
decline of industry, and for movements by migrants
across national frontiers: they were more likely to
be shaped by a Communities perspective, if one
developed, which could be at the expense of
individual states.   In this respect, therefore, the
Fund was liable to surveillance by members which at
this point had established another defence
mechanism against the Communities.   In contrast,
Article 5 activties within regions of structural
unemployment were unlikely to have implications for
the development of common policies and were less
closely controlled.
        A final reason for the Funds' rather weak

attempts to shape an unemployment support policy
which might be ventured was the paradoxical one
that it did not wish to act in such a way that
governments would be moved to take away those
freedoms which it had acquired. The member states
had not been allocated quotas of support from the
Fund: its officials used their judgement within the
stated guidelines about which enterprises to
support and where. (Even the guidelines were
largely its own creation.) In order to keep these
freedoms it was necessary for it to adopt a tactful
posture: to allocate according to a perceived
consensus among the governments and to avoid
treading on any government's toes. The
organisation had therefore developed an interest in
protecting its freedom which tended to increase its
reluctance to develop policies which could bring it
into conflict with governments. Paradoxically,
therefore, its freedom had been one of the causes
of its weakness. One particularly foolish problem
in the way of improving the Fund's role in helping
young people in the United Kingdom and elsewhere
was that it could not act until they were
technically unemployed. There could be no help
from the Fund until they had left school and joined
the dole queues!
    From the point of view of the governments of
member states there were a number of difficulties
in the way of an expansion of the size or role of
the Social Fund. The Fund was, of course, a victim
of the reluctance of the states, particularly West
Germany and Britain, to see any expansion in the
size of the Communities' Budget. West Germany had
indeed taken the lead in the late 1970s in
insisting that there could be no increase in the 1%
ceiling imposed on members' contributions to <u>own</u>
<u>resources</u> from Value Added Tax. And any success of
the British Government in the early 1980s, in
'clawing back' from the Communities a proportion of
its contributions, such as that of 1980-82, would
have the effect of further increasing the level of
demands upon the Communities' Resources: in view of
the difficulty in limiting agricultural expenditure
(see Chapter 8) the Funds were particularly
vulnerable. Most governments were under pressure
from their farming populations to maintain the
level of agricultural interventions. Some
governments' perceptions of their electoral
interests, (especially France, Ireland and Denmark)
led them to oppose any reduction of the
Communities' contributions to agricultural support.

There had also been in the 1970s an increasing
reluctance to accept redistribution through the
Communities' Budget and a propensity to insist upon
a just return or a fair national share.(37)
Accordingly the measure of redistribution following
from the Fund's activities was likely to be
acceptable to the major donor states only if it was
on a relatively small scale. Their insistence upon
fair national shares tended to reduce the scale of
funds available for redistribution. This tendency
was reinforced by the increasing wariness of
governments about the level of social spending in
their own countries as well as at the Communities
level: there had been a welfare policy backlash in
a number of member states which reinforced their
antipathy towards redistribution both vertically
among groups within states and horizontally between
regions and states. This antipathy was, of course,
accompanied by a wish amongst governments to see
the proportion of gross domestic product passing
through central budgets, be they at the national
level or the Communities level, reduced.(38)
     But perhaps the most important reason was that
the Social Fund would need to be expanded to a very
considerable extent before it could become capable
of making any real impact. The scale of the
increase necessary was itself a disincentive to
making the attempt. And if such an expansion were
to take place governments would be unable to avoid
the thorny problem of agreeing upon the policies
which it would pursue: a large Social Fund would
require an effective Communities employment policy,
and a more developed associated industrial policy.
This potential was clearly in the minds of those
who in the early Seventies had thought that the
Social Fund could become a planning agency in the
future.(39)   The member states were in the grip of
a kind of collective <u>schadenfreude in this context
in the late 1970s: worsening circumstances seemed
to reinforce their determination to do things for</u>
themselves even though there was a realisation that
this might prove to be impossible. One reason for
this was that each government seemed to wish to put
itself in such a position that it could take
advantage of any competitive edge it might obtain
if conditions began to improve. For these reasons,
then, the member governments of the European
Communities could not bring themselves to face the
policy implications of creating a Social Fund which
was adequate to its task. In 1961 Jean Boissonat
had argued that 'the Social Fund and the European

Investment Bank, if properly used, may lead to a central European planning agency."(40)   By the end of the decade the "Future Planning Agency" had become rather marginal in terms of its resources and its ability to develop Communities' policies even in the rather narrow area of unemployment.   In some ways, indeed, it survived because it had become somewhat marginal.   The Fund did however come to provide a particularly interesting focus for governments' attitudes towards the Communities in the late 1970s.

3.   Limits on the expansion of the Communities involvement in Social politics
      As was mentioned earlier in this chapter the increasing divergence in the economic circumstances of member states of the European Communities was not the only factor which placed limits upon their involvement in common social policies and structures.   The nature of the limits which governments imposed upon transfers of responsibility for social policy to the Communities are fascinating but difficult to pin down in precise terms.   They were frequently the product more of a "gut feeling" among national politicians and officials rather than of any rational strategy. They do, however, provide a useful if somewhat impressionistic indication of the extent of the functional terrain which governments and other agencies had staked out as being essential to state sovereignty in the 1970s.   In this section I discuss four categories of social policy activities which are based upon the four roles performed by the Communities in social policy which I discussed earlier in this chapter.   I should perhaps point out again that I am not concerned here to examine the effectiveness of the various Communities' policies in this area, but rather to bring out the nature of the states' resistance, or lack of it, to their expansion.
      The first category involved the establishment of minimum standards which were consistent with existing expertise in relation to individual safety and health, and sometimes in relation to a somewhat less tangible quality of life.   This included much of the Communities' activities in relation to the environment, and also a proportion of those intended to remove non-tariff barriers on trade between members, in particular, where they were based on health or safety specifications.   These included actions to eliminate administrative or

legal barriers to trade and were the subject in
particular of Article 100 of the Treaty of Rome:
the process of removing such barriers was generally
referred to as the "harmonisation" of national
legislation. In this case the line between
measures designed essentially to liberalize the
market, and those intended to protect the interests
of citizens, was very difficult to draw: the two
purposes in Community policies were frequently
inseparable. By 1980 several hundred directives
had been adopted in toto under the general
programme for harmonizing national legislation,
though the proportion of these which were concerned
with social questions, as I have defined them, can
only be estimated at around 20%.(41) In July 1981
the Health and Safety Section in Britain's
Department of Trade and Industry had 'the lead',
i.e. main responsibility in Communities
negotiations on about 70 issues compared with a
total of between 300-400 "Art. 100" issues in the
charge of the Department. In addition, in the
period 1973-1980, the Communities had adopted 58
legislative texts on pollution, 15 on water
pollution, 10 on air pollution, 7 on waste, 8 on
noise pollution, and four on the protection of the
environment, land and natural resources.(42) These
various acts constituted by far the largest
proportion of the Communities' legislation on
social questions in the second half of the decade.
    After the middle of the decade these
activities tended to be arranged on a fairly
pragmatic basis and not according to any overall
plan or carefully structured programme. Dashwood
pointed out that although there had been a
programme to eliminate non-tariff barriers, which
was approved by the Council of Ministers on the
28th May, 1969, this had been abandoned by the
mid-1970s.(43) It had just not been possible to
keep up with the timetable, and doctrine had to
give way to 'the logic of events'.(44) The
all-embracing plan was finally abandoned when the
British and Danes joined the Communities in 1973
whose 'attitudes varied from the politely sceptical
to the stridently hostile'.(45) In this way, too,
the new states helped to impose limits upon the
incursions of the Communities into the activities
and the structures of the states.
    In the Communique issued after their meeting
of December 1974 the Heads of State and government
explicitly decided that progress in harmonizing
social security systems should be maintained

"without requiring that the social system obtaining in all member states should be identical". (Paragraph 28) The policy on the environment, which had been announced at the Summit Conference at Paris in October 1972, and adopted and incorporated in an Action Programme in November 1973, was always less structured and comprehensive than typical Communities' programmes of the 1960s. This less structured approach, which meant tackling problems as they arose, and as economic and political circumstances permitted, was characteristic of the Commission's less fundamentalist attitude towards integration in the second half of the 1970s. But it was also a reflection of other changes: 'a survey of proposals for directives submitted to the Council before 1973 shows a distinct preference for detailed measures designed to govern exhaustively the matters in question, to the exclusion of the previously existing national rules".(46) After that date, there was a greater tendency to harmonize to the extent necessary to sustain the Common Market or to promote a level of safety and health consistent with prevailing expert opinion. There seems to have been a change in the mid-1970s in the political intentions of the Commission and their philosophy of integration. On environmental policy the Commission asserted in May 1980 the principle that 'the most appropriate geographical level (local, regional, national, community or international level) must be sought for each type of action. More specifically the Community will step in only if action at national level needs to be placed in a wider perspective to become fully effective or if it involves a common interest (safeguarding of water for example) or when the adoption of divergent national measures would cause major economic or social problems".(47) In conformity with this principle, the proposal on taximeters was optional, whilst that on the classification, packaging and labelling of paints, varnishes, adhesives and similar products, required total harmonization in view of the dangerous nature of the substances involved. (48) By the middle 1970s, therefore, the principle of total harmonization within a centralized Community system had largely been abandoned. Instead, there had emerged a more pragmatic approach of tackling problems at the level which seemed appropriate, and to the extent necessary, which accorded quite well with the approach of David Mitrany.(See Chapter 1.)

The Communities success with the first
category of policies was reinforced by certain
features of the policy-making process in that
context. The position of experts tended to be
relatively strong in this area. In formulating its
proposals on the harmonization of legislation the
Commission was advised by working groups which
included experts nominated by the governments of
member states. As Dashwood points out: "given that
harmonization is regarded as a largely technical
matter, on which governments will normally accept
the advice of their experts, the position of the
latter is strong."(49) Expert groups had also been
established in each industrial sector to approve
any updating of existing legislation by the
Commission which may have become necessary in view
of technical developments; if the group rejected
the Commission's 'update', the Council of Ministers
was required to decide within three months; if the
Council did nothing, the Commission's view
prevailed. This is not to argue, however, that the
experts always agreed. The Commission presented in
1980 a perceptive account of the difficulties it
encountered with expert opinion on pollution
questions which applied equally to the rest of the
category, and indeed generally to the Communities'
work on technical matters: there was insufficient
'reliable and unchallengable data' ... 'Unanimous
agreement was always difficult' ... with the result
that it may be 'tempting in some cases to use this
as a reason for restricting the severity of the
measure proposed', the 'costs and benefits of a
particular measure were difficult to evaluate in
their impact on particular firms' ... 'there were,
for instance, two different approaches to measuring
the toxicity, persistence and bioaccumulation of
substances in water: this could lead to measures of
'unequal stringency'; and, lastly, 'the differences
between measurement techniques and methods
sometimes made it difficult to arrive at common
standards'.(50) One of the results of these
difficulties was that: 'protracted discussion at
the preparatory stage provides no guarantee that
different standpoints will not be adopted by
national delegations when the measures which had
been drafted eventually reached one of the
Council's working groups'.(51) Nevertheless the
main condition of progress in this area seemed to
be the extent to which consistent scientific data
was available and different experts in agreement.
Given a sufficient consensus at the expert level,

the political barriers to further progress seemed to be relatively malleable.

One of the dynamics of this process was the subjecting of officials and experts to what has been called a 'radiation' effect from the Communities which contributed to changes in national legislation even before the Communities had acted. One aspect of this was the emerging 'collegiality' among fellow professionals in the various member states. Experts and officials involved in discussions at the Communities' level became aware of the views of their colleagues and more frequently pushed for changes in national legislation, or the shaping of new legislation, in line with shared preferences. In the case of the environmental policy steps were taken to reinforce this radiation effect with the Information Agreement of March 1973 by which 'member states undertook to send the Commission their draft national environmental legislation before adoption'.(52) This procedure allowed the Commission to advise members about their legislation, and sometimes the Commission was able to persuade states to postpone action so that the Commission could propose Community measures for adoption by the Council in the particular field. The Commission concluded in 1980: 'there is thus a kind of osmotic interaction between the various national laws through the agency of Community regulations designed to extend to the rest of the Community national schemes to improve the environment.'(53) Since 1973 the Commission had received over 250 such notifications. The existence of the Community system provided a central harmonizing mechanism: it also gave encouragement, acted as the driving force and as a focus for dialogue, and exchanges of views between national administrators, members of Parliament, industrialists and ecologists.

The relative success of the Communities in this area was probably encouraged by the adoption of a more pragmatic, less politically intimidating strategy by the Commission in the mid-1970s; by the fact that this area was not generally politically contentious, and that informed groups were beginning to push for action; by the possibility of developing a technical consensus amongst experts, though this could be slow to emerge; and by the Commission's encouragement of 'osmosis' and 'radiation'. It was an area where on the whole progress depended upon the accumulation of a weight of expert opinion.

A further supportive factor, however, was that the policies were largely supported by economic arguments, even in a period of declining economic performance in member states. The Organisation of Economic Cooperation and Development (OECD) produced a <u>Report</u> in April 1979 which demonstrated that public authorities' environmental expenditure accounted for a minimal proportion, between 1 and 2%, of the gross domestic product, whereas damage caused by pollution amounted to between 3 and 5% of G.D.P. The inflationary effect of environmental policies had on average, been around 0.2% to 0.3% each year using the consumer price index as a basis for measurement; and the short-term impact of environmental policies on employment seemed to have been a net creation of jobs.(54) The costs had therefore, been rather small, though, of course, they were not always borne equally by those firms or businesses which were affected. Nevertheless a balancing of cost and benefits overall suggested that benefits could indeed exceed costs. There was, therefore, perhaps surprisingly, no convincing economic argument which could be used by those who were opposed to environmental policies: the same argument presumably applied to much of the Communities' work in the area of establishing minimum safety and health standards for products which directly affected the general public. There were, however, greater difficulties in introducing stronger measures for protecting the safety of workers in factories and elsewhere, where the damage could be more easily concealed. On the whole, however, the Communities were, as I have said, relatively successful in this area of social policy. It remained to be seen, of course, how far success here would affect government attitudes towards the extension of the Communities' influence in other more politically sensitive areas.

Whereas in 'category one' social questions there appreared to be a window through which the Communities could further develop their role, in 'category' four questions, at the other end of the earlier typology, there were a number of definite though frequently intangible political barriers. In consequence the Communities achieved less success in the late Seventies, and their activities were usually confined to recommendations, opinions or proposals, rather than directives or regulations. It was an area of pressure but success in the sense of the movement or weakening of the political barriers established by states was difficult to evaluate. Though in both category one and category four cases the economic cost of allowing a greater role to the Communities was low, and such a development could arguably have bought economic benefits, in relation to category four questions states and their agencies on the whole preferred to stress the benefits of sovereignty over those of integration. Such a reaction was not, of course, confined to the area of social policy. The British Government in particular had frequently been accused of attempting to preserve its sovereignty ahead of economic advantage.(55) In reacting against Communities' initiatives which fall into this category actors within the state seemed more frequently to be motivated by psychological or cultural consideration. My point here is that some types of Communities' social policy came up against rather irrational prejudices about the extent to which interventions in their own nation by outsiders could be tolerated. National reactions in this context may be divided into a number of rather loose, and interconnected categories; they also affected, though less directly, states reactions to incursions from the Communities on category three questions, though, as I will explain, in this case economic costs were a more powerful disincentive.

States found difficulty in accepting symbols which seemed to challenge their status, or which conversely apparently enhanced the status of another member state or that of the institutions of the European Communities. A good example of this was the argument about the introduction of the European Passport: the colour of its cover, and the closeness of its shade to that of national passports, were politically sensitive issues; the question of whether the words 'European Community' would appear above or below the name of the issuing state was also highly controversial. It had already been established that the new passport should not involve any changes in the rights of citizens, but that it should be essentially a common package for the various national passports. After considerable procrastination it was eventually agreed that the words 'European Community' should be on top of, and in the same typeface, as the name of the state. But one commentator concluded: 'British patriots need not, however, be unduly alarmed, since only the most eagle eyed among them will notice the change when

it eventually comes to pass.'(56)   That would not
be until after a further considerable delay - in
1985.   Other questions of 'symbolic' importance
included, of course, the siting of the proposed
political Secretariat, which the French Government
had wanted in Paris: as I pointed out in Chapter 5
most of the others preferred it to be peripatetic
and hesitated to accept any symbol of French
leadership in questions of European foreign
policy.(57)   There was also opposition to the
extension of the observable 'presence' of the
Communities within states which seeemed to be based
upon views about what was necessary in order to
preserve national cultural values: this seemed to
have been motivated by a sense of cultural
superiority in some nations.   One of the problems
with the Communities' comprehensive approach to
Category four questions in 1969 and the early 1970s
- and one of the reasons why it had to be abandoned
- was that it came up against traditional tastes
and cultural pride: the British did not want
Euro-beer or bread and preferred their traditional
poisons, and wished to avoid the appearance of
having given in to an external agency such as the
European Communities.   Cultural barriers were also
encountered when the Communities proposed to
introduce a common system for admittance to
universities, or a common curriculum for schools,
or attempted to persuade member states to establish
a health education policy, 'the main areas of which
would be to reduce tobacco consumption and improve
the eating habits of the public at large'.(58)   The
Communities had indeed achieved little success in
obtaining legislation in any of these areas, though
it had made relevant proposals.   There was,
however, success in an area in which cultural
biases were also evident: an agreement on the
equivalence of doctors' qualifications was obtained
and they were allowed freedom of establishment in
the Communities on prescribed conditions.   Another
example of resistance to a Communities' proposal
for reasons which were largely cultural or
traditional concerned Trade Unions' opposition in
some member states, such as the United Kingdom, to
the so-called Fifth Directive. The Communities had
strongly supported the introduction into all member
states of the German system of involving
worker-representatives in management.   This had
been part of the Communities' proposals for
reforming Company Law and for introducing law to
facilitate the creation of European companies.

British trade unions took the line that this form
of cooperation with management was incompatible
with the performance of their main tasks. Although
worker-directors were appointed to the Board of
British Steel and British Leyland they remained
controversial and ineffective. (See Chapter 8)   In
1982 the matter was still under discussion. Unions
were generally rather resistant to any proposals
which challenged their traditional ways or which
threatened the position or the authority of
leaders. Very frequently leaders' individual
interests became confused with interests which were
attributed to the group as a whole.
     An area in which the barriers within states
between themselves and other members were
particularly visible was that of the civil rights
of migrant workers. In this area states showed the
extent of their determination to assert national
control over public life, and to prevent
non-nationals from increasing their powers. There
were a number of differences between the various
member states' toleration of foreign citizens in
positions of authority. In some states, such as
France and Germany, university teachers, for
instance, were classed as civil servants and it was
very difficult for non-nationals to obtain
appointments on terms which were equivalent to
those offered to nationals. In Britain, in
contrast, non-nationals could be appointed to
university posts on terms which were equivalent to
those available to nationals. There had indeed
been considerable success in establishing the
transferablitiy of social security benefits, and
the rights of workers and their dependents to
reside and seek employment in other member states.
It was not until February 1976, however, that the
Council of Ministers agreed a resolution which
extended to EEC migrants the status of eligibility
'for the administrative and management posts of
trade unions'. (It became possible after that date
for the General Secretary of, for instance, the
British Trades Union Congress to be a German,
though the workings of union politics made this
highly unlikely.) But there remained various
difficulties, some of them very serious, in the way
of a further extension of these rights. Migrants
were excluded from posts which involved the
exercise of official authority which in some states
included a rather broad group of positions, some of
which would normally be occupied by trade union
officials when these were nationals. In 1979 the

Commission was reported to be looking at the problems which restricted migrants' rights to occupy a wider group of public service posts. For instance, in some states a non national could not become Director of a social security office, or of a hospital.(59)   There were also serious difficulties in the way of allowing migrants the right to vote in elections, though some work had been done on the question of their participation in local government elections. In February 1979 the Council had approved a Resolution which sought to accelerate progress towards the extension of voting rights to immigrants, but working groups which were subsequently established to consider these questions were hesitant and produced no public reports. The Belgian Government had apparently committed itself to allowing voting rights in local elections to migrants by 1982, but subsequently backpeddled. Many states were worried about the impact of a large number of migrant voters - around 3 million in Germany and 2 million in France - upon the outcome of elections, particularly where there were sensitive coalitions. The West German Government was reported to be reluctant to allow voting rights in Land elections and both the West Germans and the French thought there would be constitutional difficulties in the way of allowing voting rights to migrants. There were, in other words, a number of indications that migrants' rights were moving into areas which were extremely sensitive to member states, and where firm barriers against their extension could be erected very quickly. Not least amongst the states' fears was one which has traditionally been a powerful incentive towards the protection of sovereignty: that of being ruled by foreigners. A related fear was probably crucial in the states' hesitation about the introduction of a common passport: there was considerable anxiety in some states in relation to some groups about the need to avoid seeing the passport as a way of increasing the rights of foreigners in national territories, and conversely of lessening state control over the movement of foreign nationals. I do not, however, intend to deal here with the complications of immigration law.

    States' reactions against this category of communities' social policies were also affected by what might be called a 'cuckoo-in-the-nest-syndrome'. They were generally hesitant to accept any communities presence within their frontiers which seemed capable of striking the attention and sympathy of citizens, at the expense of national loyalties: governments were opposed to any attempt by the Commission to bring the 'human face' of the Communities closer to individuals and to make it more appealing. The conscious choice by some Communities' institutions of what might be called a public relations strategy was probably a mistake in that it alerted governments and agents within the state to the dangers of such activities. An opinion by the European Parliament in 1978 that a European Foundation should be created to mobilize public opinion in favour of European policies and objectives fell on stony soil, and only in part because of the expense involved. And, in the same year, a Commission proposal to the Council that steps should be taken to develop the study on the 'advisability and possibility of Community assistance in the field of unemployment benefits', was also taken no further; it had considered, amongst other questions, the idea of setting up Community offices in towns and cities to issue unemployment benefits, which would have been identified as part of an EEC system. Such a scheme seemed to be increasingly unrealistic as the number of unemployed in the European states increased rapidly in the late Seventies, and there were, of course, powerful financial and economic arguments against developing a Communities' role in this area. But one of the problems was certainly that governments disliked the idea of Communities institutions having direct contact with citizens in the performance of a welfare task. There was the possibility of strengthening support for the Communities by this mechanism, which had indeed probably been one of the Commission's intentions.

There were, therefore, a number of difficulties in the way of strengthening the role of the Communities and of increasing the foreign penetration of states in the context of this category of social policies. Commission proposals in this area in the late 1970s tended, therefore, not to be taken to the point of Directives or Regulations, but rather remained as proposals, or opinions, or recommendations. There were also relatively few proposals in this category, and they tended to date from the middle years of the decade, a period of greater enthusiasm for more advanced schemes for integration in Western Europe.

The third category, which related to efforts to raise standards of social provision in the

Communities, was also affected by barriers of a psychological and cultural kind, but economic cost was probably a more powerful disincentive to progress in this case. Although the Communities had largely given up any idea of moving towards a unified system of social security by the mid-1970s, there remained a number of proposals for raising the standard of provision in the various national systems, which usually dated from the period before the more obvious decline in the economies of the member states in the late 1970s. One area where there was however striking progress followed from a principle which had been enshrined in the Treaty of Rome, namely that of establishing equal rights for men and women. In December 1975 the Council of Ministers adopted a Directive that women should be given equality with men in access to employment, vocational training, promotion and work conditions; and in December 1978 the Council directed that there should be a progressive implementation of the principle of equal treatment for men and women in matters of social security. In many of the member states the full implications of these Directives were still being examined at the time of writing. On the other hand a number of other attempts to raise standards on the part of the Communities were abortive. A decision in 1975 to adopt a Communities' Poverty Programme was not followed through because of its cost. A similar fate met a 1975 Communities' scheme on the 'dynamization' of social security benefits. The proposal was that they should be adapted to any increase in the prosperity of member states.

In the late 1970s the Communities became more involved with a different kind of standard raising: this was in connnection with the attempts to cope with the increasingly severe problems caused by the declining economic circumstances of states, in particular, that of unemployment. In this case, however, the improved standards which were set forth were not in the area of increases in positive benefits, but rather in the 'improved' organisation and pattern of work habits. There were a large number of discussions and proposals in various Communities' institutions - the Council of Ministers, Tripartite Committee, the Economic and Social Committee, and the Standing Committee on Employment, about such changes as work-sharing, early retirement, the limiting of overtime, and flexible working hours. But the whole exercise had an air of unreality: by the end of the decade no such improvements in the standard of work patterns had been introduced. There really seemed very little chance indeed that national governments and trade unions could take steps which relied so much on the 'Community way'. (See my discussion of some associated problems in Chapter 2). As with the other Communities proposals in this category, one of the major problems was the economic one: it was difficult to convince management and governments that these were not more expensive ways to cope with unemployment than the dole queue. And individual workers, when they had a job, could see no economic benefits, and a number of costs, in work-sharing or early retirement. The Communities' various efforts to improve standards in welfare and labour organisation in the mid-late 1970s, therefore, met with difficulties which were largely, though not entirely, economic. The Communities seemed to be more successful in raising standards where the economic cost was negligible. As I have pointed out, in areas where individual health or safety was affected, the Communities had been relatively successful. But they also achieved a number of improvements in the late 70s in consumers' rights in the event of goods being faulty, and in labelling and packaging.

I do not propose to say very much here about the second category of Communities' social policies which were those related to the further liberalisation of the movement of workers and the self-employed within the Communities. In this area the Communities achieved a high degree of success: it was an objective which was fundamental to the goal of creating a common market and was enshrined in the Treaty of Rome. As with the Communities' other policies in liberalising transnational movements this policy contained, however, both a negative and a positive aspect. The removal of barriers in the way of the movement of workers was relatively straightforward. But there were greater difficulties in creating a positive framework for the mutual recognition of professional standards and qualifications, though by the end of the decade, a wide range of professionals had been granted the right to practise their skills in member states other than their country of origin. As I have mentioned, however, the granting to migrant workers of a range of civil rights had run into difficulties by the end of the decade. In contrast it seemed possible in 1980, that EEC citizens would be granted the right of residence in any member state regardless of whether or not they were employed there. In this sense the liberalisation process had been carried beyond the terms of the Rome Treaty which stressed the primary goal of creating and protecting the common market. One British left-wing politician was reported to have said that this measure had been proposed as a Charter for the rich who wished to buy houses in the South of France: life would be so much easier for them if they had an automatic right of residence! In contrast a Communities' proposal for improving the education of children of migrants achieved little success. On the whole, as I have said, the Communities were successful in achieving the goal of negative integration in removing barriers to the movement of workers and self-employed, but they were less successful in the goal of achieving the positive integration of those who moved across national frontiers into other national systems. In the late Seventies the goal of the assimilation of migrants into other nations in the Communities acquired greater importance in view of the abandonment in a number of areas of attempts to create a common Communities system. Communities' social policy was no longer focused upon the grand goal of creating a European society: in this area too the confederal principle had prevailed.

Conclusions

The preceding arguments have both explained and described the limitations upon the Communities' involvement in social policies in the 1970s. These limitations are reflected in the tendency to produce much procedure, many guidelines, but little legislation in areas of greater political sensitivity; in the attempt to focus upon the problems of unemployment policy in this period of economic recession, though without adequate resource provision by goverments at the Communities level; and in a reaction against the greater ambition for developing a Communities' social policy as they emerged in the early and mid-1970s. Indeed, one of the reasons for the limitations imposed by governments was probably the Communities' choice of the era of social policy as a political instrument for integration, and the national governments' reactions against this in the economic circumstances of the later period.

Although economic considerations were sometimes a significant difficulty in the way of the improvement of standards, government reactions, and those of other actors in the member states, were often influenced by less tangible factors such as the fear of losing identity or control. Attempts to improve standards merged imperceptibly into activities to promote the Communities at the believed 'expense' of the states, or to strengthen the position of foreigners in what were believed to be national preserves. Questions about national assimilation became particularly important in view of the Communities' abandonment of the attempt to build a European society in the mid-1970s: integration was now no longer a matter of adjusting everybody to a Communities' norm, and fitting them into a supranational system, but rather of adjusting national systems to allow a minimum necessary overlap. As the decade wore on, economic constraints increasingly limited attempts to introduce higher common standards but they also seemed to be associated with the strengthening of psychological cultural and political barriers to integration. In crude terms: economic decline reinforced nationalism.

There was, however, considerable success in the achievement of minimum common standards in such areas as health and safety, in the environment, workplace and the specification of goods. The range of activities in the form of Communities' legislation in these areas is frequently underestimated. Its implications for the erosion of the socio-psychological and cultural barriers in the way of further integration were, however, uncertain. The evidence from the latter part of the decade would suggest that the amount of legislation in the first category increased, and that in the second category continued at a steady pace, whilst barriers in the third and fourth categories were becoming firmer and more difficult to penetrate. This is not very encouraging from the point of view of the Functionalism which suggested that cooperation in areas of lesser salience would have favourable implications for integration in more politically sensitive ones. It should be stressed though that in this study I have not dealt directly with mass attitude changes, which were a primary focus of Functionalism, but rather upon possible consequences of such changes for the empirical frontiers between the zone of transnational penetration and the zone of national retrenchment.

NOTES
1. See Gunnar Myrdal, _Beyond the Welfare State,_ Methuen University Paperbacks, London, 1960, pp. 12-43.
2. See Paul Taylor, "Functionalism: the theory of David Mitrany" in Paul Taylor and A.J.R. Groom (Editors), _International Organization: A Conceptual Approach_, Frances Pinter, London, 1978, pp. 236-252.
3. See Richard Titmuss, _Essays on the Welfare State_, 3rd ed., London, 1976, esp. Chaps 1 and 2.
4. See third section of this chapter.
5. Victor Petaccio, "The European Social Fund: Phase I in Positive Retrospect", _Journal of Common Market Studies_, March 1972, p. 249. For a comprehensive account of the development of the Communities social policy see Doreen Collins, _The European Communities: the Social Policy of the Ist Phase_ (Vol. 1); and _The European Economic Community 1958-1972_, Martin Robertson, 1975.
6. For an account of the pattern of economic divergence in the Communities in the mid-late 1970s see Michael Hodges and William Wallace, _Economic Divergence in the European Community_, Allen & Unwin, London 1981.
7. Michael Shanks, _European Social Policy Today and Tomorrow_, Oxford, Pergamon Press, 1977, p. 13.
8. Denis Swan, _The Economics of the Common Market_, 3rd edition, Harmondsworth, 1975, p. 147.
9. Petaccio, _loc.cit.,_ p. 259
10. _ibid_, p. 256
11. _ibid_, p. 253
12. _ibid_, p. 250
13. Juliet Lodge, "Towards a human union: EEC social policy and European integration", _British Journal of International Studies,_ Volume 4, No. 2 July 1978, p. 116.
14. _Resolution on the Position taken by the European Parliament in regard to the fundamental problems of European Community Policy_ ..., 3 Nov. 1969, Para. 2.C. (Quoted _Third General Report on the Activities of the Communities_, 1969, Brussels-Luxembourg 1970, p. 483.)
15. Petaccio, _loc. cit._, p. 265
16. Sergio Barzanti, _The Underdeveloped Area within the Common Market,_ Princeton, Princeton University Press, 1965, p. 162.

17. See President Ortoli's "Introduction" in Sixth General Report on the Activities of the Communities, 1972, Brussels-Luxembourg, 1973 esp. p. XXVI.

18. See Michael Shanks, loc. cit., pp. 24-25

19. ibid, p. 15

20. Juliet Lodge, loc. cit., p. 111

21. Michael Shanks, loc. cit., p. 16

22. ibid, p. 14

23. Lodge, loc. cit., p. 16

24. See account of this in Chapter 2.

25. Figures taken from "Changes in Community expenditure by sector during the budgetary procedure", tables in General Reports on the Activiites of the Communities, 1978, 1979, 1980

26. Commission of the European Communities, Seventh Report on the Activities of the European Social Fund, Financial Year 1978, COM (79) 346 Final, Brussels June, 1979, p. 20

27. General Reports, loc. cit.

28. Thirteenth General Report on the Activities of the Communities, loc. cit., p. 46.

29. Fourteenth General Report ... loc. cit., p. 46

30. Seventh Report on the Activities of the Social Fund, loc. cit., Annexe 1/1

31. ibid, Annexe 1/3

32. ibid, p. 10

33. ibid, Annexe IV

34. c.f. Petaccio's figures, above.

35. Personal interviews, July 1980

36. See Michael Shanks, loc.cit., p. 24

37. See Chapter 3 above

38. Geoffrey Denton, "Reflections on Fiscal Federalism in the EEC", Journal of Common Market Studies, Vol. XVI, No. 4, pp. 283-301

39. See Petaccio, loc. cit., p. 266

40. Quoted ibid, p. 266

41. According to information gained from personal interviews July 1981.

42. Commission of the European Communities, Progress Made in Connection with the Environment Action Programme and Assessment of the Work Done to Implement it, Brussels, May 1980, COM (80) 222 Final, p.2.

43. Alan Dashwood, "Hastening Slowly: the Communities' Path towards Harmonization", in Helen Wallace, William Wallace and Carole Webb (Eds), Policy Making in the European Communities, John Wiley, 1977, esp. pp. 290-291.

44. ibid, p. 290

45. ibid, p. 291
46. ibid, p. 288
47. Commission of the European Communities, Progress Made in Connection with the Environment Action Programme ... , loc. cit., p.2.
48. Dashwood, p. 289
49. ibid, p. 291
50. Progress made in Connection with the Environment ..., loc.cit., p.5
51. Dashwood, loc.cit., p. 291
52. Progress made in Connection with the Environment ..., loc.cit., p. 4
53. ibid, p.4.
54. See Doc. OECD ENV/MIN (79) 5, 6 April, 1979
55. See Chapter Six.
56. The Guardian, Tuesday, June 23, 1981
57. See William Wallace and David Allen, "Political Cooperation: Procedure as Substitute for Policy", in Wallace, Wallace and Webb (Editors), loc. cit.,
58. Thirteenth General Report on the Activities of the Communities, loc.cit. pp. 229-230
59. Information in this section was acquired through personal interviews with officials in Brussels, July 1980.

Chapter Eight

THE CRISIS OVER THE BUDGET AND THE AGRICULTURAL
POLICY: BRITAIN'S RELATIONS WITH HER PARTNERS IN
THE LATE 1970S AND EARLY 1980S

This is the last chapter which focuses
primarily upon the limits of integration as
reflected in policy disagreements in the European
Communities. I examine the sources of what had
become by the late 1970s and early 1980s a major
division in the Communities: that between Britain
and the other member states. The disagreement
between Wilson and Callaghan's Labour and, after
May 1979, Thatcher's Conservative governments, and
the others, seemed to revolve around a perceived
inequity in the scale of Britain's contributions to
the Budget of the Communities, and the adverse
effects of the Common Agricultural Policy (C.A.P.)
upon Britain. But these were only the most
pressing of a range of problems. They were a
symptom of a number of more fundamental
difficulties, not only in Britain's relations with
the Nine, but also in relations in general between
the member states of the European Communities.
Davidson portrayed the problem in these terms:
"Dissatisfaction with the way the Community works
is almost universal, but for many years the member
states have seemed to prefer on balance to use the
institutions as a mechanism for handling, if not
resolving, their competing national interests,
rather than make a more profound commitment to the
implied objectives of the Community. Fortunately
(or unfortunately, according to one's point of
view), the time for this static option is fast
running out: if the Community does not move
forward, it will move back."(1)   The Economist on
March 20th 1982 gave its view of the situation on
its cover with the words, embossed on the picture
of a tombstone: EEC born March 25th, 1957, moribund
March 25th, 1982, capax imperii nisi imperassett.
(It seemed capable of power until it tried to wield

231

it.)

There were, indeed, three different levels of
the difficulties between Britain and her partners.
At the more superficial level were the difficulties
which were apparently perceived by the government
and sections of the informed elite in Britain to be
the more pressing, which were those concerning, in
particular, the Budget and the C.A.P. These were
the most frequent sources of complaints about
Britain's relations with the Communities in the
early 1980s and threatened to disrupt a number of
meetings of the European Council. On a second
level, however, were a number of problems in
Britain's circumstances, compard with those of her
partners, which both contributed to the first set
of problems, and which led them to be perceived as
such by the British. These included the increasing
divergence between the performance of the British
economy and that of her partners, and the nature of
public attitudes in Britain towards membership.
And, thirdly, there were a number of long term
problems which accounted for the persistence of the
weaknesses in Britain's economy and her failure to
exploit the opportunities of membership, such as
the pattern of investment and the absence of what I
have called a consensus strategy about the
development of Britain's industry. The second and
third levels of problems tended to sharpen the
complaints about Budgetary contributions and the
Common Agricultural Policy.

The general conclusions which are reached in
the following discussion are first, that the scale
of the specific 'grievances' in Britain which might
have been found in the Communities' budgetary and
agricultural arrangements, have been grossly
exaggerated by the British Government, and some
commentators, beyond any necessary utilitarian
implications. Put more simply, the hue and cry was
not worth what it cost Britain; secondly, that much
of the perception of grievance was attributable to
Britain's continuing relative failure as an
industrial state when compared with other members
which had been more successful in economic terms;
and thirdly that Britain's style of diplomacy
tended to make it more difficult for Britain's
partners to accept necessary alterations in the
C.A.P. and possible adjustments in Britain's favour
of the budgetary mechanism. Indeed British
diplomacy - though more in its style and the
underlying attitudes which it revealed than in its
specific objectives - increased the reluctance of

the member states to accept a range of more important and far-reaching changes, in, for instance, industrial policy, a common energy policy, and more concerted efforts to adjust to the changing international economic context. As Davidson also pointed out, the squabble about the C.A.P. and the budget in the late 1970s and early 1980s was "superficially just another case of those haggles about money that have become so tiresomely familiar. But the heart of the matter is that it is really a disguised argument over whether the Community should be more integrated or less integrated."(2) Although Britain's economy would have benefitted more from integration, her policies and diplomatic style tended to reinforce pressures towards disintegration. The specific complaints were, indeed, a concentrated expression of complex and multilevel international relations between Britain and her partners, and also between the latter, and involved both tangible, utilitarian questions and less tangible questions of a psychological and perceptual kind.

I explain and develop these questions first, in the next section, with explicit reference to the budgetary and agricultural problems; then, in the second section, in the context of the longer term problems in Britain's economy and attitudes; and thirdly, in the final section with reference to the persistence of weaknesses in Britain's industry and the failure of the British to develop a coherent strategy for overcoming these. I develop here the thesis that the lack of a positive British attitude towards developing a set of policies at the Communities level for industrial regeneration and management, was in part a reflection of the lack of such policies in Britain itself, and that the "haggles about money" were symptomatic of a deeper immobilisme in the Communities which British attitudes and difficulties tended to reinforce.

*****

This is not the place for a detailed account of the Budget of the European Communities(3) or of the Common Agricultural Policy.(4) It is important to point out, however, that the then Six member states agreed to a budgetary system in a Council decision of 21st April 1970 according to which the Communities would have a legal right immediately to what are called own resources, and that these would be collected in their entirety according to an

agreed Community system after 1975.(5)   Between
1970 and 1975 all levies on imports of food from
outside the Communities, and an increasing
proportion of tariffs on manufactured goods would
go to the Communities.(6)   From 1975 on all levies
on imported food and all tariffs on imports of
manufactured goods would accrue to the Communities'
Budget; in addition a sum of up to the value of 1%
of Value Added Tax (VAT) in the member states would
be added each year though the precise level of this
would be agreed annually in the course of
constructing the Communities' Budget.
     There were two complications in the process of
introducing the system.   The first was that the
tranche related to Value Added Tax could not be
added in 1975 as had been agreed in 1970 because
that tax, when it was introduced by member states,
was not held at a standard level by them throughout
the Communities.   (A formula for its incorporation
was eventually agreed and it was introduced in
1978.)   The second was that special arrangements
were made for the states – Britain, Denmark,
Ireland – which acceded in 1973 according to which
they would pay an increasing percentage of what
they would have paid, had they been full
participants in the system, up till 1978.   After
that date the Communities system applied to them in
full, with the limitation that for two further
years their total contribution was not to vary by
more than an agreed amount compared with the
previous year's level.   It was, therefore, not
until 1980 that the Communities system applied in
full to all the members of the Communities; after
that date the scale of their contributions was to
vary automatically according to the levels of their
imports from third countries and the amount
generated within their economy by Value Added Tax.
The one 'accidental' element in this system was
that Britain and the other member states retained
the ability to manipulate to some extent the costs
deriving from the Common Agricultural Policy until
1980 because they could adjust the so-called green
currencies – in Britain's case, the green pound.
     There were a number of reasons for the
introduction of a Communities budgetary system in
this form.   Its various components were not chosen
at random.   In the context of the debate about the
links between agricultural expenditure and the
revenue-raising mechanism, and the British
assertion that the Budget could be rearranged
independently of the C.A.P. – and the French

assertion that the price levels in the Common
Agricultural Policy could be adjusted independentl
of Budgetary Reform - it is important to remember
that in the experience of the Six the creation of
own resources was linked with the need to find a
way of financing the Common Agricultural Policy.
The French Government had laid particular stress
upon the latter objective. The Treaty of Rome
stipulated that a fund for the guidance and
guarantee of the agricultural market should be
introduced (Article 40, para. 4), and on a number
of occasions in the 1960s there had been proposals
to achieve this from own resources. Although the
French had judged it premature to introduce such a
system when it was proposed by the Commission in
1965, particularly as the proposed arrangement the
was linked with the strengthening of the control o
the "supra-national" Commission and Assembly over
the Budget, nevertheless they had regarded the
system in use before the 1970 arrangement as a
temporary one. By the time of the 1969 Hague
Summit they had accepted the own resources method
and this was made clear in the final communique of
that meeting. As the Common Agricultural Policy
was in essence a system for maintaining domestic
market prices for food at a predetermined level by
imposing levies on imports of food from the world
market, and buying surplus domestic products to
maintain a relative scarcity, it was logical to us
the levies to pay for the market intervention. It
was easy for member governments to accept that
levies on agricultural imports should be a
component of own resources, particularly as even
before April 1970 the funding of food market
interventions had become the dominant item on the
expenditure side at about 70% of the total.
        There were equally powerful reasons for addin
the other two items. The Treaty of Rome had
indicated in Article 201 that there should be a
Communities budgetary system once the Common
External Tariff had been finally introduced, which
was achieved in 1969. The reasoning here, which
came to be known as the Rotterdam Principle, was
that once the European Communities existed as a
single market it would be possible for a large
proportion of the goods imported from outside the
EEC, which were eventually sold, for instance, on
the German or French markets, to enter the
Communities through, for example, Rotterdam in
Holland; in this situation there was no reason why
tariffs should accrue to the Dutch Government

alone. It was much more equitable and practicable for revenues thus raised to be transferred to a central fund. It followed then, that tariffs on imports of non-agricultural products were also acceptable as components of own resources.

There was, however, the further problem that returns from tariffs and levies were likely to be insufficient to pay for the range of Communities expenditure including that on the Common Agricultural Policy; they were unpredictable in the short term, because of such variables as the size of the harvest, and in the long term were likely to decrease as the increasing world demand for food led to price rises outside the Communities, and member states increasingly traded with each other in the Common Market in both food and manufactured goods. It had also been agreed that there would be a common system of taxation as different national tax systems could impose an unequal burden on national industries and thus undermine the principle of free competition. Again it seemed sensible to make up any shortfall in the Communities' revenue from levies and tariffs by a standard cut of such a common tax system: this would have the additional benefit of creating a link between Gross National Product and the scale of national contributions to the Budget. The more prosperous states would generate more VAT, and their 1% share would be proportionately greater than that of the less prosperous states. In 1980 the VAT tranche made up 54% of the Budget; agricultural levies were 14% and 32% came from industrial tariffs.(8) Thus the VAT component became a vital source of finance for the Common Agricultural Policy upon which the French laid so much stress.

This then was the system of raising the Communities' finance which applied to the British – and the other states which acceded in 1973 – when the various transitional exemptions ceased to be applicable in 1980. It is not necessary to deal here with the complex politics of the introduction of the system, except insofar as they affected the British complaints of the early 1980s. It is important to stress, though, that the introduction of the Communities' Budget was closely linked with the development of the Common Agricultural Policy. It was not until the major market mechanisms had been established, and the central principles – particularly concerning financing interventions out of the Communities' funds – had been agreed, that

the French Government would accept the system of
own resources. And by then it was clear to the
member governments and the majority of commentators
that the major item of expenditure from the Budget
for the forseeable future was likely to be
agriculture. Among the original Six it was clear
also that West Germany would be the major
contributor to the Budget, and that France and
Holland would be the main recipients of support.
Italy was the deviant case in that it was a net
contributor, although its per capita GNP and the
circumstances of its agricultural system would have
suggested that it should ideally have been in net
receipt of funds.
     The main reason for this pattern of net
contributions and receipts was that net importers
of food paid contributions in the form of levies to
the Budget, but received little in terms of
expenditure from the agricultural intervention
mechanism of the Communities, because of the
absence of food surpluses on the domestic market
(West Germany and Italy). Net exporters of food,
on the other hand, tended to pay little in the form
of levies to the Budget but to benefit from
expenditure via the intervention mechanism through
which surpluses of domestic food were bought and
stored (France and Holland). In both cases, of
course, the purpose was to manage prices in the
marketplace so that they approximated to a target
price, which was fixed by the Council of Ministers
in March and April of each year, in order to
generate satisfactory incomes for farmers.
Excessive surpluses - butter mountains and wine
lakes - would accrue if the target price was too
high, which was often the case, as ministers tended
for political reasons to fix prices at a level
which would provide an adequate income for less
efficient farmers.(9) It was, however, one of the
original objectives of the Common Agricultural
Policy that European agriculture should be
restructured, and inefficient farms removed, so
that the task of fixing a target price, which would
provide adequate income to the farmers without
leading some to over-produce, would be simplified:
despite a number of ambitious proposals little
progress had been achieved in this direction by the
early 1980s.
     The British complaint was occasioned by the
perceived relationship between the pattern of its
contributions to the Communities' Budget, according
to the agreed automatic system, compared with the

pattern of its receipts mainly, but not
exclusively, through interventions in the
agricultural market, when compared with those
patterns in other member states. In 1980 Britain's
gross contributions to the Budget were not
particularly unreasonable compared with her gross
national product, and compared with the
contributions of other states. The British share
was 20.5% (19.8% of gross domestic product in 1977
at current purchasing power parities), whilst that
of West Germany was 30.1% (28.1%), France 20.0%
(23.2%), Italy 11.5% (15.7%), and Holland 8.4%
(5.8%).(10) Britain tended, however, to receive a
relatively smaller share of Communities
expenditure: in 1980 it received only 8.7% of the
total Communities spending compared with 20.2% for
France, 23.5% for Germany, 16.8% for Italy and
10.5% for Holland.(11) Figures for the balance of
contributions and receipts between Britain and the
Communities tended to vary, but in 1980 they ranged
from a deficit of around £600 million, to one of
£1,300 million. The method of calculation by which
the latter figure was produced indicated that West
Germany had a deficit of £1,082 million and Italy
£24 million. Other members were all in credit,
France at £480 million and Holland at £887
million.(12) (I describe the per capita balance,
which gives a somewhat different perspective, later
on.) Britain was, therefore, judged to be the
biggest net contributor to the Communities budget
by some way in 1980. At the same time it was noted
that the value of its per capita GNP expressed as a
percentage of the unweighted mean at 1977
purchasing power parities, was only 92, compared
with 113.5 in France, 118.5 in Germany and 108 in
Holland.(13) These figures, which compared the
balance of Britain's receipts and contributions
with those of the other member states in relation
to the value of per capita GNP, were the source of
Britain's complaints about the inequity of the
Communities' budgetary system. It should be noted,
however, that its gross contributions were not
unduly out of line, but that receipts were rather
low compared with the others. This was mainly
because Britain, as a food importer with an
efficient agriculture, which nevertheless produced
relatively few surpluses for purchase out of
Community funds, tended to attract little
expenditure through the intervention system of the
Common Agricultural Policy. At the same time the
largest item by some way in total spending out of

the Communities' Budget in all states was
agricultural intervention at 62.19% of the total in
1981.(14)
　　The response of the British Government to this
perceived inequity was to put pressure upon her
partners to adjust the Budgetary mechanism. The
Labour Government had sought to do this in the
renegotiations of the terms of accession, which
preceded the Referendum on membership in 1975; this
led to a settlement at the Dublin meeting of the
European Council in March 1975.(15) The
negotiations about the European Monetary System
(EMS) in 1978 were another occasion on which the
British Labour Government sought to reduce
contributions to the Budget though, on this
occasion partners refused to make concessions, in
particular at the somewhat acrimonious meeting of
the European Council in December 1978 at which the
EMS was established. It is noteworthy that the
Labour Government's response to the problem was
broadly to seek to reduce the scale of Britain's
contributions: the 1974-75 negotiations had
produced a complex formula for adjusting
contributions in line with the level of GNP. The
Thatcher Conservative Government concentrated much
more on the level of returns to Britain, since the
level of contributions did not seem to be
particularly high compared with that of other
states and the 1965 mechanism had not been
triggered by 1982 and it did not seem likely that
this would happen. The different policy might also
be attributable in part to the relatively stronger
inclination of Labour to reduce Britain's
involvement with the European Communities to a
minimum practical level. In the early 1980s the
Conservative Government staged a number of
confrontations with the partners about this issue.
In 1980, after bitter disagreements, a formula for
rebates was agreed which was to apply until the
first quarter of 1983 and which had the effect of
returning to Britain a sum equal to about a third
of her contributions. In 1982 the disagreement
returned with new vigour as the end of the term of
the 1980 agreement approached.
　　The Commission produced a <u>Report</u> in June 1981
in response to a Mandate assigned to it by the
Council on 30th May 1980, and proposed that in the
long term the solution to Britain's Budgetary
difficulties should be the transfer to the British
of a sum "assessed by comparing the United
Kingdom's share of the Community Gross National

Product with the proportion it obtains of European
Guidance and Guarantee Fund Guarantee Section
expenditure".(16)   A transfer evaluated in these
terms would be taken from own resources.   But as
these would be insufficient to cover the cost of
such a transfer until a decision had been taken to
create new own resources which exceeded the 1%
limit on Value Added Tax - a change which West
Germany and Britain opposed - the alternative short
term measure was proposed of compensating the
United Kingdom "via abatements of their receipts
from the Community" on the part of member states
which benefitted more from the C.A.P. than their
British partner.(17)   In other words the French and
other net beneficiaries were asked by the
Commission to give back some of their money
received from the Communities.   In early 1982
diplomacy about the Budget became increasingly
strident.   The West Germans and French insisted
that no rebates to Britain should be paid by
national governments, but that they should come
from the Communities' Budget.(18)   It was reported
that at a meeting of the Foreign Ministers on 15th
- 16th January 1982 there was agreement on the
principle of a rebate to Britain and that the
settlement should be related to the difference
between Britain's share of the Communities' gross
national product and the proportionate value of her
share of the Budget.   The size of the rebate was
not agreed.   A further meeting of the Foreign
Ministers ended in disarray on 25th January with no
agreement on the scale of the rebate and on a
number of related issues.   The British also
insisted that the arrangement for rectifying the
imbalance should be permanent and that Communities
policy should be adjusted - in particular the
C.A.P. should be reformed and a ceiling placed on
agricultural expenditure - so that the British paid
less and received more.   The French argued,
however, that the arrangement should be regarded as
a departure from the norm of the Communities
practice, and the French, Danes and Irish led
opposition to the idea that there should be an
effective ceiling on agricultural expenditure.
      On 28th January the British Foreign Secretary,
Lord Carrington, was reported as having said that
no other member would accept such a poisoned
chalice.(19)   Claude Cheysson, the French Foreign
Minister, said that the "United Kingdom sought a
juste retour which was not a Community idea.   The
British and we are not speaking of the same

Community."(20)   The main Communities commentator
of the authoritative <u>Financial Times</u> retorted that
Cheysson's comment "was one of the most misleading
statements of the year(21) and later noted "the
strange web of prejudice and ideology France has
wrapped around its reluctance to dip deeply into
its pocket to help the United Kingdom."(22)   The
British responded to the impasse by refusing to
agree to higher target prices for food, and on 23rd
March 100,000 angry farmers moved into Paris and
mounted the biggest demonstration seen in that city
since May 1968.

In late March there was a further attempt to
find an acceptable formula to settle the Budgetary
problem.   On 24th March Commission President Thorn
and Belgian Foreign Minister Tindemans put forward
the idea that there should be a fixed rebate for
two years for the British of one billion E.C.U.s;
this would be adjusted if it departed by more than
10% from an "objective indicator" which was the sum
the United Kingdom would have paid if her
contributions were in the same proportion as the
relative value of her gross domestic product.   A
further refund would follow if Value Added Tax
revenue from the UK exceeded its share of Community
GDP.(23)   The key rebate would be renegotiated in
1984.   The UK reacted favourably to this proposal,
and the first reactions of the French were not
entirely discouraging: but at a further meeting of
the Foreign Ministers on 8th April the French
Government simply refused to discuss the proposal
and its representative accused the British
Government of using "terrorist tactics" when it
again responded by refusing to agree to higher
target prices for food.

At the time of writing, in late May 1982 the
Budgetary dispute had been overtaken by the crisis
in the Falkland Islands: it was, however, reported
that in view of their acceptance of a trade ban in
support of the British against the Argentines,
Britain's partners were expecting a softening of
demand for a long term deal to reduce the Budgetary
contributions as a "<u>quid pro quo</u>" for the economic
sacrifices which the ban would entail.   The dispute
reached crisis proportions when the other member
states voted to increase farm prices on the 18th
May and ignored the attempt by Britain to impose
its veto on this.   This procedure was against the
terms of the Luxembourg Agreement of January 1966,
which allowed a state to block a vote if it was
deemed to be a matter of important national

interest, although it was in accordance with the principles of the Rome Treaty. The question of whether or not Britain's partners acted legally in going against the terms of the Luxembourg Agreement was still under consideration at the time of writing. This step was, however, a measure of the other's increasing irritation with British attempts to generate pressure on her partners to allow a satisfactory Budgetary rebate by refusing farm price increases. The others had come close to forcing the issue to a vote at a meeting of the Agricultural Council on the 11th May; but the Foreign Office was reported to have assured the Government that their veto would not be circumvented. The British had indeed warned on the 12th May that if there was any attempt to circumvent the British veto on farm prices, and to "ride roughshod over our rights", "there would be very serious consequences indeed". (The Times, 14 May, 1982) On the 24th May, however, the British accepted a temporary settlement which involved a rebate for one year of under £500,000,000. This was much less than the minimum annual rebate of £600,000,000 which they had sought, but, more importantly, there was no longterm alteration of the Budgetary mechanism in Britain's favour, and there was no ceiling on agricultural expenditure as the British had demanded.

It looked rather as though the British had accepted the settlement for the current year because of the pressing events in the Falklands, but that battle would be rejoined in Europe in 1983. It also looked as if the Foreign Office had under-estimated the strength of feeling of the partners, and miscalculated the likelihood that they would circumvent the British veto. The attention of the new Foreign Minister, Mr Pym, and Mrs Thatcher, had been focussed away from European questions, on the Falklands, and one commentator said that the British representative in Brussels, Sir Michael Butler, seemed "completely to have lost his balance over the Community Budget issue ... and advised that Britain's partners would not dare to over-rule her veto on farm prices". (David Watt, The Times, 28 May 1982) There was, in contrast, considerable evidence in the previous week that the partners could be moved to risk seriously offending Britain.

British diplomacy on the Budgetary problem was extremely forthright and pressing. Indeed the tone of the Government and of the majority of

commentators was one of extreme self-righteousness
about the absolute justice of the British demands
and the extreme deviousness and short-sighted
selfishness of those who opposed them. The French
in particular were often accused of unworthy
motives, and condemned for their reluctance to give
way. The British Government, with the backing of
both major parties, seemed prepared to push their
claims to the extent of seriously jeopardising the
future of the Communities, and it was impossible to
find in the British press any account of the case
against satisfying the British claims.(24) The
issue was a catalyst for the expression of a number
of prejudices and fears about Continental Europe
and membership in the Communities which had
hitherto been barely suppressed: many of the
psychological adjustments recognised by crisis
analysts, such as tunnel vision, could be
observed.(25)
        There was, however, a good case for the view
that the British had over-reacted to the perceived
imbalance in their account with the European
Communities, and that in the medium or long term
they stood to lose more than they could gain by
such a vigorous course of action. The French
Government, and the other opponents of Britain's
claim, were not being merely stubborn in resisting
an indisputable British demand. Although there was
undoubtedly scope for altering the Common
Agricultural Policy, as the Commission had argued
in its 1981 Report, and the Budgetary mechanism
could have been altered to suit Britain, the style
of the British approach tended to raise the hackles
of the French in particular, so that any adjustment
became more difficult. The case against Britain
can be considered from three inter-related
perspectives. First, the scale of the inequity
needs to be considered: was the relative value of
the sums involved in proportion to the reaction?
Second, were there valid French and other interests
in opposing the claims in addition to the short
term one of simply preventing a return to Britain
of around £600 million a year: were there, in other
words, larger and long term interests for the
French too? And thirdly were there positive
advantages for Britain in not pressing her case on
this matter, to be set against the case for so
doing, which outweighed the immediate benefits of
increased receipts from the Communities.
        The scale of Britain's deficit needs to be put
into perspective: it was certainly enormous when

judged against personal expenditure or the budget of most businesses. I will here assume that the worst case figure as presented by Godley of a deficit of around £1,300 million a year was the correct one. This sum was equal to about 5.8% of the total value of income tax collected in Britain in the early 1980s. But it should be recalled that income tax was only 36% of total revenue collected,(26) and that the total value of the Budget of the Communities was less than 1% of the value of the GNP of member states, and about 2.6% of the value of the monies which passed through the budgets of the governments of the member states.(27) Indeed the value of Britain's net contribution was around 3.5% of the total value of the British budget in the early 1980s. This compared with other items of expenditure in Britain in 1979 such as that of defence at £9,000 million, education £9.5 thousand million, social welfare £18.5 thousand million and £400 million on the libraries and museums.(28) In other words the sums involved, though not negligible, are fairly minor in proportion to other items of expenditure in Britain, and in comparison with the total budget in Britain. The perception of grave injustice was therefore very much attributable to the comparison of Britain's contributions with that of other states rather than upon a careful and detailed calculation of what the sums meant for Britain in British terms. Commentators such as Wynne Godley demonstrated that the transfer system was arbitrary and perverse, which may be true, but they had not examined too closely the precise scale of the disadvantage. One measure was the Macdougal Report calculations that the scale of the European Communities Budget would need to be increased to between 2 % and 3% of the value of GNP before the pattern of its expenditure need have any implication for the management of national economies.(29) Another was that a casual adjustment of the tax system in Britain in 1981 decreased the tax burden of the 350,000 most wealthy individuals in the country by around £230 million per annum: this sum was approaching 50% of the amount of the deficit with the Communities which was most widely accepted - around £600 million.

The British reaction in the late 1970s and early 1980s to this order of deficit should also be contrasted with the government's acceptance of a cost of this order of magnitude when Britain

acceded in 1973. It was the kind of sum which they
had expected to pay for the privileges which had
then been extended to them. For instance, the
White Paper, <u>Britain and the European Communities</u>,
Command 4289, which was published in 1970 as the
official prospectus for United Kingdom entry, held
that "trade effects and financial charges
consequent upon accepting the C.A.P. were likely to
be around £175 - £250 million per year".(30)
Ritson also pointed out that the "balance of
payments" of the C.A.P. was estimated at between
£300 and £400 million, a sum equal to around £1,000
million at 1981 prices.(31) The predicted cost of
British membership in the Communities was close to
the actual cost in the early 1980s. This evidence
about the scale of the amounts involved, and the
expectations of Britain and her partners in
relation to this, should be set against the amount
of diplomatic energy expended on the recovery of
the sums and the risks taken in terms of souring
relations with Britain's partners. The
transnational comparative element tended to
dominate in the minds of commentators above the
details of the contract entered into and the scale
of the sums in British terms. Ritson points out,
rather, that among the reasons for the impatience
of the British were the fact that the costs in the
mid-1970s had been less than they had expected
because of world food prices and the scale of
domestic harvests, and because green currencies for
agricultural produce had in effect allowed the
British government to mitigate the effects of the
C.A.P. by adjusting the value of the green pound.
In the early 1980s, however, the value of the green
pound and of the normal pound had moved close
together so that according to the rules of the
system of monetary compensation amounts the scope
for manipulating the value of the green pound had
been considerably reduced.(32) This way of
avoiding the effects of the Budgetary mechanism had
therefore been blocked.

I now turn to an examination of the reactions
of Britain's partners to the claim. The key
position was that of the French government which
was most consistently stubborn in opposing any
reduction; there was little to suggest that much
effort had been made in Britain to understand the
reasons for this position. The French government
could, however, be forgiven for reacting rather
strongly against any attempt to undermine the
arrangements of the Common Agricultural Policy,

which was seen by them to be the major benefit for France of membership in the Communities. It should be recalled that the construction of the C.A.P. had been a major objective of French diplomacy through the 1960s, and that its attainment had been a key part of the bargain made with West Germany which lay at the heart of the Treaty of Rome. The Germans were to have a common market for their industrial goods whilst the French would have a market for their food products. In order to obtain their C.A.P. the French had had to take the risk of opening their domestic market to West German competition in manufactured goods, a risk which they survived after adjustments which had often been difficult. Financing market interventions out of Community resources was also an indispensable aspect of the C.A.P.; it was the channel through which benefits were transferred to France, and inevitably, to the extent that Community resources were reduced, as for instance by returning revenues to Britain, so the possible return to France from the C.A.P. would be scaled down.

For the French the Budget was necessarily and inextricably linked with the main prize which they thought they had obtained from the Communities: indeed their argument in March 1982 that the question of the level of agricultural prices should be discussed independently of that of the arrangement to compensate Britain was apparently based upon the recognition of that umbilical link.(33) Increasing C.A.P. prices would be more likely to commit funds from the Budget which would then not be available for return to the British.

From the French point of view the C.A.P. had the major disadvantages that it was a rather complex structure of arrangements and that the distribution of benefits from it was rather too easy to identify. In contrast, the major West German gain, the Common Market, was a relatively simple apparatus involving as its main component the mere removal of barriers, and the benefits to West Germany which accrued from them were less visible though without doubt substantial. It was, therefore, rather too easy for those who lacked sympathy for the French to argue that all benefits went to them. In addition, of course, it was easier to see how a machine such as the C.A.P. could be adjusted and tampered with to satisfy others' complaints. The West Germans became more prepared to accept such adjustments as they would not critically affect their major benefit from the

Communities, the Common Market. The West Germans
also became more prepared to take steps to mollify
the British in order to keep Britain in the
Communities, a course which held both economic and
political advantages for West Germany. This plan
also fitted in with their decision to avoid
increasing any further their own contributions to
the Communities Budget. By the late 1970s and
early 1980s, therefore, the French Government was
faced with an attack upon their major acquis from
the Communities, by a state - Britain - which was
entirely without sympathy for French judgements of
its value and with an older partner - West Germany
- which was prepared to accept rather more readily
than itself adjustments in a C.A.P. which had now
outlived its usefulness as a carrot to get the
French to give them their share of the bargain. It
was not surprising, then, that the French tended to
resist alterations in the C.A.P., even when they
were practical rearrangements, when the approach
and attitudes of their partners suggested the
danger that any change could lead to its
substantial alteration, and possibly to its loss.
The British simply failed to project any perception
of the importance of the system to the French, and
indeed tended to compound the problem by implying
that their earlier "deficit payments" system was a
superior way to subsidise the production of food.
The French could not, however, complain too openly
about the West German stand lest that pushed the
Germans into more aggressive support for the
British. This is not to underestimate the pressure
from the French Government which derived from the
powerful French agricultural lobby: at the same
time, in view of what they had quite properly won
from the Communities, and in view of the
surprisingly creditable performance of French
industry in the face of West German competition in
the Common Market, why should they have sought to
reduce drastically the size of the population on
the land and the strength of that lobby?

It was not, however, that the French were
making excessive profits out of the European
Communities or out of Britain as was frequently
implied in the British press. Criticism of the
Common Agricultural Policy which pointed to the way
in which it encouraged over-production of some
foods, such as dairy produce, were frequently mixed
up in Britain with a prejudice that it was a way of
"ripping off" the British in favour of her
partners. There were, of course, difficulties of

over-production which needed to be corrected; but
in general British farmers benefitted from the
C.A.P. and British governments had tended to play
around with the value of the green pound and the
target price of food products according to their
judgement of which particular constituency needed
to be comforted, either consumers or the farmers.
And although there was a degree of inequity in the
distributive effects of the C.A.P., it was hard to
see how the benefit to France could be judged as
grossly unreasonable. This point is reinforced by
a consideration of the benefits to the various
member states on a _per capita_ basis. It was
estimated that French _per capita_ receipts (net) in
1980 were plus £9, whereas those of Belgium -
Luxembourg were plus £49, Denmark plus £86 and
Ireland an astonishing £154.(34)   The West German
balance of a deficit of £18 _per capita_ could be
justified in terms of the benefits to West German
industry of the Common Market. Italy, however, had
a deficit of £1 _per capita_, and the United Kingdom
one of £24 per head. Although the British had the
largest _per capita_ deficit, nevertheless it is not
surprising that the French should seek to resist
British attempts to reduce the scale of their
rather modest _per capita_ benefits from membership,
particularly when these had been hard fought for
over the years and were a part of the bargain which
had been at the heart of the European Communities
and was enshrined in the Rome Treaty. This
reaction was further justified by the observation
that concessions had already been made to the
British during the negotiations which had preceded
the Referendum in 1974-75, and that, as I have
shown, the scale of the British loss was not
entirely unpredictable or even unreasonable when
measured against a range of economic criteria and
the opportunities offered to Britain by membership
in the Communities.
     The third perspective on the crisis which
suggests that Britain was acting insensitively and
probably unwisely in pushing so vigorously for the
adjustment of the perceived inequity in their
contributions to the Communities Budget, was that
of the positive advantages to the United Kingdom of
not so doing. British diplomacy did not seem to
take into account the argument that perceptions of
the deficit were one product of the relative
failure of British industry in the Common Market.
When Britain acceded in 1973 the bargain had been
understood to be that Britain would incur a cost in

the form of Budgetary contributions, and the cost
of the C.A.P., but that in return British industry
would receive the benefit of the Common Market:
" . . . there would be substantial (unquantified)
benefits if British industry exploited the
opportunities that would arise for securing
economies of scale and increasing specialisation,
and so for achieving faster growth".(35)   The
difficulty was that British industry was unable to
take sufficient advantage of membership as to make
up for its costs.   There is evidence to suggest
that there was some "gain to United Kingdom exports
from Community membership".   It has been suggested
that by 1977 UK exports in manufactures were
perhaps as much as 5% larger than they would have
been had Britain not joined the Communities.(36)
But there was, nevertheless, an increase in the
deficit of manufactures with the Six original
member states, though this seemed to be "the result
of a geographical shift ... associated with a
larger surplus with the rest of the world than
would otherwise have been the case.   Since the Six
had a larger share in UK import manufactures than
in UK exports, and since total imports had
increased more rapidly than total exports, the
deficit was bound to widen in any case."(37)   In
1978 there was a "horrifying" deficit of £2 billion
in trade with the Communities on manufactured
goods, so this could not be "a simple consequence
of Community membership".   The overall conclusion
seemed to be that the EEC was one of the contexts
in which British industry had failed in the 1970s,
but that there was little evidence to suggest that
membership was in itself a cause of that failure.
     The hesitancy of Britain's partners about her
claims in the mid-late 1970s and early 1980s are
therefore explicable in part as a natural
reluctance to return the membership fee because the
member had failed, through no fault of theirs, to
enjoy the amenities of the club.   But Britain's
diplomacy, in that it helped to sour relations
between members, and consistently focused their
attention upon short-term interests, rather than on
the prospect of long term gains, detracted from the
chances of enlisting the support of the Communities
to help modernise and restructure her industry.
Britain appeared as a supplicant, or as an
insensitive bully, rather than as a partner in a
great enterprise committed to common gain.   The
complaints about the Budget were themselves in part
a symptom of deeper attitudes in Britain, which are

discussed in the next section, but they were the
occasion of expressions of adversary attitudes
towards the partners, and equally importantly they
were a distraction from the more important
problems.

As William Wallace has pointed out there were
a number of areas where the Communities could be of
assistance to British industry: there was scope for
assistance on the model of the European Coal and
Steel Community for industrial adjustment; the
Communities could have been encouraged to provide
larger, low-interest loan facilities to help
investment in specific areas, particularly those
involving high technology; the British also stood
to benefit from an expanded regional fund; and
could also have benefitted from massive financial
and technical assistance for the retraining of
labour.(38)   The Commission's Report following its
May 1980 Mandate had also carefully linked
Budgetary reform with proposals for more active and
co-ordinated policies for the Communities as a
whole in regional development, in assisting with
the "geographical and occupational ability of
manpower", and in developing more quickly a number
of advanced technologies and associated industries
in the Communities, such as those involving data
storage and dissemination, and in developing and
conserving sources of energy.(39)   The Commission
also proposed then a number of reforms of the
Common Agricultural Policy, although it insisted
that its central principles should be maintained.
But instead of devoting resources and energy to the
construction of coalitions with Community partners,
including the Commission, in support of measures
such as these which could have helped British
industry to avail itself of the advantages of
membership, the British government chose to pursue
the return of relatively minor sums in a manner
which deeply antagonised some partners and
suggested even to those who were more sympathetic
that Britain did not understand either the history
or the purpose of the Communities.

There was, however, another kind of cost for
Britain in devoting so much energy to the restoring
of the deficit.   It became in the early 1980s an
evasion of a challenge, and could be seen as
symptomatic of a weakness in the British will to
succeed.   Indeed, the government seemed to wish to
encourage the British public to focus attention
upon it as a source of grievance and did not direct
their attention to positive ways of redressing the

balance. There had been a view among pro-membership elements in both the Labour and Conservative parties at the time of accession - as there had been in France in 1957 - that the Communities would provide a healthy, regenerative challenge to industry. Now, however, one aspect of that challenge, that of recouping the membership fee, through industrial performance, was defined as a burden and it seemed that it was to be lightened in order to avoid the necessary action involved in industrial reform. In other words, the British Government's policy of pursuing the restitution of her Budgetary contributions was not only an unnecessary distraction in the way of pursuing more positive Community policies, but was also a symptom of the absence of more positive, regenerative policies at home. It represented a small but real further step in the process of national decline. I discuss in general terms the nature of Britain's industrial problems, which are an important reason for the pursuit of the restoration of the Budgetary deficit, in the third section.

At the time of writing few concessions had been made towards the British in favour of their proposal that there should be a permanent alteration in the Budgetary mechanism to ensure in Thatcher's terms "a modest net contribution to the Budget". The May 1982 "settlement" was for one year only and for a sum much less than that demanded by the British. Regardless of the outcome there were, however, three major inter-related weaknesses in British diplomacy on this question. It was excessively vigorous in relation to the benefit to be obtained; it undervalued the importance of the concessions that were being demanded of the partners from their point of view particularly for the French; and it was not addressed to the root of the imbalance, given the nature of the original bargain, namely the need to help British industry to make more use of the opportunities of membership. In sum, there was an excess of costs in terms of distraction, internally and externally, and the antagonism of other members, over benefits, namely the restoration to Britain of, at best, around £600 million per annum.

*****

British attitudes in the late 1970s and early 1980s towards the Communities' Budgetary and agricultural arrangements were a product of

specific grievances, but also a symptom and focus
of a more general discontent in Britain with the
Communities which had grown through the 1970s.
This was a consequence of the frustration of many
of the expectations which the British had of
membership in the early 1970s: Britain's economic
circumstances compared with those of the other
member states, continued to worsen through the
period. The expected economic benefits simply did
not appear. And as attitudes towards membership
were essentially calculative and utilitarian,
rather than suggesting a commitment to solidarity
and participation in the longer term enterprise,
this was a crucial disappointment. The Labour
Party, which was in office from February 1974 until
May 1979, did little to alleviate these doubts,
partly because of a long-standing ideological
opposition to the Communities on the part of its
more left-wing members, and partly because of the
electoral advantages of siding with the opposing
elements in the country, as revealed, for instance,
at the time of the Referendum, which tended in any
case to be concentrated in areas where its support
was strongest, such as industrialised areas in
northern England, Scotland and South Wales.(40)
     Public opinion polls reflected the different
pattern of involvement of the new member states
with the Communities compared with the original
Six. The latter laid their foundations for reasons
which combined practical, utilitarian interests
with the sense of participating in a great
enterprise. It would be wrong to assert that
France or West Germany had always been committed to
working for political unity, but nevertheless at
the minimum there was a feeling that the
Communities were contributing towards the
fundamental alteration of the traditional pattern
of relations between the two states. In the
earlier days in particular they had stressed the
overall importance of solidarity above the short
term satisfaction of their interests. From the
beginning, however, the British and the other
acceding states tended to expect more specific
benefits to accrue in the short term because of
membership. Whilst an average of 63% of the
citizens of the Six thought the Common Market was a
good thing in 1973, only a little over 30% were
prepared to agree with this in Britain.(41)
Through the 1970s support for direct elections to
the European Parliament was significantly lower in
the United Kingdom than among the Six; and between

the Spring of 1977 and the Spring of 1978 an
average of 55% of the British felt that European
MPs should "support the interests of their country
all the time, regardless of whether or not they
were good for Europe as a whole"; around 35% of the
Germans subscribed to this view, and 40% of the
French in the same period.(42)

In the information on public attitudes in
Britain from 1970 to 1972 reviewed by Zakheim there
is little to suggest that the British were
interested in membership for other than short term,
utilitarian reasons.(43)   In a Gallup poll of 1971,
23%-26% stressed that British industries and
agriculture could benefit and expand as a result of
membership, whereas only between 6% and 11% pointed
to the opportunity which membership would provide
for developing closer political links with the
partners.   In an NOP poll in 1971 29% of those who
favoured joining said that membership would be good
for trade and exports and 31% said it would help
employment and competition and 10% that it would
help to get "us" out of economic trouble.   Only 15%
said they favoured joining the Common Market
because of the opportunity this would provide for
"closer alliance with Europe".   These attitudes
were reflected during the negotiations for
accession by British statesmen when they explicitly
supported the Luxembourg Agreement of 1966 which in
effect abandoned the prospect of majority voting in
the Council of Ministers in favour of unanimity.
It should not be assumed that British leaders who
supported accession all stressed essentially short
term interests as opposed to longer term economic
and political gains.   There was a group around
Edward Heath who showed a sense of embarking upon a
path of building unity with other members, and in
the Labour Party, Roy Jenkins and Shirley Williams
sometimes seemed to stress the community model in
their thinking about Europe.   Nevertheless, for
most of those who chose to join, support was either
defensive - what else is there? - or part of a
rather short term economic strategy for obtaining
tangible returns for the British economy sooner
rather than later.

I have already explained that in Britain's
trade with the European Communities these positive
returns were hard to identify.   But - even worse
from the point of view of public attitudes towards
Europe - in the years after accession the
performance of the British economy according to a
number of indicators continued to go steadily

downhill compared with that of her partners. For
instance between 1960 and 1976 Britain's per capita
GDP at current prices and exchange rates dropped
from the second highest among the Nine to the
seventh, above only that of Italy and Ireland.(44)
Between 1962 and 1978 Britain's annual rate of
growth was the lowest of any of the Nine on six
annual occasions; its exchange rate fell by 37.9%
between 1973 and 1978 (minus 47.2% for Italy; minus
24% for Ireland; minus 12% for France; plus 42% for
West Germany).(45) Its per capita GDP as a
percentage of the EEC average calculated on the
basis of purchasing power parities, fell steadily
from 112% in 1960 to 93% in 1976 and 91% in
1979.(46) It was difficult to avoid the conclusion
that British citizens were getting fewer and fewer
benefits from their economy compared with their
fellows in other EEC countries, and that this
tendency could be detected from before the date of
accession. Other figures taking a longer term view
confirmed that Britain's gross domestic product had
increased more slowly than that of a range of
comparable developed states since 1870: taking 1970
as 100 for the United Kingdom, the British economy
moved from 35 in 1870 to around 105 in 1978; the
USA went from 29 to approaching 200 in the same
period; France from 21 to 160, West Germany from 20
to 165 and Japan from 3 to 140.(47) Jones
concluded that "not only had there emerged a
substantial difference in levels of productivity in
Britain and her European partners in recent years,
but also that the slower rate of growth of
productivity in Britain (was) by no means a recent
feature: indeed, in relation to her main
competitor, Germany, it had been apparent for at
least a century ..."(48) A further conclusion is
therefore again indicated that Britain's economic
performance in the Communities was not attributable
to membership.

Nevertheless the British did tend through the
mid-late 1970s to become more critical of the
Communities as the condition of her economy
declined. The Communities were perceived to be the
culprit. There is some evidence to suggest that
there was an initial period of increasing optimism
which reached a peak in the autumn of 1975,
following the Referendum when 67% approved of
membership,(49) but that this was followed by a
steady erosion of support down to 30% and below in
the late 1970s and early 1980s. The failure of
membership to generate tangible returns was a

decisive factor in this decline: there did not develop any sense that membership was bound up with grander principles, such as commitment to a common destiny, the building of a European community in the socio-psychological sense, or the fusion of the sovereignty of the participating states, which could have countered the short-term disappointment.

Two developments tended to reinforce this rather utilitarian attitude towards Europe in Britain. First, the other member states had themselves moved some way in that direction by the mid-1970s: for instance, as I have pointed out elsewhere, the Germany of Helmut Schmidt was much more "nationalist" and prone to stress short-term interests in Europe, than that of his predecessor Brandt.(50) Underlying economic tendencies undoubtedly contributed to this development. Its consequence was that pressures upon the British to accept the community model and to seek longer term gains were relatively weak by the start of the second half of the 70s because of the changing example of the partners. Second, the Labour Government which came to power in February 1974 was itself profoundly divided about the desirability of membership, and was strongly disposed, because of public attitudes and related electoral considerations, its own ideology and doctrines, and Britain's economic circumstances, to see the scale of short-term returns from Europe as the only worthwhile test of the value of staying in. Indeed the fashionable orthodoxy in the Labour Party became one of scepticism and antagonism towards the European Communities. In pursuing their returns the Labour Government tolerated no Communities' policy which seemed to threaten British sovereignty, even when there was an apparent economic advantage. And little or no effort was devoted to the task of developing a greater preparedness among Britain's partners to help to put right the various problems in her economy. Indeed, the broad strategy of the Labour Government revealed, for instance, in the negotiations on the European Monetary System in 1978 (see Chapter 6), was based upon their view that co-operation was likely to be of greater benefit to the others than to itself, but that in return for Britain's accepting this the partners should be persuaded to pay it a fee. One form which that fee took, as demanded by the Callaghan government, was the reduction of Britain's contribution to the Budget.

Mrs. Thatcher's Conservative Government

elected in May 1979 inherited a number of pressures
and expectations about the adjustment of Britain's
contribution to the Budget of the European
Communities. The previous Labour government had
responded to and encouraged attitudes which
regarded this as an important matter, and these
attitudes were to be found in the informed media,
and in the administration. Had the new government
been disposed to adopt a more positive approach
towards the extension of the role of the
Communities in economic questions it would
certainly have come up against a problem of
steering: there were bureaucratic pressures towards
continuing the battle and mass expectations that
held that this was a fight that must be won
regardless of its merits. There was, therefore, a
positive incentive to continue with the British
demands in the general character of British
expectations about membership which had been
magnified and encouraged in the context of
Britain's declining economy by the previous Labour
government. There was also, however, a negative
element in that there would have been a real
political risk for the government of antagonising
the electorate if it appeared to be supporting what
might have been interpreted as a soft line with the
Communities.

But the Conservative government might also
have been encouraged to carry the battle forward by
two further related factors. Their adoption of
monetarist economic policies made them more prone
to count the small change and to seek financial
savings, however small, wherever possible, and
their style of operation internally and externally
was frequently aggressive and inflexible. Their
attitude towards perceived waste in the Communities
was likely to be rather like that shown in reaction
to waste, for instance, in nationalised industries
within the country, and their style of seeking
correction rather similar. The nature of the
Conservative Party's staunch commitment to
monetarist doctrines also meant that they were
likely to be rather intolerant of any attempts by
outsiders including the Communities to effect the
working out of their internal economic plans.
Indeed there is some evidence to suggest that the
economy ideology of the Thatcher government made
its members as disinclined to deal softly with the
Communities and accept Communities intervention in
their economic affairs as were the ideologists of
the Left. Secondly, there was a clear political

advantage for the government in continuing to focus
attention upon the external struggle in that it
provided an ideal excuse for possible failures in
its economic management at home. Given that
attitudes were as they were, there was no need for
the government to make this explicit: but it suited
the government to give the impression in the early
1980s that it was fighting a battle to reduce the
damage being done to the British economy by the
European Communities, and that this was part of its
overall economic strategy. It was striking that
neither the Conservative government, nor the Labour
government before it, had sought to give any credit
whatsoever to the European Communities for the
contributions that it had made, for instance, in
regional development or in the training of the
young unemployed in the United Kingdom through the
Manpower Services Commission. The British public
therefore remained relatively insulated from any
activities initiated by the Communities which could
have won public sympathy. For the Conservative
government it was useful to have around a
ready-made scapegoat to cover the risk of failure
of its rather adventurous internal economic
strategy. So the idea of the Communities as
potential opponent rather than as long-term ally
was perpetuated.
      These are at least some of the underlying
reasons why successive British governments in the
1970s and early 1980s failed to develop a more
positive approach to the European Communities and
why they became fixated on redressing the Budgetary
imbalance. Opportunities for pursuing economic
regeneration in Britain in the Communities
framework were therefore lost and British diplomacy
became an element in generating a more general
disinclination among the partners to develop a new
range of co-operative initiatives. Indeed, British
government behaviour became an element in a rather
complicated self-fulfilling prophecy. Britain was
dissatisfied with the Communities because of the
absence of utilitarian returns; the level of
utilitarian returns was low because of the poor
performance of British industry; in seeking to
increase the level of utilitarian returns the
government acted in such a way that the Communities
framework was not used to develop policies to help
British industry, and attitudes amongst the other
member states, which were also hesitant about such
policies, were strengthened by British tactics; the
failure to regenerate industry reinforced attitudes

in Britain which saw utilitarian returns as the
only worthwhile indicator of the value of
membership.

*****

It seems safe to assert that Britain's policy
towards the Communities Budget was a symptom not
merely of its economic failure in the Communities,
but of its economic failure in general. The
Communities were, as I have said, the context of
her failure and the Budgetary policy one form in
which it was expressed. In the second section I
discussed some of the consequences of this failure;
in this I consider some of its causes. This is not
the place for a detailed discussion of the British
malaise in the 1970s and the early 1980s; yet some
account is called for as it seemed to be
contributing towards a more general incapacity
among the member states of the European Communities
to adjust together to the economic challenges of
the 1980s. Britain's own immobilisme was at least
a lost source of pressure for intelligent
adaptation in the Communities, and at the worst, a
positive reinforcement of immobilisme at the
regional level. One of the roots of the failures
of the Communities, of which Britain's claims, and
the Communities' response to them, were one aspect,
must be as Peter Katzenstein has implied the
internal structures, attitudes and ideology of the
dominant member states.(51) The explanation of the
immobilisme of the Communities in internal policies
could be approached from the perspective of each of
the Communities members, but in this chapter my
concern is primarily with the British contribution.
The essence of the problem was that in Britain
the mechanisms for initiating and directing the
process of economic and industrial adaptation and
regeneration were profoundly flawed, while the
pressures which were opposed to change remained
quite strong.(52) This had the consequence that at
the Communities level the British also failed to
engage with any process for developing and applying
more positive policies, and, rather as if
responding to the law of positive entropy, in the
absence of any inclination to the contrary, tended
to insist upon policies which reinforced the status
quo. Put more clearly, as there was no clear view
of the way forward internally, there was no view of
the way forward externally either: therefore the
inclination was to hold on to what was in sight,

like the £500 million from the Communities' Budget.
The British economic malaise expressed itself
particularly in the industrial area where it was
manifest in three different areas. First there
were traditional, rather low technology industries
such as the manufacture of textiles where new
producer states had various advantages such as
cheaper labour, but where nevertheless the British
sought to protect their industries by holding out
cheaper imports through such devices as the
Multifibre Agreement. The British had been
instrumental in obtaining a more protectionist
Multifibre agreement when it was renegotiated in
the late 70s than had been preferred by the other
members of the European Communities. Secondly
there were a range of engineering and electrical
industries with rather well established
technologies where the British problem was that the
sophistication of their product compared with its
competitors tended to decline. Christopher
Saunders showed that unit values of engineering
exports were broadly comparable between France,
Germany and the United Kingdom in the early 1960s,
whereas by 1975 German and French unit values were
about 60% and 40% higher respectively.(53) And
thirdly there were the new high technology
industries particularly involving the micro-chip
and its wide range of applications, in which
Britain was lagging compared with its competitors.
As Jones pointed out: "Britain is in the awkward
position of being left behind by the technological
leaders in more advanced products while at the same
time facing growing competition from the newly
industrialising countries in more mature
price-sensitive products."(47) The British
practice was to defend existing long-established
industries long after the time when their
competitive advantage had been lost, and practice
which was reinforced by the distribution of the
electoral strength of the Labour Party, and the
difficulty for governments in general in coping
with the welfare consequences of deliberately
phasing them out. The need, however, was for
carefully considered strategies for improving the
quality and technological input of "mature"
products, and actively encouraging the development
of the new high technology industries. The
Commission had frequently presented proposals to
meet this need, but the British Government seemed
unwilling to take them up actively, or to propose
alternative policies of its own.

Among the reasons for the failure were the divergence of interests which followed from the divergence of economic performance among the member states, which I have discussed elsewhere. But there were also a number of problems concerning the structure of British industry which led to a failure in Britain to evolve what could be called a technologically informed consensus-strategy for industrial management. There were a number of fractures in the systems for controlling and directing industry which had not appeared to the same degree in Britain's major competitors. These have been widely discussed, and this is not the place to examine them in detail but it would be useful to place them briefly together in a general picture. Their effect was to make it difficult for British industry to move purposefully into new areas of production with sufficient technical knowledge, investment resources and market awareness as to be reasonably sure of success. They could not pursue the strategy of what has been called by Haas, that of "fragmented issue linkage", which seemed to be the most appropriate way of proceeding in industrial development(55): it involved devoting resources to moving forward on a concerted basis into an unknown territory but being responsive to unforeseen features of the environment and introducing necessary adjustments of strategy and direction.

The fractures were revealed in the extent to which the various parts of the production process were out of touch with each other: the production and marketing processes in Britain were "sub-system dominant". There was a low level of concertation and direction. The Civil Service tended to be relatively lacking in technical expertise, and in knowledge of production and the market, compared with that, say, in France. Commentators have frequently pointed to the relative unresponsiveness of British officials when approached by industrialists. This was in part a product of a tradition of equal-handedness towards all existing interests and industries, but also the result of a recruitment policy which still undervalued technical and specialist expertise and overvalued that of the traditional arts and classics. The problem was compounded, as Jones pointed out, by the lack of "an interchange of staff at all levels between industry and ministries".(56) This problem rather encouraged a linked difficulty: a tendency on the part of the Government to follow industrial policies rather than providing any central thrust to improve industry's performance and that of the economy as a whole".(57)   In other words the government lacked the reservoir of expertise, and the inclination, to become closely involved with developing and expanding new technology industries, or to develop a more directing role in other areas. This may be compared with the situation in Japan where government and industry were closely involved with each other in evolving a highly sophisticated consensus-strategy.

These problems were further associated with a difficulty that was ideological rather than structural.   The approach to the market on the part of both right and left tended to be uninformed and ineffective.   The Right of the political spectrum tended to treat the market as if it were a kind of magical black box, and because of this, right-wing governments had difficulty in coming to terms with the need for long-term development and investment programmes which could not be related to the rather short-term market pressures.   The left-wing, on the other hand, was ideologically inclined to downgrade the effects of the market which was dismissed too easily as a piece of Conservative ideological baggage.   The need, however, was for both sides to invest much more in research into long-term trends in the market, and to direct more investment in reflection of such trends.   This did not necessarily mean, of course, investment in grand, high technology programmes such as Concord: the technology needed to be developed not merely because of its intellectual or artistic appeal but because the market showed that it held the promise of profit in the long-term.   This was of course not an easy task and needed considerable sophisticated expertise.   On the other hand without an accurate and sensitive awareness of market development in the long-term no industrial regeneration programme could be effective.   These, then, are the first set of fractures within the British system: those between government and administration and industry, and between them and the market.   A powerful potential motor for regeneration was as a result relatively enfeebled in Britain.

Even a cursory glance at a range of Britain's competitors revealed a second range of fractures. Britain's investment institutions, the banks, the insurance companies and pension funds, tended to be relatively less involved with industrial management compared with the practice in West Gemany or Japan.

Britain and her Partners

In West Germany it was common practice for the banks to be closely involved with developing industrial strategy, and to be directly represented on the boards of companies. The pension funds in Britain – a massive source of investment capital – had only begun to take a more active interest in industrial management in the early 1980s. One source of expertise about the market and technology was therefore lost in Britain, and, as has often been pointed out by critics of the British banking system, the banks tended to pursue a global investment policy which was sometimes at the expense of somewhat riskier investments within the United Kingdom. British production and selling also tended to be relatively insulated from each other compared, say, with the situation in Japan. British retailers tended to buy in the cheapest market rather than being closely involved in a particular production-retailing process. One of the few – and highly successful – exceptions to this was the retailer Marks and Spencer. This fracture was one aspect of the appalling record of the British in marketing their products. Time and time again a good product was not sold effectively because of inefficient sales techniques, or because it was slightly "out of tune" with current market needs. The basic technology may have been excellent but the packaging somewhat deficient; for example, this was true of the British motor cycle industry, the high fidelity audio equipment industry, and the industry in photographic equipment, where the British lost out to the Japanese in the 1950s and 1960s mainly because of deficient marketing.

A final set of fractures was to be found in educational and cultural areas. Differences of purpose and the lack of reinforcement of mutual needs in the educational system and industry led to rather low levels of training and expertise amongst both workers and management. Workers in Britain tended to be relatively unqualified and less skilled than their German and Japanese equivalents: training and apprenticeship systems were under-funded and less well developed. Management, too, tended to underrate specialised professional qualifications and many large companies consistently under-valued and dismissed the specialist skills of university graduates in relevant subject areas and blandly insisted upon experience on the job. Some skills were undervalued because of rather intangible cultural

preferences: engineering, for instance, was
consistently awarded a rather low social status
compared, say, with classics or philosophy.
Successful university students tended to wish to
stay in the university system rather than move out
into industry. There was a national prejudice
against areas of expertise which could have been of
particular benefit to industry.

Another fracture of the cultural/ideological
system affected the pattern of involvement of
labour in consultation with government and
industry. On the one hand British workers and
their representatives tended to be rather hostile
to forms of co-determination, such as worker
directors, in large part because this would confuse
the lines of battle about wages and conditions of
work. There was also some evidence to suggest that
British workers consistently rejected what were
understood to be middle class values and had little
wish to be elevated to management positions
compared, say, with their French equivalents. On
the other hand trade unions consistently pressed
for closer consultation at the level of national
government as a means of furthering their interests
in that battle: the Labour government in the late
1970s welcomed close consultation and enshrined it
in the concept of the "social contract". The
Conservative government of the early 80s decreased
the level of consultation with the unions, however,
as part of their strategy of keeping as far as
possible out of wage bargaining and of leaving the
economy more exposed to the short-term movement of
the market. Both under Labour and Conservative
governments the same general problems could,
however, be observed. The difference was where the
line of battle between management and labour was to
be drawn. It was, therefore, very difficult to
involve labour in any process of producing a
consensus strategy for industrial management and
regeneration. Workers and unions were a continuing
potential source of opposition to any policy for
industrial recovery which might be devised because
they insisted on staying, to some extent, outside
the system.

The various sub-systems of the industrial
marketing process therefore remained relatively
isolated from each other and it proved impossible
to link them to each other in the construction of
the kind of consensus-strategy which I have
outlined. Government, administration, market,
investment, labour, education, remained relatively

discrete components and could not be made to work together. The system was therefore difficult to steer, and indeed, the Conservative government of the early 1980s rather withdrew from the task of trying to steer or develop a consensus. These problems together meant that, compared with other developed countries, Britain's economy tended to lack any effective guidance system, and, from a number of points of view, it continued its long decline.

*****

As the European Communities were limited in their ability to act together externally, in the absence of a range of agreed policies between members, so it seemed unreasonable to expect that such intra-Communities policies could be agreed if actors within the states could not agree that they were necessary. The British had found it impossible to agree upon policies to encourage national industrial economy recovery: this seemed to be largely a function of the divisions within the British economy and British society. How then could they be brought to accept such policies at the Communities level? If they did not know what they wanted themselves they could have no positive reaction to what the Communities proposed. A series of Commission proposals about industrial development had therefore fallen on stony soil: the Colonna Memorandum of 1970, the Spinelli Report of 1973,(58) and, as seemed likely in 1982, the Commission's proposals of 1981, which were explicitly linked with Budgetary reform, all had little positive effect. "Advanced schemes for Community involvement in promoting and restructuring advanced technology sectors, such as aerospace and computers, came to nothing in the face of national resistance."(59)

It is, of course, not the case that Britain was the only source of opposition to such enterprise in the Communities. But Britain, which could have been a particular beneficiary of cooperation, was a factor in the development of a more general reluctance to move forward among the member states. Britain's internal divisions and immobilisme contributed to the more general malaise. To some extent the Communities' failure to move forward in the late 1970s and early 1980s was an expression of Britain's weakness in tackling her own problems.

The British claim about the Budget and the
C.A.P. were one consequence of Britain's industrial
weakness: had British industry succeeded, as had
been expected at the time of accession, the claims
would almost certainly not have been made. Though
perceptions of the inequity of contributions and
returns, compared with those of other states,
provoked their expression, they were much more a
result of the fundamental problems of Britain's
industrial structure and the attitudes towards the
Communities which had been sustained by a number of
factors in the 1970s. As I pointed out at the
beginning of this chapter, Britain's claims about
the Budget of the European Communities, and the
other member states' response to this, were an
expression of a complex and multilevel pattern of
relations between Britain and her partners. As
Davidson pointed out they involved the more
fundamental question of whether the Communities was
to become more integrated or to become less
integrated.

NOTES

1. Financial Times, Monday, February 22,
1982, p.13.
2. Ibid.
3. For a useful discussion of the development
of the Budgetary mechanism see Helen Wallace,
Budgetary Politics: the Finances of the European
Communities, University Association for
Contemporary European Studies and George Allen and
Unwin, London, 1980.
4. See John S. Marsh and Pamela J. Swanney,
Agriculture and the European Community, University
Association for Contemporary European Studies and
George Allen and Unwin, London, 1980.
5. For details of the decision see Sweet and
Maxwell's European Community Treaties, London,
1972, pp. 239-242.
6. Ibid., Article 3.
7. See Treaty of Accession, Articles 127-132.
8. Reported by Wynne Godley in William
Wallace (ed.), Britain in Europe, Heinemann,
London, p.73.
9. See J. Marsh and C. Ritson, Agricultural
Policy and Common Market, European Studies No. 16,
London, Chatham House and Political and Economic
Planning, 1971.
10. Figures taken from Godley, in William
Wallace (Editor), loc. cit., p.73.

11. Ibid., p.75.
12. Ibid., p.76.
13. Ibid., p.79.
14. See Commission of the European Communities, 5th General Report on the Activities of the European Communities in 1981, Brussels, Luxembourg, 1978, p.54.
15. See Helen Wallace, loc. cit., p.59.
16. Bulletin of the European Communities, Supplement 1/81, Report from the Commission of the European Communities to the Council pursuant to the Mandate of 30 May, 1980, Luxembourg, 1981, para. 42, at p.16.
17. Ibid., para. 44, p.16.
18. Financial Times, 15th January, 1982.
19. Financial Times, 28th January, 1982.
20. Financial Times, 26th January, 1982.
21. John Wyles in the Financial Times, 28th January, 1982.
22. Financial Times, 2nd April, 1982.
23. Financial Times, 1st February 1982.
24. See report of debate in the House of Commons, The Times, April 8, 1982.
25. See K.J. Holsti, International Politics: A Framework for Analysis, Prentice-Hall, Englewood Cliffs, 1977 (3rd Edition).
26. See figures in A.R. Prest et al (ed.), The UK Economy, Weidenfeld and Nicolson, London, p.308.
27. The latter point in Helen Wallace, loc. cit., p.17.
28. Figures presented in Europe 81 No. 4, April 1981, p.8.
29. Commission of the European Communities, Report, The Role of the Public Finance in European Integration, (MacDougal Report), Brussels, April 1977.
30. Godley, in W. Wallace (Editor), loc. cit., p.80.
31. Christopher Ritson, 'British Interests and the Common Agricultural Policy', in ibid., p.99.
32. For an examination of Monetary Compensation Amounts, and 'Green Pounds' see R. Irving and H.A. Fearn, Green Money and the C.A.P. Occasional Paper 2, Centre for European Agricultural Studies, Ashford, 1975.
33. See The Times, April 7, 1982.
34. Figures reported by Godley, loc. cit., p.79.
35. Ann D. Morgan, 'The Balance of Payments

and British Membership of the European Community', in W. Wallace (Editor), loc. cit., p.58.

36. Ibid., p.66.
37. Ibid., p.67.
38. William Wallace, loc. cit., pp.15-17.
39. Commission's Report, loc. cit., pp.9-11.
40. See Stephen L. Bristow, 'Partisanship, Participation and Legitimacy in Britain's EEC Referendum,' Journal of Common Market Studies, No. 4, Vol. XIV, June 1976, pp.297-310; see also Roger Jowell and Gerald Hoinville, Britain into Europe: Public Opinion and the EEC 1961/75, Croom Helm, London, 1976.
41. See Commission of the European Communities, Euro-barometre, No. 9, July 1978, p.27.
42. Ibid., p.42.
43. Dov S. Zakheim, 'Britain and the EEC: Opinion Poll Data 1970-1972', Journal of Common Market Studies, March 1973, Vol. XI, No. 3.
44. Figures compiled by E. Hallet, Research Department, Foreign and Commonwealth Office, for a Seminar at Chatham House.
45. OECD Economic Outlook, July 1977 and July 1978.
46. From the Commission, European Economy, November 1978 and November 1979.
47. Figures from Daniel T. Jones, 'British Industrial Regeneration: the European Dimension', in William Wallace (Editor), loc. cit., p.117.
48. Ibid., pp. 116-117.
49. See Jowell and Hoinville, loc. cit.
50. See Paul Taylor, "Intergovernmentalism in the European Communities", forthcoming.
51. Peter Katzenstein, 'Domestic Structures and Strategies of Foreign Economic Policy', International Organization, Autumn 1977, Vol. 31, No. 4.
52. For an interesting account of Britain's foreign economic policy and its links with domestic problems see Stephen Blank, 'Britain: the politics of foreign economic policy, the domestic economy, and the problem of pluralistic stagnation', International Organization, Autumn 1977, Vol. 31, No. 4.
53. Christopher Saunders, Engineering in Britain, West Germany and France: some Statistical Comparisons, Sussex European Papers No. 3, University of Sussex, Brighton, 1978.
54. Jones, loc. cit., p. 122.
55. Ernest B. Haas, 'Turbulent fields and the

theory of regional integration', <u>International Organization</u>, Spring 1976, Vol. 30, No. 2. The alternative strategies, in Haas' view, are <u>incremental</u>, in which there is involvement in an existing course of action, and the commitment of resources to its successful conclusion; and <u>rational analytic</u>, in which all options and relevant information are scanned and the optimum course chosen. Fragmented issue-linkage has the advantage over the other two in such areas as planning industrial policy in that it does not assume that the present course is largely the right one (as with incrementalism), or that all options and relevant information can be known at the point of decision (as with rational analytic). Fragmented issue-linkage involves rather trying a variety of approaches in the absence of complete information, and investing in the more successful ones: it describes the best course through unknown territory.

56. <u>Loc. cit.</u>, p. 125.

57. P. Mottershead, 'Industrial Policy', in F.T. Blackaby <u>et al</u>, <u>British Economic Policy</u> 1960-74, London, Cambridge University Press, 1978, p.

58. See Michael Hodges, 'A Directorate General in Search of a Role', in Helen Wallace, William Wallace and Carole Webb (eds.), <u>Policy-making in the European Communities</u>, Wiley, London 1977.

59. Jones, <u>loc. cit.</u>, p. 129.

Chapter Nine

THE CHARACTER OF COMMUNITIES LAW

        In this chapter I summarize from a legal
perspective the implications for integration in the
European Communities of the argument of the
preceeding chapters. The question is asked of
whether the programme of integration has had
implications for the sovereignty of member states.
I also focus here much more explicitly than
hitherto upon the consequences for international
integration of the dynamics which were stressed in
the Functionalism of David Mitrany: how far had a
new base of sovereignty developed which transcended
the previous national bases? Was there a
noticeable change in attitudes and behaviour which
would support the view that sovereignty had been
transferred to a new centre? I should stress that
I am not here dealing with the dynamics of the
process of integration from a Functionalist
viewpoint, but rather with the primary effects of
that process, namely the transfer of authority and
legitimacy to the higher level. The extent of that
transfer may be considered in legal terms, which is
the method of this Chapter though in Functionalist
eyes it is essentially founded upon the development
of socio-psychological community as discussed in
Chapter One.
        I examine the contention that 'on balance the
emerging European Community fits, in the light of
the EEC Treaty, better into a federal, than
confederal form'.(1) This claim is of interest not
only to students of law, but also to students of
politics: it refers to a possible development of
considerable political importance, namely the
emergence of a central authority in the European
Communities. The student of politics should,
therefore, accept the challenge of examining and
evaluating the legal arguments which have led some

lawyers to this conclusion. This task acquires the character of an obligation when it is recalled that so many political and constitutional aspects of the Communities seemed in the late 1970s and early 1980s in flat contradiction of these legal judgements. The modest question which is put here - with apologies to international lawyers - is therefore: how far short of a modern federal model are the Communities' legal arrangements?

Four features of federalism seem to recur in discussions about how that system differs from Leagues or Confederations.(2) They are, first, the constitutional immunity of the federation against dissolution by the secession of its constituent regions; second the existence in the system of an independent sphere of central authority; third, the exclusive control by the general government of foreign relations and defence; and, fourth, the possibility of the amendment of the federal constitution without the consent of all the constituent regions. In this chapter I deal with aspects of the first two features; each has been adapted however to allow a fuller discussion of related circumstances in the European Communities and to permit an account of the major developments which might be expected before they are acquired. The question of the right to secede and the related question of the right to nullify legislation are examined. The question of whether the centre has acquired the character of an independent sphere of central authority is then discussed with particular reference to its ability to enforce legislation in member states. These are but a small, primarily legal, selection of the dimensions in relation to which the Communities 'federal' character could be examined, but they are of central importance.

In the next section the practice of existing federations in these areas is briefly considered: this provides the model with which the experience of the European Communities may be compared. In the second section arguments concerning the rights of states to nullify legislation in the Communities are evaluated. In the third section the nature of the enforcement procedures in the Communities are discussed in comparison with the federal model.

*****

There are two dominant views about the value of not allowing secession under the federal constitution. On the one hand there is the view

270

that it is logically incompatible with the federal
principle because 'if such actions are permitted
the general government is subordinated to the
regional governments'(3). For similar, but
opposite reasons, the general government cannot by
itself dismiss a constituent state: this would also
contradict the principle that the powers of the
general and constituent governments should be
co-ordinate but independent. This position is
illustrated by the absence of the right to secede
in major modern federations, such as Canada,
Australia, Switzerland or the USA, although in the
latter case an ambiguity in the constitution was
only clarified by the painful experience of the
Civil War. The Supreme Court decided after the War
that 'the Constitution in all its provisions looks
to an indestructible union composed of
indestructible states'.(4) In Western Europe, the
'constitution' of the European Political Community
presented to the foreign ministers of the Six after
the deliberations of the Ad Hoc Consultative
Assembly in 1953 contained no reference to the
'right of secession', and this was regarded as a
'victory of the more radical proponents of the
federalising of Europe'.(5) There are, however, a
few nominal federal constitutions where the right
to secede is allowed: the Soviet Union,
Yugoslavia, and Burma between 1947 and 1957. In
these instances, however, it may be safely
concluded that practical considerations were
thought to obviate the constitutional possibility.
   On the other hand it was also argued that,
though the refusal of the right to secede might not
be a necessary feature of federalism, it was
nevertheless desirable in that it contributed to
the stability of the system. What mattered was not
so much the constitutional situation as the
practical one: as Friedrich has put it, 'at the
beginning of the federalising process the ability
to secede (regardless of the formal right) will
obviously exist; it will decline as the process
goes forwards and will tend to disappear as the
inclusive community is extended to ever-widening
spheres of the common life'.(6) Kenneth Wheare is
careful to distinguish between the right to secede,
and the right to nullify the legislation of the
federal government. Secession in his view is not a
challenge to the federal principle because it
involves a decision to reject the legislation of
the central government 'entirely and without
exceptions'(7), whereas nullification does

271

challenge that principle because it involves placing the general government in a subordinate position to the regional governments within the union: the governments are no longer co-ordinate and independent. But Wheare stresses, nevertheless, that 'while the existence of the right to secede unilaterally, or a right to expel unilaterally, may be quite consistent with federal government, it is not, I believe, consistent as a rule with good federal government.'(8) The use of the threat to secede may in practice weaken the position of the general government.

The question of whether or not the regions' possession of the right to secede is logically compatible with the principle of federalism is clearly still a matter for debate among constitutional lawyers. But there seems to be a large measure of agreement that it is a practical necessity in the working of federal government in the modern world, a view which is reflected in the arrangements which have been made in the leading existing federations. But it is not enouogh to ensure that secession will not in fact take place: political pressures may impose themselves on constitutional requirements. It is as well, therefore, to examine not only the constitutional aspects in this respect of the European Communities, but also the so-called political realities; is secession still a right and is it also a practical possibility? These questions necessarily lead on to a further question which is perhaps more fundamental: which government, regional or central, is ultimately responsible in the Communities? Kenneth Wheare's sharp distinction between the implications of the retention by the regions of the right to nullify the legislation of the central government, and their possession of the right to secede, is in the context of the attribution of responsibility seen to be a somewhat artificial one. Both suggest that the constituent regions have retained responsibility: they illustrate the power of the regions to impose conditions upon their preparedness to accept federal legislation. In this sense secession is merely an extreme form of nullification.

Secession and nullification refer to the powers of the regions in relation to the centre. The centre's powers in relation to the parts may also be examined as an aspect of the power of centre to <u>enforce</u> its laws. The first requirement

here is the obvious one that there should be courts
throughout the union which have been invested with
jurisdiction in the sphere of federal law. It is
not necessary that there should be a separate
system of federal courts (this is the
case in the USA, but not in Australia, Canada or
Switzerland), but it is necessary that, "when any
question arises concerning the federal law there is
the power for a supreme court of the general
government in the last resort to hear and determine
the appeal. There exists always some form of
safeguard for the general government in the
appellate jurisdiction and, in some matters, in the
original juridiction, which has been conferred upon
the Supreme Court of the general government".(9)
It is necessary not only that there should be
courts to enforce federal laws but that they should
enforce the same versions of these laws in the
various parts of the union. Without this
centralised mechanism for the interpretation of
points of ambiguity, the authority of the centre,
in relation to the activity of law enforcement,
would be threatened because each constituent region
would apply that version of the federal law which
it preferred. The federal legal system would have
lost its coherence: the central government's role
would have been weakened to this extent.

A second requirement is that there should be
in the hands of the central government a reserve
power which can be used to uphold, "the privileges
and immunities of citizens of the federal system,
the rights of member states in their relations with
one another", and to keep "the government's member
states in their proper place".(10) The power is to
be used if there is no other way to counter the
challenge to the constitution, or to enforce the
federal laws. As Holcombe points out, the founders
of federal constitutions have sometimes hesitated
to be too explicit about granting such powers,
which ultimately involve, "the use of military
force by the general government of the system for
the purpose of compelling member states to perform
their duties under the constitution of the system".
The problem is that: "if a federal government
possesses a constitutional authority to intervene
by force in the government of a state for the
purpose of ensuring that state's performance of its
duties as a member of the federation, there is no
adequate constitutional barrier against the
conversion of the federation into a centralised
state by a vigorous and resolute central

government. If it does not possess such a therapy,
there is no adequate assurance that the federal
government can maintain the character of the system
when vigorous and resolute state governments take
full advantage of their constitutional freedom to
go their own ways".(11)   Modern federations would
prefer, therefore, to stress the processes of
judicial review as the primary mechanism, and the
one which is spelled out most explicitly for
settling such differences. Nevertheless, it seems
to have been generally accepted, however cautiously
and implicitly, that the federal government should
be permitted to use force as a last resort.
      The mechanism through which this power is to
be exercised is the responsibility of the general
government for the organisation and command of the
armed forces. The police force is very frequently
organised and controlled locally, but armies,
airforces and navies are either exclusively federal
(as in Canada and Australia), or are raised and
maintained by constituent regions, but subject to
supervision and general command by the centre.
Where regions were originally allowed to raise
their own armies, as in Switzerland or the USA, the
tendency has been towards increasing the control of
the centre. Hence in the USA, the states were
allowed to raise a militia, but the National
Defence Act of 1916, apart from changing their
title to that of National Guard, also incorporated
them as a reserve component of the national Army.
In an emergency, the command of the National Guard
may be taken over from state authorities by the
President of the federal government (Article 1 of
the Constitution provides for, "calling for the
Militia to execute the laws of the Union, suppress
insurrection and repel invasion"). Among recent
examples of the exercise of this power by the
President, was President Eisenhower's use of the
National Guard in 1960 to enforce a court order to
desegregate schools in Little Rock, Arkansas; this
action was judged to have "affected the balance of
forces in the federal system because it proved that
in an eventual confrontation between the national
government and the state, on the question of civil
rights, the state must comply".(12)   Congress is
also authorised to call forth the Militia "to
execute the laws of the Union".(13). The general
rule, however, is that federal constitutions
contain provision for the exercise of reserve
powers by the central government, and either
explicit or implicit provision for the use of armed

274

forces in this connection. The constituton drawn
up by the European Movement, for the new United
States of Europe in the early 1950s, was no
exception in that it also included the provision
that the Federal Executive could find that coercion
was necessary, though the approval of the Union
Parliament was required for this to happen".(14)
     The contribution of the possession, by all
inhabitants of the union, of federal citizenship to
the central government's ability to conduct this
activity, perhaps should be stressed at this point.
Where there is common citizenship, the courts are
not being asked to exercise the law of a foreign
power: their officers, and indeed, all those who
administer federal laws, are acting on behalf of an
authority of which they are themselves,
individually, subjects, and which they themselves
helped appoint. They are therefore normally not
influenced by divided loyalties. Similarly, when
members of an army or militia are asked to enforce
laws of the federation, they are more likely to
obey the orders of the centre government, even
against members of their own state, because of the
possession of common citizenship. It would be
impossible to exercise the reserve powers if
citizenship were local rather than general: in
such circumstances the problems which would be
experienced by the citizen of one region, who
attempted to command troops from another, would
probably prove insuperable. The danger of mutiny
would be endemic.

                    ****

     The features of federalism which have been
discussed will now be examined with reference to
the European Communities. I examine, first, the
questions of, "could the states secede?", and,
"could they nullify Community legislation within
the European Communities?". In this context, it is
necessary to look at the interaction between
relevant legal arguments and facts, and relevant
political arguments and facts. The argument that
the states still have the power, and that they
therefore could impose themselves on the centre, is
obviously an over-simplification, not only because
it leaves unexamined many of the relevant aspects
of the nature of power but also because it takes no
account of ways in which the exercise of political
power is liable to be modified in some
circumstances by legal constraints. On the other

hand, it is also necessary to guard against the
opposite conclusion: that because an act such as
secession or nullification is illegal, it therefore
cannot be done. Frequently, however, the political
analyst of the European Communities has faced the
development of the Communities' legal order with
bafflement and with the feeling that it was largely
irrelevant to political realities. He has found it
hard to understand some lawyers' assertions of the
federal character of the Communities' legal system
which, at first sight, seem inconsistent with the
political realities. Indeed, the political
implications of the development of a legal order in
the Communities, within which priority is given in
the working system to the laws of the center over
the laws of the constituent governments, need
considerable further consideration. Little work
has been done in this area since the pioneering
efforts of Stuart Scheingold in the late 1960s.

It was suggested earlier that secession should
be seen as an extreme form of nullification. The
argument that the character of the legal system of
the EEC allows member states to nullify Community
legislation - a circumstance which would reflect
the retention by states of primary responsibility
for their affairs - is hard to reconcile with the
argument that they had yielded the right to
withdraw from that organisation, which suggests, in
contrast, a powerful limitation upon that
responsibility. Before considering more closely
the question of whether nullification was
compatible with the character of Community law, I
first briefly examine directly the question of the
legality of secession.

The argument that withdrawal was excluded was
frequently based upon Article 240 of the EEC
Treaty, which held that, "this Treaty is concluded
for an unlimited period", and is supported by
reference to the character of the Treaty as an
'integrating Treaty'.(15) The Vienna Convention of
the Law of Treaties, of 23 May 1969, held in
Article 56(1) that there was no provision for
withdrawal in a Treaty (as is the case with the
Treaty of Rome); this was allowable only where "a
right of denunciation or withdrawal may be implied
by the nature of the Treaty".(16) The nature of
the founding Treaty of the European Economic
Community, in that it was believed to have been
intended to produce integration, was thought in
this argument to preclude that possiblity.

The opposing argument holds that, on the

contrary, the form of words used in Article 240 did not amount to a 'perpetuity clause'; it is suggested only that the Treaty was intended to apply for a period which had not been determined beforehand.(17)   Where founder states had definitely intended to exclude withdrawal, they had used much more explicit language: for example, the Act of Union between England and Scotland (1706-07), and that between Great Britain and Ireland (1800), had stressed repeatedly that they applied, 'for ever and after' and 'in all times coming', and should remain 'binding for Parliaments to come'(18) (unlike the European Communities' Act of 1972, by which Britain accepted the law of the Communities within her territories). The omission of any withdrawal clause from the Treaty of Rome is not nearly enough to suggest that the founders intended to exclude such withdrawal, though their reluctance to spell this out was natural in the circumstances of the negotiations in 1957; there is an analogy with the reluctance of guests at a wedding to discuss the subject of divorce.

The argument that the integrative nature of the Treaty excluded withdrawal may be countered by reference to the rather modest duties of the institutions of the Communities in developing their independent powers, and by the efforts of the founders to protect the sovereignty of member states at several points in the Treaty. Of particular importance in illustrating this caution were the procedures for modifying the Treaty contained in Articles 235 and 236. Amendment is only possible with the 'common accord' of the member states and after ratification by all governments, which confirmed that the sovereignty of members was not impaired by adherence to the Treaty, and strengthened the hand of those governments which wished to protect the status quo. Individual governments were not bound by amendments and remained masters of the Treaty: they might withdraw as an alternative to accepting amendments. This would not have been the case had amendment not required unanimity or if it could have been effected by a 'community' institution. Dagtoglu concluded that, "it is the individual sovereign Member States who have the last say, not the Community. An amendment machinery of this type cannot be declared to be incompatible with the right of withdrawal".(19) Dagtoglu adds the important point, however, that before withdrawal a state had an obligation to attempt to use the

machinery for amending the Treaty: "that is
probably the minimum stipulation resulting from the
integrating character of the European
Communities".(20)
     Professor J D B Mitchell has presented a
number of legal arguments which support the
doctrine of the supremacy of community law over
national law: the context of his arguments was the
judgement of the European Court of Justice in the
so-called Simmenthal case, in which it was held
that a national court "must within its jurisdiction
apply Community law in its entirety and protect
rights which the latter confers on individuals, and
must accordingly set aside any provision of
national law which may conflict with it, whether
prior or subsequent".(21) The implication of this
was that the powers of national parliaments, in the
United Kingdom and elsewhere in the Communities,
have been limited by membership, and that those of
central government in the Communities had been
correspondingly increased. The central theme of
Mitchell's argument — one which he shares with a
number of other constitutional lawyers — was that
there had evolved in the Communities a legal order
which represented a "higher constitutional norm",
and which had the essential characteristic of
superiority over national legal orders.(22) The
root of this higher constitutional norm can be
found, in Mitchell's argument, in the Treaty of
Rome, particularly in Article 189, which holds
that, "the Council and the Commission shall in
accordance with the provisions of this Treaty make
regulations ... (which) shall be binding in
entirety and directly applicable in all member
states"; in the practical requirements of economic
integration which included that of a consistent and
uniform system of rules throughout the region; in
the decision of the European Court of Justice which
had developed and sustained the necessary
principles of the direct affect of European
Communities' law, and the concomitant primacy of
that law in the states; and in the preparedness of
national courts to accept and apply these
principles.(23) This system, which required the
primacy of Community law, was one which the British
implicitly accepted at the point of entry, as the
other states had accepted it through their
membership over the years.(24) It was a
constitutional system which followed necessarily
from the political fact of membership.
     It followed that any specific act by national

parliaments to establish that primacy, such as the
European Communities Act in Britain, was
superfluous, though such an act might be expedient,
"simply to facilitate the recognition of
'enforceable Community rights' by the courts".(25)
These rights, which followed from the primacy of
Community law were not, however, created by the
Act: they merely "derived legal consequences from
a pre-existing situation".(26) It is itself
derivative, "unlike the situation with a normal
statute". Professor Mitchell argued further that,
"essentially whatever binding effect there be
flows not from the European Communities Act but
from entering the new legal order", and "any repeal
of the European Communities Act would be
immaterial".(27) Three inter-related points should
perhaps be stressed in summary and conclusion of
this argument: first, that the European
Communities were seen to have emerged as a
constitutional system which included the principle
of primacy, and that member states committed
themselves to that principle by the political act
of entry (The British and the other states had
simply joined that kind of thing.); second, that
national parliaments were thought to have played no
part in creating any rights that followed from the
new constitutional order: the implication of this
was that they could not legally remove any of them,
as they were not conditional upon the decision of
the law making entities within the state ("what
does stand out is, first the degree to which the
results are derived not from national
constitutional law, but from Community law
itself"(28)); and third, that national courts, as
is evidenced in the Simmenthal case, are seen to
have of necessity the right to decide in favour of
the applicability of Community law as opposed to
national law, in the event of a conflict between
the two. This represents a further limitation upon
the exercise of sovereignty by national
legislatures.

There are three ways of qualifying or
challenging these arguments: first, there are
alternative explanation of the constitutional
events treated by Professor Mitchell, which support
the opposing argument - that Community law is not
in reality superior, though it might be accepted as
such for the time being; second, there are aspects
of the superior constitutional norm argument, of
which Professor Mitchell's is here taken as
illustrative, which seemed to limit its

implications; and third, there are a number of
developments, or conceivable developments, in the
Communities in the 1970s and early 1980s, which
also implicitly contradict the thesis. The
existence of these qualifications and challenges
itelf deserves to be treated as a political fact by
the student of politics: the absence of consensus
amongst constitutional lawyers could indicate that
in the European Communities a political decision to
re-assert national superiority could find
appropriate legal backing. The continuous
assertion by a distinguished group of lawyers that
Community law is superior may also be seen as part
of a political process of realising that
possibility.

The main element in the arguments which extend
a different interpretation to the same
constitutional events treated by Professor Mitchell
seems to be that supranational law was effective in
the states because it was introduced by the process
normally followed in adopting international
treaties. According to Schlochauer, it follows
that the supranational law is "ranked in respect to
national law" by a decision taken according to
national constitutional norms, which therefore
remains superior to the Communities' constitutional
norms:(29) the Communities' system is an extension
of the judicial arm of the state. The European
Comunities Bill in the United Kingdom was not,
therefore, merely a way of making it easier for the
courts in the UK to use Community law, but an
indispensable part of the process of making the
terms of the Treaty, and the law derived from it,
accessible to English courts. A comparable
situation is seen to have existed in other states
in the European Communities, although the details
differed according to the various constitutional
procedures for ratifying treaties. Professor
Mitchell implicitly acknowledged the strength of
this argument when he complained that the French
Court de Cassation, in accepting the obligation to
test, in the light of the Treaty, the applicability
of _Une loi_, which was subsequent to the Treaty,
placed "too much reliance on Article 55 of the
Constitution". Article 55 was the part of the
French Constitution which made treaties superior to
law: the implication seems to be that by using this
procedure the essential dependence of Communities
law upon conditions decided within national systems
was being unduly stressed.

According to Schlochauer, the only way to

overcome the problem of the dependence of Communities law upon national constitutional norms was for there to be an "express provision in a constitutional instrument" (30) which extended superiority to the central government such as existed in the constitution of the USA or West Germany. Article 189 of the Treaty of Rome as the only part of the Treaty which was conceivably a candidate for this role, but it was judged not to be such a supremacy clause because it was part of a treaty between sovereign states, and because it did not enumerate powers which were to be conferred to the centre.(31) If these powers were not enumerated, as is required in a federal constitution, the question of whether any particular power had been transferred, and legal superiority extended in that connection, could therefore always be disputed, and the transfer denied in the member states of the Communities. Furthermore, in the absence of an express provision, which in effect created a superior power at the centre, supranational law must always be limited, according to Professor Scelle, by the implications of what he called the <u>dedoublement fonctionel</u>; "national institutions exercised both national sovereignty, and, as a collective body, powers on behalf of the Community, the one function being the counterpart of the other; as a result a treaty establishing a supranational community, or acts issued thereunder, can never be unconstitutional under national law".(32) It follows from this circumstance that Communities laws should be seen as having been made separately by the national governments which happen to be acting together in the Communities' institutions, that is, in the Council of Ministers. The Communities' legal system must therefore have the character of a series of adjustments in national legal systems made by national actors, who happen to be working together, rather than be the result of the introduction of a superior system. Some authorities have added the further point that it is illogical to expect that states should establish within themselves a superior power.

Enough has been said to illustrate the general nature of the alternative accounts of the constitutional events which link national and supranational law in the Communities. The student of politics should note that there are at least two views of the matter, and that each has a distinguished following. A discussion of the

logical implications of the thesis that a higher
constitutional law has evolved in the Communities,
which required the superiority of supranational law
(the Mitchell thesis), provides a second source of
support for the judgement that states would not
necessarily be acting illegally or
unconstitutionally if they decided to nullify
Communities legislation, and yet retained
membership in the Communities, or if they decided
to secede. This was, of course, a very important
political fact in the Communities in the late 1970s
and early 1980s, especially in view of the British
Labour Party's decision to withdraw from the
Communities if returned to power.

The argument that the legal system of the
Communities has the essential characteristic of
requiring primacy over national systems, and that
the act of membership involved accepting that
character, depends upon two different kinds of
assumption. First is the straightforward
assumption that if the economic community was to
work its rules had to be uniform in character: the
Communities system is seen to be as it is because
that character is judged to be functionally
necessary. Second, however, is the assumption
that it is as it is because of the acceptance of
this character by the institutions which are
involved in operating the system, in particular by
the courts and national legislatures. The problem
with the second assumption, however, is that it
does not necessarily involve the recognition by the
institutions of anything fundamental about the
system; rather it involves a number of judgements
about what was convenient, or practical. A great
deal of stress is rightly placed, in Professor
Mitchell's argument, upon such factors as the
goodwill of the courts, or the political sense of
assemblies or governments;. but such judgements
suggest more a preparedness to act as if the system
had primacy rather than an acknowledgement of its
essential character. The second assumption is
indeed a tautology; the system is seen to be like
this because this is what relevant actors were
prepared to believe it was like. The conclusion
follows that if the courts or legislatures had
chosen to interpret the character of the system
differently, then it would have been different.
Furthermore, if the institutions of a new member,
such as the British Parliament, or Courts, chose to
act after accession as if the character of the
Communities' legal system did not require primacy,

then it follows that, for the British at least, that character would *ipso facto* be altered in that way.

The central problem in the second assumption is that it involves a mixing of views about what is necessary with views about what is conditional or optimal. Professor Mitchell argues, on the one hand, that, "implicitly the opponents of membership maintain their opposition (to the European Communities' constitutional system) because it is opposition to that current fact (of membership) just as the Jacobites fought for old days and old ways".(33) (Meaning: if the British are 'in', they must recognise the character of the Communities'; if they reject that character, they must reject membership.) On the other hand, however, the Italian Courts, by implication, have the option within the Communities of not following the European Court's judgement. In the Simmenthal case: "there is nothing in the past history of these decisions in Italy to suggest that this most recent decision will not be accepted".(34) This is a much more cautious, conditional evaluation based upon observation of practice hitherto, rather than anything which is necessary. Furthermore, the right of national courts to decide upon the applicability of law, which involves the right to grant primacy to the law of the European Communities in the event of a clash, may also be seen as resting upon the assumption that national legislatures would avoid passing legislation which contradicted communities law, as a matter of good political sense, but that if they chose to do this, national courts would probably follow the national parliament. The British Parliament could do this by using normal legislative processes, but some courts on the continent of Europe might have to use the special procedures required for constitutional amendment, because of their diferent ways of accepting international treaties. Geoffrey Howe's comment about the effects of the European Communities Act probably apply in some form to all member states of the Communities. He wrote that the British Parliament, "could revoke the section of the European Communities Bill which asks the British Courts to give precedence to 'enforceable community rights' and that if this happened the Courts would follow that law".(35) The student of politics must conclude therefore that the argument that communities law is necessarily superior to national law is not without its weaknesses, and that a number of arguments point in the opposite direction; they suggest that if, say, for political reasons, a national legislature decided to limit the effect of a Communities Regulation, or to nullify it, and if this intention was made plain to the national courts by the legislature, that the national courts would not apply the Communities law. If this happened, one would be entitled to conclude, quite simply, that the character of the Communities' legal system had been altered.

A number of recent developments, or conceivable developments, in the Communities provide a third basis for challenging the view that the laws of the Communities now necessarily have primacy over those of member states, and that the powers of national legislatures have been reduced as a consequence. There are two interrelated arguments which need to be briefly examined in this context; the first concerns the kinds of powers which recent developments suggest or imply, have been retained or yielded by national systems; the second concerns the kind of use to which these powers could conceivably be put in present political circumstances. The first argument emerges from the debate in the 1970s about the role of the European Parliament in decision-making in the Communities in relation to that of national parliaments. The second deals with the attitudes towards the Communities and the extent to which political resources could be mobilised against it.

National legislatures have generally as yet not developed ways of closely supervising the legislation of the Communities, either during its preparation or after it has been passed by the Council. Administrations and executives have more usually formed the primary mechanism for supervising the national input into, and response to, Communities' decision making.(36) These circumstances have made it easier for the supranational primacy argument to retain its credibility, and have also encouraged those with federalist inclinations to argue that the only way to strengthen popular control over European legislation was by developing the European Parliament. Had national legislatures generally developed the kind of supervisory mechanisms which are used, say in Denmark, the ability of national parliaments to impose conditions upon Communities' law-making would have been much more difficult to deny.(37) It is important to stress, in this context, that control of legislation as it is being made in the Council, by such procedures as closely instructing Ministers, is a functional alternative to the act of nullification after Communiies laws have been passed. National legislatures are probably unlikely in practice to nullify legislation because of the de-doublement fonctionel: the Ministers who approve it in the Council of Ministers are also involved in managing national governments, and their supporting majorities in national assemblies. This is not to deny, however, that a national legislature could nullify, and would do this, say, in the event of a change of government, or in the event of a Minister's losing his political support. But the main point to be made here is that it is still very much a conceivable option for national legislatures to strengthen their supervision and scrutiny of Communities legislation, and that had they done this effectively earlier the argument that they had in some sense lost sovereignty would have been seen to be much weaker.(38)

This possibility is indicated by the imposition by the British Parliament, when it approved the legislation governing direct elections to the European Parliament, of the requirement that no new powers should be allowed to the latter without its approval, and by the French Conseil d'Etat's decision that such new powers would be unconstitutional.(39) There are two implications of these decisions, which are relevant here. First, they required that no powers should be given to the European Parliament which were not the subject of the terms of the Treaty of Rome, unless they were granted in a new treaty which had been approved according to national constitutional provisions. The limitations are, therefore, a reassertion of the principle that the Communities system is dependent upon national constitutional norms and not superior to them. Second, they implied that the Council should not yield powers which it currently held in the Assembly, in the manner discussed, for instance, in the Vedel Report. This limitation suggests that the British Parliament, and the French Court, were anxious to protect the rights of national institutions to impose themselves if they chose upon the law makers either by increasing supervision or by scrutiny. A transfer of Council powers to the Assembly would have made it much more difficult to exercise that right, and by undermining the de-doublement fonctionel it would have greatly strengthened the

federal character of the Communities. The
limitations are, however, an indication of the
extent to which powers have been retained at the
national level, rather than transferred, though
many may be latent, and of the use to which they
could be put by national legislatures. Again, the
conditionality of the 'primacy' of the
supranational legal system is revealed.

The second aspect of circumstances in the
Communities in the 1970s, which tends to confirm
this conclusion, concerns attitudes towards
membership which, at mass and elite levels, are
generally well-short of what some have seen as an
essential condition of federalism, namely a
'sentiment of unity'. This is not the place for a
detailed analysis of such attitudes, but it should
be noted that support in the original Six, for
effective centralised government in some task-areas
at around 60%, is high but not near the
overwhelming level of support found in stable
federations.(40) Support for membership is
consistently high too, but again short of
irresistible. In the new member states, support
for membership and for stronger central government
is generally lower. In the latter, the issue of
membership still has a political significance - it
is an issue in national elections - which it may
have lost in the original Six. Political resources
are indeed devoted to the objective of secession,
particularly in Britain and Denmark. The
Referendum in Britain in 1975 was one consequence
of the existence of these resources; it resulted in
a decisive defeat for those who were opposed to
membership, but from some points of view it was not
an unqualified success. First, support for
membership was large but not overwhelming; it was
not large enough to amount to an expression of a
'sentiment of unity'; and, second, the Referendum
could also be seen as a confirmation of the
political fact that secession was indeed possible.
If it had occurred, it may be assumed that
appropriate legal backing would have been easy to
discover. Far from confirming unity, it was a
measure of the extent to which the Communities
legal system is short of that of a federation.

****

I now turn to a more specific examination of
the ability of the Communities to enforce its
legislation. The questions discussed here are, of

course, closely connected with those already examined: but the perspective is different in that the powers of the centre, rather than those of the 'regions' (states), are the primary focus. As was suggested in the earlier consideration of this feature, there are two related aspects of enforcement, namely the activity of the judicial review of the laws of the Union, and the activity of the use of sanctions to uphold those laws.

From the point of view of judicial review, the Communities might be though, at first sight, to come rather close to the federal model. As Lasok and Bridge have pointed out, "this weapon (of interpretation of Communities' laws) has been taken away from the signatories of the EEC Treaty and so they cannot resort to legal subterfuge".(41) This is according to Articles 177 and 164 of the Treaty of Rome. Article 219 reinforces the terms of these articles by requiring that member states will not submit any dispute concerning interpretation or application of the Treaty to any method of settlement other than those provided in the Treaty. These Articles established the Court of the Communities as the only body in the Communities which was permitted to hand down an interpretation of Community law, and any court may use this procedure; the highest courts, however, must do so. In this way, the signatories of the Treaty of Rome sought to ensure a uniform application of the Communities laws throughout the Union. Lasok and Bridge point out also that the founders also sought to protect this principle against those states which might wish 'to flout the Treaty overtly'.(42) Under Article 213, the Commission, "for the performance of the tasks entrusted to it", "may collect any information and carry out any checks required within the limits and under the conditions laid down by the Council". There are a number of other Articles which require member states to give the Commission information which it requests.

The student of politics must agree that a system of judicial review certainly exists in the Communities, which looks at first sight rather like that which is normally found in federations. But there is some evidence which suggests that the practice might be rather different: at least one authority has concluded that the Court behaves in reality rather more like the International Court of Justice at the Hague than is usually supposed, although there is no equivalent in the Communities legal system of the optional clause in

international law. Stuart Scheingold suggested,
for instance, that "the federal rhetoric cannot be
taken at face value because the pattern of
constitutional coercion and the hierarchical
ordering of relationships associated with a federal
system are not taking place".(43) The Court has
certainly asserted constitutional principles, about
such questions as the supremacy of Communities law,
but it has tended to avoid the policy issues when
there is a chance of sharp dissent, and to leave
such issues to the political process. "Judges do
not appear to have been very active federalisers
and the most important controversies are seldom
litigated".(44) Scheingold also argued that this
hesitancy at the top is matched by a corresponding
hesitancy among lower national courts: they have
been surprisingly reluctant to use the procedures
made available by Article 177. He quotes research
by Richard Buxbaum, who considered that in the
context of the development of a single regional
anti-trust policy, "the more sensitive and
political the issues, the more marked the
divergence". "National judges send forward only
the less important problems".(45) Scheingold
reinforced this point by pointing out that a
surprisingly small number of references to the
Court had taken place under Article 177: between
1958 and 1968 there had been 366 cases involving
European Communities' legislation before national
courts, of which only 47 had involved the request,
under Article 177, for an opinion by the Court of
the Communities.(44) Lasok and Bridge reported in
1976 that English courts and tribunals had adopted
"a generally restrictive approach to requests for
preliminary readings".(47) There was, in other
words, a de facto equivalent of the optional clause
in the behaviour of the courts.
    The critical underpinning of the system is
not, as is implied by many lawyers, the
legally-agreed division of powers and
responsibilities, but rather the less tangible
socialisation of national legal officers and the
extent of the development of the authority of the
central court. This authority is rather fragile
compared with, say, the Supreme Court of the USA.
Scheingold concludes that, though "the judges may
have authorised enforcement action by the
Commission against member governments that resisted
the application of various community rules ... the
federal prerogatives have been employed very
sparingly and then not so much in the service of

coercive patterns which typify the federal model,
as in the support of 'consensual politics'".(48)
Indeed, a large number of suits against member
governments, such as occurred in 1969, "may be
taken as a sign of the breakdown of community
bargaining procedures, and a failure of executive
leadership, rather than of the federalising process
at work".(49)

It is also the case, however, that from the
point of view of the effectiveness of the
enforcement of the Communities laws, a further
problem had begun to emerge in the late 1970s. The
Commission had experienced increasing difficulties
in supervising the operation of Directives issued
by the Council, and in using Article 213 on the
collection of information to reinforce its
jurisdiction effectively.(50) Directives,
according to the Treaty, are binding in terms of
the ends to be obtained, but usually leave the
means to be used to national legislatures. They
have been used in such areas as the elimination of
technical barriers to trade (for example safety
requirements, performance standards, nomenclature)
in food and manufactured goods. In these areas,
the rate of technical change has required a
continuing up-dating of established standards,
which has imposed a burden in addition to that
required by introducing new directives. The
Commission has found the task of checking whether
national legislatures were acting in accordance
with Directives increasingly difficult to perform
because of the shortage of suitable administrators
in its Departments, in relation to workload
involved. The feeling seemed to be fairly
widespread in the Commission that there were indeed
instances of deliberate avoidance of Directives at
the national level, though more often failure was
the result of misinterpretation. This applied
particularly to Italy, though other states were
also guilty. The Court was sensitive to the charge
that continuously demanding compliance, and then
being ignored, would damage its own authority.
There was also concern that the Commission should
be equipped to perform this supervision function
more effectively, without detracting from its
ability to formulate new proposals. It certainly
represented a practical limitation upon the ability
of the Communities' institutions to operate an
effective system of judicial review. The danger
was stressed of the appearance of significant
differences in national standards in these areas.

As with Article 177 and 164, the implications of Article 213 on information gathering and supervision seem to be rather less than federal in practice.

The second aspect of this area of control by the Communities concerns the use of sanctions to enforce its laws in the event of non-compliance by states or by organisations, or individuals within the state: the particular question which arises here is that of whether the Communities have the power to undertake forced execution of decisions or judgements. The execution of decisions and judgements of the Communities against individuals and groups is mandatory upon member states but, nevertheless, execution takes place according to national legal and practice under the authority of national judicial power. The Communities do have the right to impose fines upon firms under all three of the founding treaties. For instance, infringements of the terms of Articles 85 and 96 of the Treaty of Rome may led to the imposition upon firms of fines by the Commission of between 50 and 1000 units of account per day.(51) The Commission may enforce such fines by withholding funds which it owes that enterprise (for example, in seeking execution of a fine under Article 92 ECSC Treaty); the Euratom Commission may enforce safety provisions by withdrawing technical or financial assistance. But, despite the existence of these powers, the Communities' ability to execute its laws within states is inevitably limited by the absence of any Community agency for this purpose: there are no Communities police and no militia, and no Communities presence within the states. Compared with these deficiencies, the enforcement powers which exist seem rather feeble. It should be recalled also that execution of laws is inevitably limited by the lack of any Community citizenship: individuals and firms, courts and administrators, may have rights and duties under the Community's legal system, but they are not Community citizens and there is no zeal in using, and applying, such law, particularly when it seems in some sense to be in conflict with national law.

The limitations upon the Communities' enforcement procedures are more apparent when applied to the member states themselves. There are indeed procedures by which a state may be found to have infringed the terms of the founding treaties. The Commission may, for instance, direct a state to abolish subsidies to its industry which had been

forbidden by Article 93 and such a directive would
be mandatory upon states: under Article 171 they
must "take the steps necessary for the
implementation of the judgement". However, "the
Court has now power to impose sanctions but its
judgement is a judicial declaration of fact and a
reminder of the obligations to comply with the
judgement".(52) The term 'mandatory', when used in
this context, is seen to be used in a rather
peculiar sense; it is not that something can be
made to happen by using sanctions adequate to that
purpose but rather that it is legally required.
There is no way of compelling a state to do what it
has been asked. Indeed, the Communities use their
legal system against recalcitrant states in a way
which is somewhat reminiscent of the behaviour of
Violet Elizabeth in _Just William_: she would yell,
"if you don't do what I want I shall scream and
scream until I'm sick, and I shall too!"(53) There
is a possibility of administrative action if a
state is in breach of its obligations. Other
states may be authorised to take counter-measures
by, for instance, counteracting the effects of a
partner's alteration of an exchange rate in a
manner inconsistent with Article 104 of the EEC
Treaty; another state may also be authorised to
protect itself against unfair competition from
another member by, for instance, imposing
countervailing duties. But this method of
'enforcement' seems to contain an important
weakness: if it is used too often, the Communities
would be effecting enforcement, paradoxically, at
the cost of its own disintegration.
This dilemma is a reminder of the delicate
balance which exists between the imposition of
rules and the building of consensus about political
and economic interests in the Communities. The
attempt to impose rules very easily spills back
into the undermining of fragile political and
economic agreements, a circumstance which is rather
more reminiscent of the practice of leagues of
separate states or confederations than of federal
unions. Lasok and Bridge wrote that "a
recalcitrant state cannot really be forced to abide
by the judgement of the court or the decision of
the Commission. This indeed is the last vestige of
sovereignty. In this respect, the Community
differs from a federal state which may have federal
means at its disposal for the execution of the
judgement of the federal court or the decisions of
the federal executive". "... if the authority of

the Community Court was to be questioned, the
matter would develop into a political crisis within
the Community, which could be solved only by
political means".(54)   This point became all too
evident in 1979-80 when the French government
refused to permit imports of lamb and mutton from
Britain, despite being found guilty on two
occasions, by the Court of the Communities, of a
breach of the rules of the Common Market.(55)   The
student of politics is entitled to comment that the
lack of machinery for enforcement action against
member states is an aspect not of the 'last vestige
of sovereignty', but rather one of its first
principles: that the sovereign state is by virtue
of its sovereignty entitled to decide upon those
laws which shall apply within its territory,
though, as the previous chapters have indicated,
members of the European Communities may be
sometimes disinclined, or lack the capacity, to do
this.   In this respect, too, the character of the
European Communities is revealed as being more like
that of a confederation or league of states than a
federation.   In the complex and original legal
procedures developed in the European Communities,
the states have carefully preserved their
traditional values.
     The shortcomings of the Communities in the
context of their legal system have been stressed.
(It is not denied that it also possesses a number
of highly distinctive strengths and virtues which
have been widely discussed.)   But a brief
examination of the aspects of the constitutional
arrangements of the Communities adds a further
dimension to the explanation of these problems.
There are two perspectives from which an evaluation
may be approached: the Communities fall rather
short of the practice of stable modern federations
in both of the areas thus illuminated.   First,
there is the manner and terms of appointment of
members of the executive agency, the Commission.
Whereas in federations no reliance is usually
placed upon the criterion of proportional
recruitment to executive bodies, from the various
member regions, in the Communities this has come to
be the practice.   The Court has attempted to
prevent the reservation of particular posts to
particular nationalities below the level of the
Commission, but the practice is nevertheless to
preserve a balance among the various nationalities,
rather than making appointments strictly on the
basis of merit, or party membership.(56)   The

implication of these procedures is that there is no
figure, and no institution, which is clearly
qualified by virtue of the manner of its
appointment to act and speak for the group as a
whole, as is the case, for instance, with the
President of the USA. Any institution or person
who claims this title and is allowed to act in this
capacity is generally limited by various advisory
groups, such as the so-called 113 Committee, which
are in effect coalitions of sovereign states.
Although the idea of loosening national control of
appointments to the 13-man Commission has been
frequently discussed and, indeed, President
Jenkins, after his appointment by a consensus of
member governments, was consulted about
appointments to this team, nevertheless, these are
still made on the basis of the general agreement of
governments. Most recently proposals have been
made to change this system in the Tindemans Report
and the Genscher-Colombo plan of 1982. It is, of
course, a requirement of the Treaty of Rome, as
modified by the 1972 Treaty of Accession, that no
more than two Commissioners should be taken from
any one nation. Both the formal requirements and
the evolving practice of appointments in the
Commission would be regarded as a serious
compromise with the political independence of the
executive in any modern federal state.
     The second perspective concerns arrangements
for the elections to the European Parliament in
1979. The Communities' institutions were not
permitted to establish uniform criteria for the
conduct of the election. The result of this was
that the timing of the elections varied (on the 7th
of June in Britain, Denmark and Ireland, and the
following Sunday in France and Italy); the
electoral system varied (proportional in some sense
in all states except for Great Britain, where the
first-past-the-post system was used); and that the
criteria for deciding upon the eligibility of
voters varied (in some states non-residents could
vote, in others not). These variations existed
despite the Treaty requirement that the elections
should be held according to a uniform procedure.
It is indeed the case in a number of federations
that the regions are given responsibility for
deciding how the elections for central institutions
are to be conducted. But they generally exercise
this function within a framework of rules agreed
upon at the centre: for instance, in the USA the
states are not permitted to exclude voters on the

basis of race, colour or sex (15th and 19th Amendments), and there are rules which govern the shape, size and contiguity of electoral districts. Wechsler pointed out that, in this context, "state control then rests entirely on the tolerance of Congress".(57) In the Communities, in contrast, it would be difficult to agree that the central instutions have played any role at all in deciding who could vote, how, where or in what framework. The matter was left entirely to the whims of governments, and indeed, of parties in the constituent states; even the one rule that was laid down in the constitution, the Treaty of Rome - that requiring a uniform procedure (Article 138) - was casually ignored. In this matter too the Communites seem to have fallen rather short of the standards of modern federations.

****

It has been shown that the judgement which was quoted at the beginning of this Chapter is contentious in that it reflects the view of only a part of the society of international lawyers and is at variance with many existing political circumstances. It seems to this student of the European Communities, however, that the arguments which support the supremacy of communities law have been particularly stressed in Communities literature - even in elite journals - in legal articles for non-lawyers. It is important to redress this balance. There were also non-legal arguments which were nevertheless important to the evaluation of the legal case. The conclusions is hard to avoid, however, that in the legal area, as in 'policy' areas, the practice of the European Communities differs sharply from the federal model. This negative judgement should not lead the reader to conclude that there are not a number of ways in which the Communities legal system is a valuable development from traditional international law. But the arguments do confirm the conclusion of the preceeding Chapters, that governments have been careful to impose limits upon their involvement in the European Communities, which stop well short of any grant of sovereignty to the regional institutions. They are also an indication of the extent to which the Communities fall short of the transfer of authority to a new centre in the manner suggested by David Mitrany.

294

NOTES

1.   D Lasok and J W Bridge, <u>An Introduction to the Law and Institutions of the European Communities</u>, Butterworths, London, 1976.

2.   I D Duchacek, <u>Comparative Federalism: The Territorial Dimension of Politics</u>, Holt, Rinehart and Winston Inc., New York, 1970.

3.   K C Wheare, <u>Federal Government</u>, Oxford University Press, London, 1951 (2nd Edition), p. 91.

4.   Quoted in I D Duchacek, <u>loc. cit.</u>, p. 218.

5.   Carl Friedrich, "Supranational Union in Western Europe", in Arthur W Macmahon (Ed), <u>Federalism: Mature and Emergent</u>, Doubleday, New York, 1955, p. 523.

6.   <u>Ibid</u>, p. 523.

7.   K C Wheare, <u>loc. cit.</u>, p.90.

8.   <u>Ibid</u>, p. 92.

9.   <u>Ibid</u>, p. 71.

10.   Arthur N Holcombe, "The Coercion of States in a Federal System", in Arthur W Macmahon, <u>loc. cit.</u>, p. 139.

11.   Holcombe, <u>loc. cit.</u>, p. 140.

12.   Harry Lazer, <u>The American Political System in Transition</u>, New York, Crowell, 1967, p. 79.

13.   K C Wheare, <u>loc. cit.</u>, p. 201.

14.   Holcombe, <u>loc. cit.</u>, p. 138.

15.   See A Campbell, <u>Common Market Law Review</u>, Vol. 11, London, 1969, No. 2284.

16.   See P D Dagtoglu, "How Indissoluble is the Community?", in P D Dagtoglu (Editor), <u>Basic Problems of the European Community</u>, Basil Blackwell, Oxford, 1975, p. 264.

17.   <u>Ibid</u>, p. 259.

18.   See J D B Mitchell, <u>British Law and British Membership</u>, Eur. 1971, p. 97, <u>et. seq.</u> (102).

19.   Dagtoglu, <u>loc. cit.</u>, p. 265.

20.   <u>Ibid.</u>, p. 265.

21.   J D B Mitchell, "The Sovereignty of Parliament and Community Laws: The Stumbling Block that isn't there", <u>International Affairs</u>, January 1979, p. 33.

22.   For a general discussion of this approach, see Peter Hay, <u>Federalism and Supranational Organisations</u>, University of Illinois Press, 1966, p. 55-56.

23.

24. J D B Mitchell, loc. cit., p. 40.
25. Ibid, p. 41.
26. Ibid, p. 41.
27. Ibid, p. 41.
28. Ibid, p. 44.
29. Discussed in Peter Hay, loc. cit., p. 54.
30. Ibid, p. 54.
31. Ibid, p. 57-58.
32. Schelle, quoted Hay, loc. cit., p. 69.
33. J D B Mitchell, loc. cit., p. 39.
34. Ibid, p. 44.
35. Geoffrey Howe, "The European Communities Act, 1971", International Affairs, Volume 49, No. 1, January 1973.
36. See Helen Wallace, National Governments and the European Communities, Chatham House/PEP, London, 1973; Anne Stevens, "Problem: of Parliament Control of EEC Policy", Millennium: Journal of International Studies, L S E, London, Vol. 5, No. 3, Winger 1976-77, p. 269-279.
37. See J Fitz Maurice, "National Parliaments and European Policy-making: the Case of Denmark", PParliamentary Affairs, XXIX, 1976, pp. 310-26.
38. cf David Coombs' argument in this contribution to Sasse et al, Decision-making in the European Community, Praeger, New York, 1977, pp. 310-331.
39. See Robert Jackson and John Fitzmaurice, The European Parliament: A Guide to Direct Elections, Penguin Books, Harmondsworth, p. 140.
40. See Commission of the European Communities, Eurobarometre: Public Opinion in the European Community, No. 9, July 1978, Brussels, p. 30-31.
41. D Lasok and J W Bridge, loc. cit., p.217.
42. Ibid, p. 218.
43. Stuart A Scheingold, The Law in Political Integration, Centre for International Affairs, Harvard University, 1971, p. 26.
44. Ibid, p. 47.
45. Richard M Buxbaum, "Article 177 of the Rome Treaty as a Federalizing Device", Stamford Law Review, Vol. 21, No 4 (May 1969), p. 1043-1045.
46. Stuart A Scheingold, loc. cit., p. 33-34.
47. Lasok and Bridge, loc. cit., p. 41.
48. Stuart A Scheingold, loc. cit., p. 4.
49. Ibid, p. 15.
50. According to interviews conducted by the author in December 1978.
51. See Peter Hay, loc. cit., p. 45.
52. Lasok and Bridge, loc. cit., p. 219.

53.   See Rachel Crompton's <u>Just William</u>,
stories.
54.   Lasok and Bridge, <u>loc. cit.</u>, p. 271.
55.   See Commission of the European
Communities' <u>Thirteenth General Report on the
Actions of the European Communities</u>, Brussels,
February 1980, p. 280.
56.   A Report by Sir Roy Denman, assistant to
President Jenkins, in early 1980 was severely
critical of aspects of Commission staffing
arrangements, including <u>inter alia</u> the practice of
reserving posts for particular nationals.

Chapter Ten

CONCLUSION AND PRESCRIPTIONS

In this Chapter, I first summarise the conclusions which have been suggested in the preceding nine Chapters, before turning to prescriptions for integration in Western Europe in the 1980s. The conclusions are about, first, the changing role and structure of the "central" institutions; second, the limits imposed by governments and other actors in the member states upon cooperation, as reflected in their policies, and in national decision-making structures; and third, the extent to which authority has been transferred to the new centre - and sovereignty relocated - as revealed in legal practice, mass attitudes, and the related habits and expectations of elites. It will be recalled that this arrangement of conclusions reflects the theoretical introduction, and the organisation of the volume. Perhaps it is worth restating that I argued that the goal of the central institutions was illuminated by both of the main "gradualist" theories; that the changing interest of governments in cooperation, and related adjustments in national decision-making, were a central concern in neofunctionalism; and that functionalism more effectively addressed the fundamental question of the conditions under which there could be a transfer of authority and sovereignty from the states to the centre. I was not, however, concerned with testing or improving these theories, but used them to arrange the empirical materials.

In the 1970s, there was a marked increase in the range and status of the inter-governmental institutions of the European Communities, and a matching decline in the authority of the Commission. In the early 1970s, there was still some encouragment for those who favoured

298

supranational Europe. To them, it still seemed
conceivable that the institutions of the First
Europe could be restored to health. But the
creation of the European Council in 1974, and the
progressive expansion of the role of the
Presidency, both reflected and confirmed the
declining status of the Commission. The increasing
importance of the machinery for political
cooperation also indicated a move of the centre of
gravity of the European institutions towards
inter-governmentalism, and the return to a position
of leadership in handling relations between
national governments and the Communities of foreign
ministers and officials. It is not the case,
however, that the pattern of work in the European
Communities which had emerged in the 1950s and
1960s had been abandoned. The Commission retained
a role as initiator, though on a less grand scale,
and was the main formulator of Communities'
policies; this was particularly evident in external
relations in the Common Commercial Policy. The
relations between the central dyad of institutions
the Commission and the Council of Ministers,
remained a central part of what had become a rather
complex system for the coordination of national
policies. Indeed, despite its decline, the
Commission probably retained an unusual authority
among international institutions and frequently
defined the "ideal" of European policy as part of
the coordination process.

The interests of member states were, however,
more often defined in the short-term, and on
internal economic issues it proved increasingly
difficult to find a way forward. In the 1970s
members needed and failed to find a new central
bargain which could be an equivalent to the
original bargain between the French and the West
Germans by which the latter got the Common Market
and the former the Common Agricultural Policy. Th
transitional phase had been completed in 1969, and
there was now increasingly a need to develop forms
of positive integration in a wide range of areas.
In the circumstances of adverse economic condition
in the 1970s, the states generally found it
difficult to move towards positive integration.
This difficulty was made more intractible as
differences of interest emerged between richer
states, and a group of poorer states led by
Britain, whose economies declined by comparison
with the former in terms of a number of indicators
The British, in particular, were hesitant about

economic integration, and combined an anxious protection of sovereignty with an essentially utilitarian approach to the Communities which was frequently frustrated. The one area of progress seemed to be that of foreign policy harmonisation, though this was not without its costs in terms of a negative impact upon internal integration; and some aspects of progress in this area were probably illusory.

This greater caution about the definition of national interest in the Communities' system and the more aggressive pursuit of those interests was reflected in the decision-making structures, within administrations and executives, and at the non-governmental level. There was little evidence of any tendency towards the development of European political parties; interest groups such as Trade Unions kept watching briefs in Brussels, but continued to focus primarily upon the major centres of power at the national level. This is not to say that the European Communities' institutions were unimportant; but they were regarded as a point of entry into a decision-making system which was in part transnational but which was nevertheless still centred on national governments. They had developed an extensive habit of consultation, and an unusual degree of inter-penetration of bureaucracies, but national civil servants saw the Communities as a framework for attempting the resolution of existing national difficulties, rather than as an opportunity for transcending them. They also tended to resist any developments at the Communities' level which could conceivably challenge their own role or that of the role of the national decision-making structures of which they were members.

There was also little evidence to suggest that there had developed in the Communities a sufficient degree of consensus at the popular level, and a refocussing of loyalties towards the Communities' institutions there, so that any claim of the latter to sovereignty could be sustained. At the end of the day, national governments remained the responsible actors, and the separate nations the main constituencies. Although there was some evidence of the emerging of a security-community in Deutsch's sense, the functionalist (and Gaullist) requirement of a socio-psychological community as a condition for the establishment of the sovereignty of the new centre remained unfulfilled. This point has been illustrated in various parts of the

300

volume. In Chapter Nine, however, one of its
primary consequences was discussed in legal terms:
that it was impossible to conclude with any
certainty that the Communities' legal system had
primacy over national ones. Though it was unusual
in many ways, the questions of "who is ultimately
responsible", and "what system prevails" could not
be resolved in favour of the Communities. It is
perhaps worth stressing that neofunctionalist
theories failed to deal with these questions
effectively, though Haas recognised this difficulty
in his contribution to the journal International
Organisation in 1971.

Now I put forward a few suggestions about how
to tackle the problems of the European Communities
in the early 1980s. My prescriptions are based
upon the assumption that there is still a need for
a more unified entity, a more organised central
'core' within Western Europe, though reasons for
this assumption are not examined closely here. It
may be that the best argument in the early eighties
was that a more unified Western Europe could
provide a stronger deterrent against further Soviet
expansion, both because of its ability to organise
a more coordinated military effort and because of
its diplomatic weight. I realise though that the
arguments in favour of reinforcing the unity of
member states of the European Communities are not
self-evident. I am also aware that prescriptions
need to be in tune with others' preferences about
goals, as well as seeming to be realistic and
practicable. They should convey a sense not only
that something needs to be done, but that it can be
done, and will lead to the desired end situation.
It is also necessary to avoid the gross error of
simply asserting that a problem once recognised
should be exorcised through the application of some
primitive magic such as 'political will'. As with
human ailments the problem may be either directly
treatable, or it may be the symptom of some
underlying tendency or conjunction of tendencies:
an illness usually cannot be cured by eliminating
its symptoms which are nevertheless the visible
contours of the problem. Prescriptions should
therefore be related to the underlying treatable
tendencies as well as, where appropriate, to
aspects of the problem itself. To state the
problem is not necessarily to operationalise the
process of providing treatment.

The European Communities have since their
inception shown three tendencies which separately

and in conjunction had generated by the late 1970s, and early 1980s, the problems which I have outlined. The first was that of centralisation. The attempt was made to transfer power to the centre by strengthening the institutions of the centre and by establishing a unified legal order. The Commission was the institution upon which the expectations of greater centralisation were focussed, though this goal also became attached to the European Assembly, particularly after direct elections in the Summer of 1979. Centralisation was also reflected in the goal of having single regimes which involved all members for the range of Communities' activities. National Governments, Assemblies, Legislatures and Executives were seen both by supporters and opponents of integration as progressively losing their traditional position as the process went forward and common arrangements were supposed to increasingly involve all states. The survival of this view was one of the reasons for Member Governments' increasing anxiety in their relations with their partners: the notion of centralisation seemed to be overambitious but its survival sometimes increased governments' doubts about cooperation. The second tendency was that of internationalisation. Those who supported European integration generally did so in part because they were generally international in outlook. For this reason the European Communities felt the necessity of adopting generally liberal policies and postures in their relations with the outside world: they were sensitive to accusations of protectionism and anxious to play their part in the various rounds of tariff reductions. They were prepared to initiate new concepts, and follow new policies in their relations with the Third World (for example, the STABEX System in the Lome Agreements).(1) Thirdly, the Communities followed the road of expansion. The Six eventually accepted the addition of Britain, Ireland and Denmark, and in 1981 they added Greece. Further expansion to include Spain and Portugal was likely.

Yet each of these tendencies from the point of view of obtaining unity led to difficulties in the late seventies and early eighties. Centralisation meant that ultimately existing powers within the states would have to reduce themselves in order to set up a new central one, a strategy that politically and psychologically was fraught with difficulties: was it ever really likely that a Government or a Parliament would accept that its

own powers should be removed? And was it likely
that the number of common regimes could be steadily
increased without sooner or later running into the
problem of the diversity of economic and social
circumstances and the wide range of related
interests in the various states? One striking
illustration of this problem was the British
refusal to join the European Monetary System in
late 1978, but through the Seventies particularly
in the Common Agricultural Policy, the practice of
amending a general regime to allow for special
cases steadily increased.(2) The C.A.P. became
hopelessly over-complex because of this problem:
but increasing divergence between the performance
of the economies of member States eventually meant
that new regimes could not be established at all.
The tendency towards centralisation must be
regarded, however, as a necessary concomittant of
the earlier expectations among Governments that
there would be increasing convergence between their
interests and structures. But, by the late 1970s
and early Eighties these expectations had been
considerably reduced as the level of politicisation
of the Communities' decision-making had increased.
There came a point at which centralisation which
had earlier seemed a natural-inseparable-adjunct of
unification, became a part of the underlying
pathology. Continuing expectations that further
cooperation could only be based on this principle -
the rejection of Europe a la carte by Tindemans and
others - had a crippling effect on the process of
initiating new proposals for unification. And the
centralised institutional frameworks and regimes
became a source of strength for those governments
and groups which were opposed to unification.

Europe's internationalism - the second
tendency - meant that she became too open to the
international system and too vulnerable to divisive
influences within it: at the same time Europe's
openness meant that she could not solve many of her
internal problems at the European level. This
tendency became a source of increasing difficulty
in the late 1970s and early Eighties, in particular
because of the growing divergence between the
economies of the member states. The interest of
members in retaining their ability to defend
themselves against adverse developments in the
international economy, and to take advantage of
favourable developments there, was increased. More
openness, which was the result of that
internationalism which had helped to create Europe,

itself contributed to the sense in the early
Eighties that she was in some ways redundant. The
third tendency - the expansion of the European
Communities to include new members - meant that the
Communities lost the dominant core of France and
Germany, and also created an increasing drain upon
their resources, and new problems (in part through
sheer numbers) for their institutions. In
particular expansion meant the admission of Britain
which as a member became probably the most
determined opponent of movement towards further
unity. By the late Seventies and early Eighties
the tendencies which had earlier seemed easily
reconcilable with the process of increasing
unification between members of the Communities
became in the one case an underlying cause of
increasing problems between them, and in two cases
aspects of the problem itself. I now concentrate,
however, upon prescriptions which relate to
problems caused by the first tendency, that of
centralisation. Problems related to the other
tendencies, though closely related to the first,
are discussed in less detail.
     I first examine the principles and
institutional implications of the alternatives.
These are suggested by the Council of Europe's
practice of concluding what have been called
partial agreements between governments.(3) The
international institution, through its Secretariat
and Assembly, work out in some detail a proposed
cooperative arrangement - in this case usually in
the social or cultural fields. Close consultations
with member governments accompany this process and
the proposal is adjusted in the light of these, but
the introduction of the proposal does not depend on
the assent of all member States. A specified
minimum number of signatories is necessary for any
particular agreement to become effective, but the
agreement may remain partial in that there are
others who have not acceded. The latter may do so
later - or not at all - though the international
institution does what it can to push them in the
direction of accession. The Consultative Assembly
set up a special Committee to check on progress in
dissenting States towards signature, which worked
particularly through links between Members of the
Consultative Assembly of the Council of Europe and
members of National Assemblies.(4) Such a system,
if introduced into the Communities, would
constitute a step of which at least one reviewer of
Europe's development, Tindemans, would be likely to

disapprove. He called it <u>Europe a la carte</u>, and
contrasted it with the arrangement favoured by him
of a 'two-tier' or 'two-speed' Europe: those who
could reach more far-reaching agreements would do
so in the expectation that the others with their
help would eventually catch up.(5) Europe a la
carte in contrast assumes that some states may
never catch up, and that it may be difficult to
decide which states are ahead, and which are behind
in the movement towards integration. Dahrendorf
seemed to support this notion of Europe a la carte
in his Monnet lecture in Florence in November1979.
     The system would require that Governments
should abstain from vetoing in the Council of
Ministers proposals which did not suit their
immediate interests. The legal bases of
Regulations, Directives and Decisions in the
Council of Ministers of the Communities would
probably need to be altered to allow for such a
possibility. They would have to be changed so that
the legal consequences of the new Regulations would
only follow for those states which had given their
assent but not for those which had abstained. Such
an amendment would have a number of great
advantages in present circumstances. It would make
it more difficult for states to establish links
between issues, and accordingly package deals would
be greatly simplified. States could argue less
frequently that they would only yield a particular
concession if other States made a reciprocal
concession — a strategy which now too often leads
to stalemate — because those states which supported
action could move ahead on their own: the system of
deadlock would be loosened. And their intentions
towards unification would not be subdued in the
inevitable compromises required in the present
system with the less enthusiastic states. It is
also apparent, however, that a state which
persistently used its veto could be more readily
outflanked in this new system.
     The Commission would also stand to recover its
own ability to initiate: it would be less
vulnerable to the pressures which tended to draw it
into the intergovernmental negotiations in the way
which I have discussed. It could produce more
detailed, general interest proposals in the
awareness that they only needed to obtain a
sensible sufficiency of support from member states
in order to become law, rather than reflect the
lowest common denominator of agreement between all
states: the introduction of a system of partial

agreements would have the same implications for the role of the Commission as would the introduction of a system of majority voting. There would be less stress upon the delicate processes of intergovernmental negotiation, which, as I have suggested, seems to have reached a crisis threshold, and more upon the Commission's development of proposals which could attract sufficient support. Over time the Commission would probably enter into a special relationship with the more ambitious states and would be reinforced in its ability to lead them further along the path of unification. The significance of states' relations with each other in determining the prospects for developing new agreements would be to some extent reduced in this new system.

Two problems emerge at this point. Would member governments be prepared to accept the system of partial agreements. And are there indeed issues on which it would seem conceivable that a small group of states would wish to move ahead of the others? It is by no means certain that the more 'difficult' states would support the changes: they would lose some of their ability to put pressure upon partners simply by being difficult. Hence Britain's and the other new members' great hostility to the majority vote in favour of increasing farm prices in May 1982 despite an attempted veto by Britain. On the other hand the nature of their intentions towards Europe would become so transparent if the issue became part of the agenda of the Communities, and if they objected, that there would be for them considerable political and economic costs. They would be judged by more pro-European groups and states as stubborn luddites. It is even conceivable that those in favour of taking further steps towards unification would be moved to exclude the dissenters from the Communities. Although the Treaty of Rome contains no provision for such a step there are interpretations of the Communities' legal system which would allow this possibility.(6) It could also be argued that by the late seventies and early eighties there were no states which would wish to move ahead of the others. This is a matter of judgement about the intentions of governments and the strength of pro-European groups within the European states which could only be tested after the introduction of the new system. My judgement is that within the original Six, with the possible exception of France, there remained in the late

Seventies and early Eighties a greater preparedness
to accept more ambitious schemes for European
unification than in the other four. The
introduction of a new system would in any case
encourage more pro-European parties and groups
within these states.

If the system of partial agreements were
introduced, and the required legal and procedural
changes were accepted, there are a number of areas
where some states could move ahead, though progress
in some cases would probably involve mini-packages.
Some states, for instance, members of the old
Snake, could move more rapidly towards Monetary
Union, particularly if special arrangements under
regional policy and industrial policy were made for
the less prosperous 'assenting' states. Those
states might also move ahead in coordinating their
budgetary policies and their fiscal policies. In
the social and cultural areas the unlocking of
issues might also allow some states to establish a
Passport Union on the Scandinavian model. The
complete elimination of controls on movements of
people across frontiers would probably be fairly
straightforward for, say, Holland, Belgium and West
Germany. There are also a number of areas of
welfare policy where harmonisation could be
relatively straightforward for some states. It
should be stressed, however, that although economic
advantage could prove a major incentive for some
states to move ahead, the main advantage of the new
system would be its contribution towards the
regeneration of the 'cement of Community spirit'.
It is necessary to find some means of moving away
from the deeply entrenched pluralism of the early
eighties towards a stronger sense of community.(7)
A Passport Union is unlikely to provide many
immediate economic advantages, but it would
symbolize a new commitment to unification and would
reinforce the position of the pro-Europeans in
members' political elites.

If a partial agreement system were to be
introduced there would be advantage in linking it
with a further innovation, which is also, itself, a
measure of decentralisation. Although the
introduction of <u>Europe a la carte</u> would have the
beneficial effect of weakening the target of
unification as a consensus objective among member
states, nevertheless it would be appropriate to
reinforce as far as possible any tendency towards
unification which might develop. A model of
procedures which could achieve such an effect in

the European Communities can be found in
Scandinavia: that of <u>parallel legislation</u>.(8)
Members of the Nordic Council do not have any kind
of centralised legislative machinery, and no
equivalent of the European Assembly. Nevertheless,
they ensure that they have a wide range of
legislation in common by passing similar laws in
the various national systems: the system is
coordinated but decentralised. In the early days
of the development of the USA a similar system of
parallel legislation among the States was used. It
would be inappropriate to introduce exactly this
system in the European Communities, and, indeed,
for those states which accepted legislation in the
Council of Ministers it would of course be
unnecessary. (The Communities' legal system is
based upon the principle of the direct
applicability of Community law.) But for those
states which had not accepted the proposed
Regulations, or Directives, the idea of parallel
legislation suggests various possibilities. The
main objective would be to attempt to organize
interests within national assemblies so that
support for the proposal might be increased within
them and pressures upon executives to accept them
generated. One possibility is for the Commission
to cooperate with national representatives in the
European Assembly so that the latter could be
helped to build support within their own parties in
National Assemblies. It seems unlikely that the
European Assembly will ever gain independent
legislative powers: it could, however, make a
greater contribution to stimulating support in
national Assemblies for European legislation.
Indeed, the passing of a law within a national
Parliament which introduced a Community decision
would have a similar effect to an assenting vote in
the Council of Ministers.
     A Commission which was more capable of
developing European initiatives might also be more
capable of making an effective contribution to the
organisation of European lobbies in national
Parliaments. This process could also be helped by
the fact that in this new context the attention of
the emerging 'Euro-lobby' would be focussed upon
particular, detailed proposals, namely, the
legislation already approved by the assenting
States. One difficulty with the organisation of
more powerful European lobbies in the traditional
system is that while legislation is being made, it
is relatively remote from the attention of national

Assemblies, and there is therefore little of
substance on which their enthusiasm could be
focussed. National Parliaments do not have easy
access to specific European 'causes' which they
could influence. Scrutiny of Community legislation
is ex post facto; debates in national Parliaments
on proposed legislation in the Council of Ministers
are rather unusual.(9) With appropriate
organisation, therefore, it is possible that
European Parliaments and the Commission together
could organize a strategy for generating support
for European legislation in at least some national
Parliaments. The process would not be rapid but
could be expected to develop rather like the role
of the Irish lobby in the British Parliament in the
late nineteenth century. It would be likely to
nudge states gradually towards unification. It is
of course possible that one result of this process
would be the introduction of compromise
arrangements between those states which had
originally assented to the Communities' legislation
and those which had dissented about the extent to
which it should apply in the latter. Nevertheless,
if the strategy were effective each State would
follow its own path towards European union.

In a system of parallel legislation the
European Parliament would still express particular
positions in the development of Europe and of
European legislation, and it would seek to exert an
influence upon the formulation of European
legislation as it does at present.(10) But it
would also develop its role as a lobby before
national Parliaments which had the special
advantage of close party links between European MPs
and those in national Assemblies. A 'creep-back'
of support for European integration would move from
the European Assembly into national
Parliaments.(11) The Assembly, of course, would
not give up its attempts to obtain more legislative
power for itself: but it would avoid the
implication that it was in any sense a rival to
national Parliaments. Its main short term strategy
would be the less challenging one of facilitating
the development of support for specific European
legislation at the national level. There would be
a shift from the present strategy, which appears
too often to stress challenging and reducing
national assemblies, to one of harnessing and
coordinating their separate powers. Given this
strategy it is vitally important that the members
of the European Parliament should develop the dual

mandate.   They would be more effective as
organisers of lobbies for Europe if they were also
members of national Parliaments.
     The second set of proposals is implied by the
first: enlargement has taken into the Communities a
number of states which hold a general posture of
opposition to the process of unification.   It may
be that some of those states would find it
impossible to adjust and that they would continue
to be difficult partners.   Europe a la carte would
make it easier for such states, if they so wished,
to extricate themselves from their entanglements,
although the procedures of parallel legislation
would generate opposing pressures.   It is, of
course, also possible, that the pro-unification
members would be reluctant to allow their partners
to withdraw from those arrangements which involved
costs whilst continuing with those that brought
benefits.(12)   Such considerations could become
important aspects of intra-Community negotiations
in the new system.   But it is also possible that
relations between enthusiasts and doubters could
reach the point at which it would seem necessary
for the latter to leave the European Communities.
The advantage of this would be that it would assist
any emerging core of European states to progress
faster.   The point is ventured rather tentatively
here: but it seems that the accession of Britain
has not been an unqualified success for the
development of the European Communities.   The
threat of her exclusion could be a salutary
experience: her absence from an organisation which
was still in the process of development would make
'completion' easier.   From the point of view of
British interests an objective judgement might
suggest that her exclusion or withdrawal at this
stage would be undesirable.   But from the point of
view of the development of Europe, British
withdrawal at this stage could be advantageous.
There may be a case in the early eighties for
stressing completion at the expense of expansion.
It all depends upon your point of view: Britain
would then later have the choice of joining or not
joining a Community which was nearer its completed
state and which was therefore less likely to be
spoilt by British pragmatism.
     The third set of prescriptions, related to the
second tendency, are discussed here very briefly
and are put forward very tentatively.   There may be
a case for reversing to some extent Europe's
interdependence in trade and other matters with the

rest of the world. The idea that Europeanism and internationalism are each implied by the other needs critical examination. Indeed, in trade it may be that European integration would benefit from a measure of protectionism. The economists' idea that international trade encouraged an international division of labour is not supported by the pattern of trade in manufactured goods between developed states which makes up an increasing proportion of the value of international trade. Trade increasingly involves the exchange of the same or similar goods rather than different ones: states send and receive similar items. Given this development, and that, in any case, European states increasingly trade with each other, it would seem possible to insulate Europe's economy to some extent from the international economy without incurring undue costs. An increasing insulation of Europe's economy would over time reduce the potential conflict between members' external and internal interests and would further simplify the calculations of members in negotiations about further integration. The reduction of members' trade, and other exchanges, with non-members could be made up by an increase in the level of exchange with other members of the Communities. There is no necessary reason why Europe's external trade dependence should be so very much higher than that of, say, the United States of America, though it might be necessary to make special arrangements for particular raw materials. I should stress again, however, that I am putting forward this proposal in a tentative way: it follows from the observation that the internal-external links of members are often in conflict, that Europeanism and internationalism are not necessarily convergent, and that other emerging states have generally been protectionist rather than liberal in their international commercial and economic posture.

*****

Conclusions

The European Communities in the early eighties seemed to many observers to be in crisis. Numerous Reports had been written, diagnoses made, prescriptions suggested. By early 1982, however, there had been no significant reforms of the Communities' institutions or their working procedures. It seems to the present writer that the process of European integration was more likely to begin again if the goal of unification were consciously abandoned in the short term and if some of its supporting doctrines were discarded. The system needed to reflect the realities that no national power, be they parties, assemblies or executives, would accept its own reduction; and that the increasing divergencies between the economic performance of member states made the development of further common or centralised regimes unlikely. There were indeed good reasons for this reluctance. It was therefore realistic to contemplate the prospects for persuading the European states to work more closely together on the basis of different procedures and principles, in a system which was perhaps less centralised but nevertheless coordinated. If the paths followed by the Communities, hitherto, had not led to unification, and seemed in the early eighties to be enhancing the prospects for disintegration, an alternative route was at least worth trying.

NOTES

1. Carol Cosgrove Twitchett, _A Framework for Development: the EEC and the ACP_, Allen and Unwin, London, 1981.
2. The prime example of this was the Monetary Compensation Amounts. See Werner Feld, 'Implementation of the European Community's Common Agricultural Policy: expectations, fears, failures', _International Organization_, Vol. 33, No. 3, Summer 1979, pp. 335-364.
3. See A.H. Robertson, _The Council of Europe_, (2nd edition), London, Stevens, 1962.
4. See A. Glenn Mower Jr., 'The Official Pressure Group of the Council of Europe's Consultative Assembly', _International Organization_, Vol. XVIII, No. 2, Spring, 1964, pp. 292-306.
5. _European Union: Report by Mr. Leo Tindemans to the European Council_, Bulletin of the European Communities, Supplement 1/76, Commission of the European Communities, p. 21.
6. See my article, 'The legal bases of the European Communities: a Political Perspective', forthcoming.
7. For a discussion of the role of a sense of community in the European Communities see my 'Interdependence and Autonomy in the European Communities: the case of the European Monetary

System', _Journal of Common Market Studies_, Vol. XVIII, No. 4, June 1980, pp. 370-387.

8. See Gunnar Nielsson, 'The Parallel National Action Process: Scandinavian Experiences', in P. Taylor and A.J.R. Groom, _International Organization: a Conceptual Approach_, Pinter, London, 1978, pp.270-316.

9. For a discussion of the British practice see Anne Stevens, 'The Problem of Parliamentary Control of EEC Policy', _Millennium: Journal of International Studies_, London School of Economics, Winter 1976-77, pp.310-326.

10. For a discussion of the work of the European Assembly see Valentine Herman and Juliet Lodge, _The European Parliament and the European Community_, Macmillan, 1978.

11. The term 'creep-back' was used by the late John Macintosh, M.P. at a Seminar on Direct Elections held at the London School of Economics in 1977. He was referring to the fear of some anti-EEC members of the British Labour Party, that involvement in the European Parliament could effect a 'creep-back' of pro-Europeanism into the Labour Party at home.

12. The French government threatened 11 January 1980 to seek a special status for Britain in the Communities - undefined - unless she adopted a more accommodating stance in her negotiations with her partners about the scaling down of British contributions to the Budget. See _International Herald Tribune_, 12 January 1980. President Mitterand made the same point in May 1982.

SELECTED BIBLIOGRAPHY

J Bryan Collester (1979) <u>The European Communities,</u>
<u>a Guide to Information Sources</u>, Gale Research.

Documents

Kitzinger, Uwe (1967) <u>The European Common Market</u>
<u>and Community</u>, Routledge and Kegan Paul,
London.
Sweet and Maxwell <u>European Community Treaties</u> (A
collection of the main relevant treaties
including the European Communities Act).
Vaughan, Richard (1976) <u>Post-War Integration in</u>
<u>Europe</u>, Arnold.

Books and Articles

Arbuthnot, H and Edwards, G. (1979) <u>A Common Man's</u>
<u>Guide to the Common Market</u>, Macmillan.
Baker, Elizabeth (1971) <u>Britain in a Divided Europe</u>
<u>1948-1970</u>, Weidenfeld.
Buchan, Alistair (1963) <u>NATO in the 1960s</u>, London,
Chatto and Windus.
Camps, Miriam (1967) <u>European Unification in the</u>
<u>Sixties</u>, New York.
Coombes, D (1970) <u>Politics and Bureaucracy</u>, Allen
and Unwin.
Dagtoglou, P D (1975) <u>Basic Problems of the</u>
<u>European Community</u>, Basil Blackwell.
Deniau, J (1968) <u>The Common Market</u>, London, Barrie
and Rockcliffe (revised edition).
Diebold, William <u>The Schuman Plan. A Study in</u>
<u>Economic Cooperation. 1950-59</u>. (A critical
bibliography), pp. 718-739.
Europe Unites (1948) The story of the campaign for

Selected Bibliography

Europe Unites (1948)   The story of the campaign for
    European unity, including a full report of the
    Congress of Europe at The Hague, May 1948,
    London, Hollis and Carter.
Fitzmaurice, John (1978) The European Parliament,
    Saxon House.
Groom, A J R and Taylor, P (eds) (1975)
    Functionalism, University of London Press.
Harrison, R J (1974) Europe in Question, Allen and
    Unwin.
Henderson, W O (1962) The Genesis of the Common
    Market, London, Frank Cass & Co Ltd.
Henig, Stanley (1980) Power and Decision in Europe,
    Europotentials Press.
Herman, V and Lodge, J (1978) The European
    Parliament and the European Community,
    Macmillan.
Holland, Stuart (1980) The Uncommon Market,
    Papermac.
Hu, Yao-su (1981) Europe under Stress, Butterworth.
Ionescu, Ghita (1973) The New Politics of European
    Integration, Allen and Unwin.
Kerr, A J C (1980) The Common Market and How it
    Works, Pergamon.
Kitzinger, Uwe (1961) The Challenge of the Common
    Market, Oxford, Basil Blackwell.
Kitzinger, Uwe (1973) Diplomacy and Persuasion,
    Thames and Hudson.
Lerner, Daniel and Aron, Raymond (eds) (1975)
    France Defeats EDC, London Thames and Hudson.
Lindberg, Leon N (1963) The Political Dynamics of
    European Economic Integration, Stanford
    University Press.
Lindberg, Leon N (1966) "Integration as a Source of
    Stress on the European Community System",
    International Organisation, Spring.
Morgan, Roger (1972) West European Politics Since
    1945, Batsford.
Palmer, M and Lambert, J (1968) European Unity: A
    Survey of European Organisations, Allen and
    Unwin.
Pickles, William (1967) How Much Has Changed?
    Britain and Europe, Oxford, Basil Blackwell.
Pryce, Roy (1973) The Politics of the European
    Community, Butterworth.
Sasse, Christopher et al (1977) Decision-making in
    the European Communities, Praeger.
Saunders, C (1975) From Free Trade to Integration
    in Western Europe, PEP/Chatham House.
Spinelli, A (1966) The Eurocrats, John Hopkins.
Stevens, Anne (1976-77) "Problems of Parliamentary

Selected Bibliography

        Control of EEC Policy", <u>Millennium</u>, Winter.
Swann, D (1978) <u>The Economics of the Common Market</u>,
        Penguin.
Taylor, P (1971) <u>International Cooperation Today:</u>
        <u>The Universal and the European Pattern</u>, Elek
        Books Ltd, London.
Taylor, P (1972) "Britain, the Common Market and
        the Forces of History", <u>Orbis</u>, Philadelphia,
        Fall.
Taylor, P (1975) "Politics of the European
        Communities", World Politics, April.
Taylor, P (1981) "The Obligation of Membership of
        the European Communities", <u>International</u>
        <u>Affairs</u>, April.
Taylor, P and Groom, A J R (1978) <u>International</u>
        <u>Organization</u>, Frances Pinter.
Wallace, Hellen (1980) <u>The Budget of the European</u>
        <u>Communities</u>, UACES.
Wallace, H and Edwards, G (1979) <u>The Presidency of</u>
        <u>The European Communities</u>.
Wallace, W and Hill, C (1979) "Diplomatic Trends in
        the European Community", <u>International</u>
        <u>Affairs</u>, January.
Wallace, A, Wallace H and Webb, C (1979)
        <u>Policy-Making in the European Communities</u>,
        Wiley.
Willis, F Roy (1975) <u>European Integration</u>, New
        Viewpoints.
Zurcher, Arnold J <u>The Struggle to Unite Europe,</u>
        <u>1940-1958</u>, New York University Press.

INDEX

317

Index

Index

Index

Index

Index